Judging Passions

European monographs in social psychology
Sponsored by the European Association of Experimental Psychology

Series Editor:
Professor Rupert Brown, Department of Psychology, University of Kent, Canterbury, Kent CT2 7NP

The aim of this series is to publish and promote the highest quality of writing in European social psychology. The editor and the editorial board encourage publications which approach social psychology from a wide range of theoretical perspectives and whose content may be applied, theoretical or empirical. The authors of books in this series should be affiliated to institutions that are located in countries which would qualify for membership of the Association. All books will be published in English, and translations from other European languages are welcomed. Please submit ideas and proposals for books in the series to Rupert Brown at the above address.

Published

The Quantitative Analysis of Social Representations
Willem Doise, Alain Clemence, and Fabio Lorenzi-Cioldi

A Radical Dissonance Theory
Jean-Léon Beauvois and Robert-Vincent Joule

The Social Psychology of Collective Action
Caroline Kelly and Sara Breinlinger

Social Context and Cognitive Performance
Jean-Marc Monteil and Pascal Huguet

Conflict and Decision-Making in Close Relationships
Erich Kirchler, Christa Rodler, Erik Hölzl, and Katja Meier

Stereotyping as Inductive Hypothesis Testing
Klaus Fiedler and Eva Walther

Intergroup Relations in States of the Former Soviet Union
Louk Hagendoorn, Hub Linssen, and Sergei Tumanov

The Social Psychology of Ethnic Identity
Maykel Verkuyten

Consumer Culture, Identity and Well-Being
Helga Dittmar

Judging Passions: Moral emotions in persons and groups
Roger Giner-Sorolla

Forthcoming Title
The Passionate Intersection of Desire and Knowledge
Gregory Maio

Judging Passions

Moral emotions in persons and groups

Roger Giner-Sorolla

Psychology Press
Taylor & Francis Group

LONDON AND NEW YORK

First published 2012
by Psychology Press
27 Church Road, Hove, East Sussex BN3 2FA

Simultaneously published in the USA and Canada
by Psychology Press
711 Third Avenue, New York NY 10017

[www.psypress.com]

*Psychology Press is an imprint of the Taylor & Francis Group, an informa
business*

© 2012 Psychology Press

British Library Cataloguing in Publication Data
A catalogue record for this book is available from the British Library

Library of Congress Cataloging-in-Publication Data
   Giner-Sorolla, Roger.
   Judging passions : moral emotions in persons and groups / Roger
Giner-Sorolla.
      p. cm. — (European monographs in social psychology)
      ISBN 978–1–84872–068–8 (hardback)
   1. Emotions—Research.   2. Ethics.   3. Social justice.
   4. Moral development. I. Title.
   BF531.G56 2012
   152.4—dc23

                                                        2011038919

ISBN: 978–1–84872–068–8 (hbk)
ISBN: 978–0–203–12387–4 (ebk)

Typeset in Times New Roman
by RefineCatch Limited, Bungay, Suffolk
Cover design by Design Deluxe
Cover image: German chancellor Willy Brandt kneeling before the Polish
National Memorial in Warsaw, 1970 © Keystone/Getty Images

To Rea, who has helped me so much with this book and everything else.

Contents

List of figures

Table

Acknowledgements

Across the decades leading up to this book, I'd like to thank Shelly Chaiken, for getting me interested in subjectivity and bias; Susan M. Andersen, for awakening my interest in emotion; Jon Haidt, for fuelling it further; Tim Wilson, for insight into fast and slow processes; and Rupert Brown, for encouraging me to write this and giving valuable feedback. Across the year leading up to it, I'd also like to thank Rea Giner-Sorolla, for time management, process improvement, layperson's perspective, and substantial encouragement; and Neil McClatchie, for help with the vast task of the referencing. Finally, the manuscript has been greatly improved by the comments of Brad Bushman, Agneta Fischer, Thomas Kessler, Greg Maio, Sophieke Russell, and an anonymous reviewer.

1 Emotions, morality, and groups: Introduction and definitions

This book deals with the intersection of three heavily studied concepts in psychology and other disciplines: emotions, morality, and groups. I argue that these three topics bear a special relationship to each other. The passions give important input to our moral judgments, providing fuel and direction for moral action. Morality is rooted in concerns about living with other people, in relationships, but also in larger groups. And groups use emotions as a stimulus toward collective action, as well as a marker of belonging. The judgments of our passions are a critical component of our life as individuals and as members of social groups.

At the same time, my title also implies that I will be passing judgment on passions. Indeed, one of my aims is to argue for a more comprehensive account of whether emotions help or harm us as moral beings and as group members. To this end I will present a functional conflict theory of emotions (chapter 2) that explains how the essentially functional nature of emotions can at times lead to malfunctions. This explains both how emotions work and how they can become botched. In this chapter, however, before defining these three key concepts, I want to address a potential criticism of the so-called moral emotions in the context of morality and groups. If emotions such as anger, guilt, and disgust are so important in moral judgment, how is it that these same emotions and judgments can lead to immoral consequences?

Take this historical example. On 1 September 1939, the news broke: after years of oppression of ethnic Germans living in Poland, things had gone too far. The Polish had invaded Germany. Polish soldiers had seized the radio station at Gleiwitz. At an extraordinary session of the Reichstag, Chancellor Hitler raised his voice in anger, roared on by his delegates. He explained how patient and tolerant he had been in the face of provocation; but now, he could take no more. "I will not war against women and children," said Hitler. "I will continue this struggle, no matter against whom, until the safety of the Reich and its rights are secured." A book in English published the following year in Berlin made the case to Americans for the moral outrage that many Germans no doubt already felt. Before the previous September, "Germans were attacked in the open country, in their homes and on the farms. From May 1939 onwards prohibition orders and punishments literally rained down on them ... Outbursts of racial propaganda could be read in the Polish press" (Schadewaldt, 1940, p. 17).

Of course, these claims of moral righteousness were cynical propaganda. The raid on the radio station had been carried out by SS operatives disguised in Polish uniform. German atrocities against the occupied Polish population eventually far outnumbered whatever Poles had done to ethnic Germans, even in the first days of the invasion, when violent reprisals undoubtedly took place. Maybe there was even an ironic taste of psychological projection in the complaints against "prohibition orders" and "racial propaganda." After all, violence and repressive measures had been openly and officially levelled against Jews in the Reich for the previous 6 years.

And yet, a queasy kind of sympathy can arise when reading some passages from Schadewaldt's report: "Why did Poles, without the slightest reason, attack the one or other German—known or unknown to them—why were they willing to take part in these indescribable atrocities?" (Schadewaldt, 1940, p. 18). This echoes the question that has been asked, over and over again, about the German atrocities. The most popular answers are comforting. Various scholars have told us that the Nazis followed an evil psychopath (e.g., Victor, 1998); they followed mindless processes of conformity and obedience (Arendt, 1963; Asch, 1951; Milgram, 1974; Zimbardo, 1971); they exploited cultural beliefs in racial and national superiority (Goldhagen, 1996); in sum, they abandoned morality entirely to enlarge their empire. Less comforting is the possibility that the Nazis convinced the mass of the German people, not just to obey and conform, but to follow a goal described in moral terms. Did they ask the same questions about the "injustices" of the Versailles treaty and the Silesian Germans as we ask of Dachau?

In culture high and low today, Hitler stands as a firmly rooted moral nadir. There is even a term for the tendency of debate on an Internet forum to eventually start comparing the opposition to the Nazis: Godwin's Law. But as hollow as they are, the moral protestations of Nazi propaganda present a problem for a caricatured view of the regime as proud Nietzschean super-villains who placed themselves "beyond good and evil." Even the Reich needed to present itself to internal and external audiences with moral concerns. It drew on the passions of the unjustly wronged and humiliated, to mobilize action within its borders, and to deflect criticism from outside. When later uncovered, the actions of the SS and the clandestine table talk of Hitler with his cronies revealed the cynical nature of these claims. But it is uncomfortable to consider that we, too, might be fanned to righteous indignation for a cause eventually revealed as unworthy; that there is nothing separating our highest, best, and most human moral sentiments from those that could support the darkest evils of history.

The field of experimental social psychology took, as an early focus, questions raised by the rise of Hitler and the uncovering of the Holocaust. The "classic" post-war experiments in social psychology argued that the essential cause of Nazi atrocities did not lie in anything innate in the human condition. Nor was there something peculiar to Germany. Rather, social psychologists pointed to the influence of collective social forces upon the way people construe reality, potentially leading to irrational and destructive behaviour. We can illustrate this with Solomon Asch's demonstration of the informational influence of conformity (Asch, 1951).

Participants in his experiments not only agreed with the majority opinion of experimental shills against the evidence of their own senses, but came to believe the socially constructed reality, even when led away from the original social group. The same conformity and obedience that led American men of the 1950s to put on grey flannel suits and go to work every day also led German men of the 1940s to don *feldgrau* and do a more sinister work.

Even in this interpretation, though, there remained the hope that moral sentiment would burst through the grey curtain of mindless social influence. A continuous counter-narrative to the classic social psychology experiments has pointed out the ability of humans to resist conformity and obedience. Starting in the 1970s, Asch's (1951) results showed a number of non-replications, and in general conformity experiments have yielded diminishing returns since the 1950s (Bond & Smith, 1996). Milgram's (1974) well-known experiments did not yield absolute obedience, and in fact many individuals resisted the orders to inflict torture on others to the end. Recently, a 21st-century take on Zimbardo's Stanford Prison Experiment, conducted and televised in Britain, yielded much less docile "prisoners" who effectively organized against cowed and doubtful "guards" (Haslam & Reicher, 2007). Some might see in these examples a triumph of moral feelings over the forces that keep people fearful. But the story may not be that simple. If moral sentiments and judgments themselves can be manipulated for evil, then the good fight may not pit morality against its absence. It may pit us, who think we are moral, against them, who also think they are moral. And with this comes the possibility that we are not actually as moral as we think we are.

Still, confronting the subjective nature of the moral sense allows us also to confront the worst outbreaks of prejudice and conflict. Material conflicts between peoples can give rise to horrific struggles. When the war is seen pragmatically, the nature of reality remains the same for both sides; the same thing motivates us and our enemy. But when war gains a moral justification, the enemy becomes contemptible and incomprehensible. Compatriots and leaders, by the same device, become ennobled. Sacrifice beyond any rational calculation becomes thinkable. It is precisely moral arguments that make modern conflicts so passionate and intractable.

This book concerns itself with three intertwined topics in social psychology: emotions, morality, and groups. As the story of the Polish invasion of Germany shows, conflict between groups is heavily imbued with moral concerns. And morality in turn is felt, communicated, and arguably even constituted through our emotions (e.g., Haidt, 2001; Prinz, 2007). Hitler sought to stir up not just an invasion, but the anger among the German people that would deliver broad support for it. Other outlets of Nazi propaganda reached lower, stirring up a physically embodied moral disgust toward Jews, Poles, and other non-Aryan peoples. And after the war, German official policy showed an exceptional degree of public self-confrontation, bringing out self-condemning moral emotions of shame and guilt, rather than the other-condemning feelings of the Nazi regime (Barkan, 2000).

Emotions don't simply aim to punish immoral action in one's own group and other groups. There are other emotions that promote and reward moral action.

Among these are feelings of moral concern for others. In the English thesaurus, these descend uncomfortably from sympathy to compassion to pity, which itself is just a step away from contempt. Feelings of moral self-approval, pride, and satisfaction provide self-praise for good deeds in the same way guilt and shame supply self-condemnation for bad. Turned outward, feelings can also approve of the morality of others. Labelled as *admiration* and *elevation*, these positive emotions are just now coming under the scrutiny of psychologists. All these feelings can operate both within and between groups, encouraging and empowering where negative moral emotions punish and forbid.

If we accept a moral sense that draws on emotions, however, we have to also accept the flawed nature of emotions themselves. Emotions, I will argue, are a paradox. They help us function in so many ways, and yet often show dysfunctional sides, irrational biases and outbursts. In explaining moral emotions in persons and groups, I find it necessary to present a theory of emotions that acknowledges multiple functions for each emotion. These functions can be categorized four ways: emotions can help us appraise new developments in the world; learn about the world in a rapid, associative way; regulate our own behaviours; and communicate our sincere intentions to others. While other categorizations of emotional functions are possible (e.g., according to level of social organization; Keltner & Haidt, 1999, 2001), my scheme, the functional conflict theory (FCT), helps explain how one function of an activated emotion can have side-effects that get in the way of others. Anyone who has tried to use the scissors of a multipurpose knife knows that they aren't very good at cutting, because the other tools in the knife constrain their design. Emotions are worse than the knife, because most of their functions require a fast and automatic activation. It's as if, while you were trying to cut a piece of thread with the knife's scissors, the tape measure, fish scaler, and magnifying glass also sprang out automatically. The times when emotions seem dysfunctional are times when the functions interfere with each other.

Before I say anything more about emotions, morality, and groups, I owe the reader an explanation of what I mean by these three terms, with a focus on the difficult and controversial concepts of emotions and morality.

Defining "group"

This first and simplest definition nonetheless involves a small degree of legerdemain that has become habitual in my field. The research and theory I am going to describe as a social psychologist do not take as their object the group itself, but the individual's ideas and feelings about social groups and their individual members. Because of this, the subtitle of this book is not merely "Moral emotions in groups"; as a psychologist, I am bound to recognize that group-level emotions have their origins and parallels in individual psychology, hence the added reference in my title to "persons." The social psychological approach to groups, then, studies mental representations of groups the individual belongs to (ingroups), groups the individual does not belong to (outgroups) and the interaction between these two.

Although a group is a social category of human beings, not every possible category forms a viable group. For example, I can categorize humans into those whose first name begins and ends with the same letter, distinguishing this special club from all the other unfortunates stuck with mismatching letters. But this category is not a true social group, because the Rogers, Annas, and Evangelines of the world lack certain essential marks of cohesion. We do not share a common fate, a common culture, widely held stereotypes, or really much of anything else in common, other than a barely noticed orthographic trait.

This collection of traits that makes a group "groupy" is present in greater or lesser extent in all true groups. The subjective sense of a group's "groupiness" has been extensively studied under the less casual (and less pronounceable) name of "entitativity" (Campbell, 1958). This group glue has proven to be an important part of another kind of idea that an individual can hold about the connection with his or her own group—social identity. It is a gross understatement to say that the strength and quality of social identity has been studied extensively. Indeed, many different facets and strategies relevant to the sense of identity have been identified. However, for the time being I am going to take a broad view of groups, similar to my broad view of emotions, that leaves open whether or not the group experiences a common social identity. In particular, there is a group of human characteristics that have been studied under the name of "stigma" (Goffman, 1971). Having a trait that is stigmatized within a given culture, such as obesity, a handicap, red hair, or being attracted to the same sex, may not necessarily lead to a group identity. At the same time, if stigma is seen as a kind of prejudice, then the psychology of those who treat a class of people badly based on a stigma is bound to be similar to those who base their prejudice on an identity. For this reason I want to be able to consider attitudes toward a "group" that exists at least in the eye of the beholder, if not in the eyes of its own members.

Defining "emotion"

Defining a difficult term such as "emotion," it is tempting to do the work of a thesaurus instead of a dictionary—to use concrete examples instead of trying to find the exactly correct abstract phrase. After all, the scope of my interest is the set of emotions involved in morality, which can be enumerated by a list of English terms: "anger", "disgust", "shame", "guilt", "sympathy", and several others. So, it would be easy to just focus on the psychological phenomena that those English words refer to, whatever they may be, and leave it at that. But it doesn't seem fair to present a theory of emotion out of context, to give a "why" for a concept lacking a "what." There should be some kind of boundary to the concept of "emotion," if only to make clear what kind of things I am *not* talking about.

In any event, my boundary is broad. I don't see it as productive to locate the core of emotion in any one phenomenon such as culture, language, cognition, subjective feeling, expressive display, peripheral or central nervous physiology. I side instead with eclectic definitions that present the emotion concept as involving all these phenomena and binding them to each other (e.g., Keltner & Lerner, 2010;

Kemper, 1987). Emotions arise from sensory and cognitive input, elaborated to a greater or lesser degree. From sources in the brain they activate peripheral nervous, endocrine, cardiovascular, and other physiological responses. At the same time they activate hard-to-control bodily expressions that can be read by other people, in our faces, voices, and posture. As with many other psychological states, humans reflect on emotions and give them names, so that emotions take on a semantic life. And humans cannot help but speak about and learn about emotions within the context of a culture, leading to cultural differences in emotion expression and knowledge.

Emotion thus can be seen as a multi-layered concept, with roots in brain and body, branching through thought and awareness, and flowering in cultural and linguistic expression. In psychology, of course, we sometimes see debates about whether or not such things as awareness, peripheral nervous system activation, facial expressions, or language terms are necessary or sufficient to the category of emotion. To me, these are as pointless as debates on whether a tiger counts as a cat. Just as an animal can be a more or less prototypical example of its lay category, so we can speak of prototypical emotional phenomena that tick off all the boxes, and contrast them to marginal emotional phenomena that are missing one or two of these tick-marks—for example, emotional activation without awareness, or feelings such as guilt that do not entail strong facial or nervous changes. Drawing the correct boundary is less important to science, I think, than understanding how guilt is and is not a prototypical emotion, or how the tiger is and is not a prototypical cat. Only this sophisticated understanding can help us understand that both a tiger and a housecat can be fed meat, but only one can be safely scratched behind the ears; or that guilt may act in some ways like an emotion, but the researcher will look in vain for a distinctive facial expression for it.

However, even fuzzy prototypes need a centre. To me, the irreducible centre of an emotion is motivational. That is, the more emotional a concern, the more systems are activated that deal with things of high relevance to the self. Abandoning the chase for a solid definition of the noun "emotion," what makes something more or less "emotional" is this sense of self-relevance. As humans, we can also extend our sense of self into personal relationships and group affiliations, feeling emotions on behalf of our loved ones or broader social identities. The lower threshold of "calling something emotional" versus "emotion" also means that a number of things that may not be considered emotions nonetheless can share important characteristics with them. So, for example, moods are often distinguished from emotions in that they are less connected to a specific situation, longer lasting, and more diffuse. But the very fact that we can talk about "sad" and "angry" moods makes them to some extent emotional, sharing key cognitive, experiential, and biological traits with their fellow full-blown emotions. An angry incident can leave an angry mood behind. A happy mood can predispose someone to react positively when a more specific occasion for a "real" emotion arises. Likewise, emotional attitudes can be defined as connections in memory between an object and a specific emotion (Giner-Sorolla, 1999; Zanna & Rempel,

1988). While they're not the same as emotional episodes, emotional attitudes can be left behind by such episodes, and can form the basis for renewed outbreaks of that emotion—as well as playing a crucial role in emotional learning, as we will see in the next chapter.

We can speak of pleasant or unpleasant feelings, but part of the interest value of emotions comes from the varieties of feeling within the "pleasant" or "unpleasant" categories: anger, fear, sadness, shame. Vocabulary also gives multiple shadings even to these specific categories; in English, an educated person can speak of irritation, indignation, frustration, and outrage as "shades" of anger, in much the same way that an artist can speak of fuchsia, lavender, violet, and mauve as shades of purple. How precisely, then, should emotions be differentiated in psychological research?

The multi-layered nature of emotion complicates the answer. It seems that the more basic the system involved, the fewer categories can be differentiated. Our internal biology makes few distinctions between specific emotions, being organized mainly around the two dimensions of core affect—pleasantness or unpleasantness, and high or low arousal (Russell, 2003). Our expressive systems, however, are able to communicate information relevant to about a half dozen emotions, although imperfectly and subject to contextual cues (Elfenbein & Ambady, 2002; Matsumoto, Keltner, Shiota, Frank, & O'Sullivan, 2008). At the top level, within each human culture, language is able to create a vast vocabulary of feeling states, with specific terms to match a feeling's basic type, context, intensity, and accompanying thoughts; one survey of the English language, for example, identified nearly 600 emotion words (Johnson-Laird & Oatley, 1989).

An important feature of this scheme is that lower levels feed up to and help categorize higher levels. So, for instance, verbal measures of feeling states generally show a two-factor structure corresponding to the pleasantness dimension of core affect; nice feelings in one factor, nasty feelings in the other. Although this has been taken as evidence against more fine-grained distinctions between emotions (Barrett, 2006; Russell & Barrett, 1999), it could also be that the lower-level distinction of an emotion's positive or negative valence is an important semantic trait that organizes higher-level expressions and language terms for more specific emotions (Osgood, Suci, & Tannenbaum, 1957). In fact, cluster analyses of emotion language do show meaningful separations beyond the positive–negative split, which functionally differentiate emotions at more precise levels (Shaver, Schwartz, Kirson, & O'Connor, 1987). When asking about someone's behaviour at a funeral, for example, the differences between "sad," "angry," and "anxious" are less informative than the difference between all three and "happy"; but still, differences among the three reactions do convey something useful.

This hierarchical view also suggests that activated emotions at a more basic level can rise up to influence more specific states. Thus, non-specific arousal carrying over from a fearful experience or from physical exercise can increase the likelihood of reporting high-arousal emotions such as attraction (Schachter, 1964). In fact, despite initial evidence that emotion words have separate effects from emotional experiences (Innes-Ker & Niedenthal, 2002), there is growing evidence from research inspired by theories of embodied cognition that the different aspects of emotion are in fact interconnected (Niedenthal, Barsalou, Winkielman, Krauth-Gruber, & Ric, 2005). For instance, the experience, expressive processing, and semantic processing of disgust activate common regions in the brain (Jabbi, Bastiaansen, & Keysers, 2008); thinking emotionally also unconsciously activates the appropriate facial muscles to the emotion being thought about, and inhibiting the muscles involved in facial expression (for example, by holding a pen sideways in the mouth to prevent frowning) also inhibits cognitive operations involving those emotions (Niedenthal, Winkielman, Mondillon, & Vermeulen, 2009).

As a final application of this definition of emotion, I also want to remark on a seldom-noted category of psychological phenomena, the *cognitive-motivational state*. This seems the best name for a number of sentiments that the English language and Western cultural usage locate inside the neighbourhood of feeling, but outside the house of emotion, or at least uncomfortably on its doorstep. When thinking and learning, we can feel confident, bored, curious, or discouraged; other people can leave us feeling responsible, reassured, obliged, or grateful. Why do these states struggle to be labelled as emotions when other similar states, such as guilt or envy, fall safely within the emotion category?

Certainly some of the marginal states I have mentioned have such a rich expressive, subjective, and physiological profile that there seems to be no objective reason to deny them emotion status. Surprise, for example, was originally classified by Ekman as one of the basic emotions on the strength of its distinctive facial expression. Doubts about the status of surprise as an emotion have rested on the fact that it is not consistently felt as pleasant or unpleasant (e.g., Ortony, Clore, & Collins, 1990), calling into question its nature as a state that can fuel lasting motivations. However, other cognitive feelings such as certainty and boredom are just as motivationally relevant and expressively distinctive as sadness or shame. It is hard to see why these states should not be considered in the same category as non-typical emotions such as envy or *schadenfreude*, which have been studied as emotions but lack distinctive facial expressions, among other peculiarities.

This division makes clear that the "emotion" concept, arbitrary in its exact boundaries if not its approximate centre, is a cultural idea (Wierzbicka, 1999). Western psychological thinkers need to at least recognize this fact. One instructive example is the Polynesian Ilongot people, whose lay psychology, first relayed to the West by Catherine Lutz (1988), puts physiological states such as fatigue and hunger in a complex with phenomena we would call emotional. We cannot ignore the lay psychology of our own culture, not while we make lay terms serve double duty for communication within and outside our scientific community. But we can certainly judge whether or not honouring lay categories creates or impedes interesting research.

In this light, I see no reason why we should not study feelings of gratefulness, curiosity, fatigue, or obligation with the same tools and theories that we use to study feelings of anger, guilt, or jealousy. All the same, there is something special about the basic prototypical emotions that are bound to come first in any lay person's list—anger, disgust, happiness, shame, fear. For some reason they seem to be more intrinsically interesting objects of psychological study than just "feelings of responsibility" or "feeling curious." Perhaps this is because all the marginal states I have described are linked to a single cognitive appraisal or physical need. Gratitude is hard to pry apart from the thought that someone has done you a good deed. Curiosity always fulfils a specific goal, that of needing to know more. However, the most prototypical emotions can be triggered by more than one kind of input. Anger can come about through any of a half-dozen perceptions, ranging from physical pain to a sense of injustice (Berkowitz & Harmon-Jones, 2004; Kuppens, van Mechelen, Smits, & de Boeck, 2003). Disgust likewise has a broad range of elicitors, ranging from things associated with disease to moral turpitude (Rozin, Haidt, & McCauley, 1993). Paradoxically, the "basic" emotions are the ones that seem the most complex, in terms of the range of things that can set them off.

This distinction has real consequences for research and theory. Pragmatically, it is just about impossible to put people in a state of gratitude without confounding it with the cognition that someone has done something good for them. The sense of being helped by another is not just a semantic association with the word "gratitude," but part of its definition. In experimentally manipulating gratitude, there is no other way but to ask the participant to imagine something that almost certainly will bring the key cognition to mind. By contrast, research on disgust is much more amenable to eliminating cognitive confounds. It is highly unlikely when a researcher infuses a room with the disgusting scent of a practical joker's "fart spray" that this causes harsher moral judgments just because it represents some cognition relevant to punishment (Schnall, Haidt, Clore, & Jordan, 2008). Disgust, here, stands on its own; the emotional feeling is the only possible connection between the odour and the judgment. A similar leap can be made when we induce happiness by means of a comedy routine, or sadness by depressing music, and trace its influence on self-esteem. The most prototypical emotions, because of the many different things that bring them about, are able to stand on their own without being tied to a single necessary elicitor.

This view of emotions guides my functional conflict theory. The negative moral emotions I have chosen as my focus—disgust, anger, shame, and guilt (chapters 4 and 5)—have very different characteristics, from the visceral impact of disgust to the highly cognitive and social context of guilt. But each of these emotions is interesting because it can arise in different ways. Each different way by itself serves a purpose, but because these different purposes are routed through the same activation system, the purposes can become confused. The advantage of this approach, too, is evident when considering the positive moral emotions (chapter 6). The various purposes of pride might muddy its uses in the moral domain. Likewise, the emotions of moral concern walk an ambiguous path between empathy and pity. Finally, given the similarities among multiple emotions of other-approval such as gratitude, admiration, and elevation, I will argue that they might be better understood by categorizing them under a larger umbrella.

Defining "morality"

The definition of morality is a very old task in philosophy and a very young one in psychology. Although moral psychology is by all accounts a booming field, it's not often that writers lead off by defining the concept of "morality"; it's one of these lay terms that gets treated as self-evident. But I think the issue of definition deserves some thought and articulation here, because it underlies a number of difficulties and controversies in contemporary research.

Indeed, the moral psychologist's task at first glance looks relatively easy. Because behaviour and subjective experience are the main *descriptive* objects of psychology, we need not concern ourselves with *prescriptive* questions of what is actually morally correct. As scholars in the psychology of morality, we need only to define the moral domain, so that we can agree on what thoughts, feelings, concerns, and actions are related to the moral context. As psychologists, we can show the internal mechanisms that allow one person to kill another, without having to prove that killing is bad. We can figure out what in the environment makes people more likely to help each other, without showing that helping is good. If a moral pronouncement makes its way into one of our papers, it is because some of us find it uncomfortable to leave value questions out of our science. But psychologists are not first and foremost ethicists.

Even this task of drawing boundaries to the moral domain is not easy, however. Many of the recent well-known treatments of morality in psychology assume that the reader knows where the boundaries lie, and pass on quickly to the specifics of its characteristic judgments and feelings (e.g., Greene, 2009b; Haidt, 2001; but for a counterexample see Haidt, 2007). "Morality" may itself be a truism (cf. Maio & Olson, 1998): a super-positive concept used as an end for arguments, but impossible to justify with further reasons—why is it good to be moral? And yet, recent disagreements in moral psychology hinge on what counts as morality. It's my belief that these disagreements have, at their core, a confusion between the prescriptive and the descriptive sense of morality. If you are studying something you describe with this loaded word "morality," the implication is that you approve of the kind of behaviour you are studying. With a clear goal to describe rather than approve, this unwelcome implication vanishes.

In psychology and philosophy, three possible views of what constitutes the moral realm can be distinguished. The first takes a very broad view based on purely descriptive premises. The other two are narrower, based on more prescriptive views of what should count as morality. Given that "morality" has the connotation of being not just good, but the best attribute of human actions (cf. Leach, Ellemers, & Bareto, 2007), it is not surprising that the argument over what should count as morality overlaps with the argument over what kind of morality people should follow.

The broadest view of morality, which I label the *mores* view, treats all prescriptive norms (by the modern usage of the Latin term *mores*) as a form of morality. The narrowest view, *single-concern*, confines morality to a specific class of norms about just and benevolent dealings with people. Finally, a number of views in the middle, congenial to my way of thinking, expand the range of morality to cover *multiple concerns*, while drawing a distinction between moral and other types of prescriptive norms.

Morality as mores

A simple approach to the problem would be to classify any social norms as belonging to the moral realm. Indeed, the *Stanford Encyclopedia of Philosophy* notes two definitions of morality, a descriptive one encompassing any "code of conduct," and a normative one "that, given specified conditions, would be put forward by all rational persons" (Gert, 2011). Keeping in mind that as psychologists we are supposed to be investigating only the descriptive aspects of morality, the former definition would seem to be an easy choice to take on.

And yet, this definition gives me pause. Specifically, it inflates the scope of moral psychology from the massive to the Cyclopean. Surely morality can't be as broad as to cover all social norms, personal habits, and religious injunctions? This would strand the psychologist's definition far away from lay people's views. We would be obliged to treat public nose-picking as a moral fault, or dressing fashionably as a moral virtue. These norms seem too petty to rate the "moral" label. It is all right to break a conventional *rule* in order to honour a moral *law*, but not the other way around. Moral concerns are seen as independent of the word of such authorities as rulers, God or society, while conventional ones are not (Turiel, 1983).

Might we then put the name of "morality" to only the highest-ranking *mores* of any person or society, the ones that take precedence over all others? Let's call this viewpoint *mores maximi* (the greatest *mores*). Ayn Rand, the Objectivist economic and political writer, promoted a morality of selfishness; the Marquis de Sade, for his part, followed a morality of debauchery. Certainly, neither of these concepts fits the traditional content of morality; altruism, not selfishness, and self-restraint, not debauchery, are much more likely to be rated as moral virtues. But at least the scope of Rand's and de Sade's "moralities" seems right, unlike the manners or fashion examples. Each of these concepts—selfishness and debauchery—is not just a convention, but a desired end-state, a value.

Values, as studied extensively by such scholars as Rokeach (1973) and Schwartz (1992), are ranked hierarchically by individuals and cultures. For example, in a right-wing ideology the value of freedom may outweigh the value of equality, whereas in a left-wing ideology, equality may justify restrictions on freedom. However, all the terminal values studied by Rokeach, as well as the values and value clusters studied by Schwartz, are ultimate ends of social concern. So, all of them are potentially moral under our *mores maximi* viewpoint.

Even individualistic values such as independence and power may be seen in some lights as moral. Work and achievement, for example, are moralized in the Protestant work ethic (Furnham, 1990), which is reflected in moral disapproval of welfare recipients or (in North America, at least) of grown men who still live in their parents' home. Likewise, the morality of power found an advocate in

Nietzsche. In *On the Genealogy of Morals* (1887/1967) and subsequent writings he set forth the "morality of the strong," a code of conduct based on the unfettered exercise of personal excellence, against the altruistic Judeo-Christian "slave morality." While I may disagree that Nietzsche's code is moral, in the sense of being morally good, it is hard to deny it a place in the realm of morality, more generally defined. Nietzsche, Rand, de Sade, each promoted a value system broad and deep enough to challenge conventional morality on its own ground.

Mores maximi also appears to explain the phenomenon of moralization as studied by Paul Rozin and others (Brandt & Rozin, 1997), in which a practice previously regarded as a matter of personal preference or social custom takes on moral value, sometimes as a virtue but more often as a vice. A moral crusade takes wing, focusing social attention on the real or purported harms of the now-immoral practice. If we define a moral concern as any kind of behaviour or goal that's seen as supremely important to attain or avoid, then the process of moralization is easy to understand. It simply becomes moving the importance of that behaviour or goal up or down in the ranking.

Some examples from the Anglo-American culture of the last couple of generations include the increasing disgust and stigma attached to smoking (Rozin & Singh, 1999); the moralization of eating and body image among women, captured in advertisements for desserts that flaunt a "sinful" taste while remaining calorically "guilt-free" (Griffin & Berry, 2003); and innumerable choices in child-rearing that have become moralized, such as breast-feeding (Lee, 2007) or food allergies (Rous & Hunt, 2004).

Moralization often arises from awareness of harm to others caused by a practice, as with smoking and morally based vegetarianism. But it can also take on a life of its own. Immoral practices become disgusting, and disgust can persist even when harm to others is irrelevant or disproven. Someone whose actions principally concern themselves, as in the case of obesity today (Townend, 2009) or masturbation in the 19th century (Hunt, 1998), can still be moralized and viewed with revulsion. Conversely, preferences such as homosexuality can lose their moral taint, and defending against them correspondingly moves down the ladder of cultural concerns. Rather than just being outcomes of moralization, greater importance and centrality to the self may in fact be defining traits of the moral domain (Leach et al., 2007; Rozin, 1999; Skitka & Houston, 2001). But is importance the only defining trait of the moral sphere? We will return to this question after considering two other existing definitions of the moral domain among psychologists.

Single-concern morality

According to a more restrictive position that has historically been promoted in both philosophy and psychology, morality has to do with a single kind of value. Using the influential scheme for classifying human values developed by Shalom Schwartz (1992), single-value views of morality in psychology generally identify it with the self-transcendent value clusters, which Schwartz labels "benevolence" and "universalism." Benevolence can be summed up as doing good things for other people and not doing bad things to them. (Or, in the immortal phrase of the religion founded by the slacker heroes of the Bill and Ted films, "Be excellent to each other.") Universalism is more concerned with doing right than doing good, embracing concerns such as justice, fairness, rights, equality, and the well-being of the environment. Of course, the exact interpretation of "doing good", "not doing bad", or "being fair" can be unpacked considerably. Philosophers—or just regular dudes and dudettes—can spend all day pondering tricky cases such as "Is it justifiable to beat a masochist?" and "Is it really morally good to keep someone in a happy fool's paradise?" However one defines what's malevolent and what's benign, the key idea of single-concern morality is concern for other people—whether it is their happiness, well-being, desires, rights, integrity, or future that we are concerned about.

Schwartz' two self-transcendence value domains hold together across a great deal of research in different cultures. Benevolent people are more likely to endorse universalism. Universalism also reinforces and multiplies the effects of benevolence; a moral person should be excellent to everyone, regardless of kinship, race, or place of national origin. This also fits with more elaborated attempts in philosophy to prescribe morality based on a universalistic rule or scenario. Thus, universal benevolence fits with Kant's definition of a moral rule as one that a rational person would wish to be followed universally. If all people were good to others in need, then people will be good to you when you need it, an offer that's hard to turn down. Benevolence is also the value achieved in Rawls' (1971/1999) definition of a morally just society, which is founded on universalistic principles. This is evident from Rawls' famous thought experiment, the *original position*, in which the architects of a society each are told that they should advocate the well-being of a particular individual without knowing that person's social or demographic particulars. It follows from this that the architects, working rationally, should make sure that any inequality in the system must ultimately benefit the least-advantaged. This difference principle reflects the essence of benevolence and universalism combined.

Psychologists have shown that not just philosophers, but adults and children, hold single-concern morality to be prescriptively *universalistic*; that is, they think that norms of fair treatment and kindness should apply to all people, regardless of culture (e.g., Wainryb, 1993). But this moral realm also seems to be actually, descriptively *universal*, in the sense that it guides conduct around the world. For example, Vauclair and Fischer (2011) analysed a worldwide survey of values and moral judgments, and found that judgments of dishonest or illegal behaviours were universally negative, with only a small amount of variance explained by the respondent's country and cultural characteristics. A systematic review of moral-developmental studies by Gibbs, Basinger, Grime, and Snarey (2007) likewise concluded that basic moral values such as life, property rights, and truth-telling are universal. It has also been argued from an evolutionary point of view that moral imperatives toward cooperation and avoidance of harm-doing are biologically ingrained in our species as an aid to its survival (e.g., Hauser, 2006).

The single-concern view of morality fits neatly with the kind of liberal-egalitarian Western worldview prevalent in the academic world. But you don't have to travel far to find a conservative religious person who strongly believes that sex between two men is by definition morally wrong—even if it harms nobody, and is safe, sane, fair, consensual, and private, therefore violating nobody's rights. You might also run into an economically minded conservative who believes it's immoral to live off other people's money in the form of government grants, or the conservative's patriotic buddy, who believes it's morally wrong to disrespect the nation's troops by protesting the war they are fighting. A political liberal, perhaps, might argue that these people are just using the term "morality" as a fig leaf to cover attitudes that are little more than prejudice, selfishness, and conformity. But a psychologist, whose job is to describe and explain subjective experience, has to admit that each of those conservatives sincerely believes that he or she is defending morality. The task of describing all moralized values, not just the ones we think constitute true morality, leads us to values that are not moralized by everyone. And this brings us to the next approach to morality—one that recognizes multiple concerns as potentially falling within the moral domain.

Multiple-concern morality

Like "morality," the term "moral relativism" is loaded with a fatal ambiguity between its descriptive and prescriptive uses. If you take the descriptive position that different cultures have somewhat different moral rules and concerns, you open yourself up to two unpleasant over-interpretations. Either you are misunderstood as saying that each of those different moral codes is equally valid, and are blasted for implying that no moral beliefs are really valid at all (mostly from the political right); or you are misunderstood as saying that, because moral beliefs are different, your own culture's beliefs are more advanced than those of others, and come under fire for cultural imperialism (mostly from the political left). Richard Shweder (1990) has argued cautiously for a form of relativism that respects the major concerns of world cultures, instead of relegating them to the status of primitive stages of moral thought. In this vein, and speaking purely descriptively, ample research evidence shows the existence of moral concerns beyond the universalistic or benevolent values. What's more, these concerns vary in their level of endorsement and specific contents across the world's cultures.

Shweder and his colleagues have shown that in many cultures, there are two important moral systems, in addition to the universalistic/benevolent "ethics of autonomy" (Shweder, Much, Mahapatra, Park, Brandt, & Rozin, 1997). Moral concerns relating to the social hierarchy of obligation are summed up under the "ethics of community" (see also Miller & Bersoff, 1992), while moral concerns relating to purity and pollution of one's spirit and body fall under the "ethics of divinity." To interpret these labels correctly, the reader needs to understand that they each describe a source of moral obligation. So, the ethics of autonomy don't mean that a person should be selfish; they mean instead that our moral obligations to others are framed as rights and contracts between autonomous individuals. The ethics of community, on the other hand, refers to the framing of moral obligations within social roles—as a family member, denizen of a particular village, older or younger person, or citizen of a particular country. Finally, the ethics of divinity do not presume any metaphysics, but refer to obligations to act in accordance with the laws of the universe—they condemn acts seen as unnatural or inhuman, as well as acts that are unholy or sacrilegious. Research in this tradition, using coding of respondents' moral justifications as well as a scale recently developed by our lab (Guerra & Giner-Sorolla, 2010), finds cultural variation in endorsement of community and divinity; while educated Western liberals care primarily about autonomy, people in non-Western countries such as Brazil or India, as well as more conservative Western populations, care more about community and divinity (Guerra & Giner-Sorolla, 2010; Haidt, Koller, & Dias, 1993; Jensen, 1998; Vasquez, Keltner, Ebenbach, & Banaszynski, 2001).

This scheme has been built on by the more recent moral foundations theory (Graham, Haidt, & Nosek, 2009), which presents both a more complex system of moral concerns and a higher-level organization of them. This theory presents a view of morality divided according to the content of moral principles, rather than the source of moral obligation. However, these principles also correspond to Shweder's moral scheme and also roughly correspond, in my observation, with Schwartz's value scheme. Autonomy is separated out into harm and fairness concerns, which appear conceptually to correspond to Schwartz' benevolence and universalism values respectively. The other three moral foundations in that scheme, corresponding to community and divinity, are called "binding" foundations because they more strongly unite people within a particular social group or religious view. These three principles share characteristics with Schwartz' conservation value cluster, rather than self-transcendence (although it could be argued that they provide an alternate form of self-transcendence). Thus, the ingroup/ loyalty and authority/respect moral foundations conceptually expand the ethics of community into respectively horizontal and vertical obligations, while the moral foundation of purity corresponds to Shweder's divinity ethics. While the exact correspondences have yet to be worked out, the set of "binding" moral concerns has obvious parallels to Schwartz's conservation values including obedience, conformity, and tradition.

Do other values in Schwartz's scheme have the potential to extend the realm of morality beyond the self-transcendent and conservation values expressed in the moral foundations scheme? The other three Schwartz value clusters are openness, hedonism, and self-enhancement. Openness includes stimulation (that is, excitement as a goal in life) but also the more readily moralized value of self-direction—encompassing more specific concepts such as freedom, creativity, and independence.

Now, it is important to distinguish the value of freedom for one's self from related values that depend on honouring the freedom or rights of others. Respecting others' freedom and independence falls, I believe, more accurately under the umbrella of benevolence and universalism. It is less clear whether valuing and affirming one's own freedom of choice can be seen as a moral goal. This position has been most forcefully stated as such by Sartre, through the negative concept of "bad faith" (Sartre, 1965/1938). Briefly stating this moral philosophy: when we act in bad faith, we create excuses for our actions or inactions. Sartre believed that to be truly authentic, humans should act without those excuses. This freedom can be achieved in the realm of morality by constantly questioning received rules, seeing even morality itself as a constant choice.

There are two problems with accepting Sartre's stance as a descriptive moral code alongside the other ethics or moral foundations. First, very few people consciously subscribe to Sartre's philosophy, and even fewer can carry it out. More importantly, though, Sartre's way to authenticity cannot be measured by consistent adherence to any given position or action. A morality of self-determination is by its nature unpredictable and subjective. Perhaps, then, openness values are a means to a flexible variety of moral ends, but not moral ends in themselves. Intuitively, too, personal failure to be open to new experiences doesn't really register as a moral failing. Everyone has the right to be boring, if not to make others' lives boring (which is more of a failure of benevolence than openness). Sacrificing the rights and happiness of others in the name of new experiences, in the manner of *Crime and Punishment's* Raskolnikov (Dostoyevsky, 1866/1945), is not generally regarded as a moral choice.

Let us move to another sector of Schwartz's value scheme that might provide us with an additional moral value—self-enhancement. I have already discussed the possibility that self-enhancement values such as achievement might be moralized by individualist philosophers and cultures. The Protestant work ethic (Weber, 2009/1904), for instance, certainly moralizes the impulse toward achievement, showing it as a sacred calling, associated with religious salvation and indirectly serving other values. However, it is arguably another tenet of the Protestant work ethic that marks it as a moral scheme—its asceticism, or renunciation of pleasure and luxury in order to achieve. Looking at the different quadrants of the values model, in fact, it seems that the least inherently moral of the values cluster around the hedonism group. Seeking pleasure for one's self is a goal that may be powerful, but it's not often set forth as a moral dictate. However, self-control is often formulated as the giving up of pleasurable short-term goals in order to achieve more meaningful long-term or socially beneficial outcomes (Fishbach & Shah, 2006; Giner-Sorolla, 2001). As such, it is often positively associated with morality (Baumeister & Exline, 1999) and some writers have discussed self-control as a form of morality on a par with the others we have discussed (Monin, Pizarro, & Beer, 2007).

Janoff-Bulman and colleagues have recently developed a system that classifies multiple moral goals (Janoff-Bulman, Sheikh, & Hepp, 2009), including some forms of self-enhancement. Moral concerns in this model fall into four categories along two dimensions. One dimension tells whether the concern is to promote something good or prevent something bad. The other tells whether the object of the moral action is one's self or others. Prevention of harm to others and promotion of others' benefit, in line with the self-transcendent values, thus form two types of morality. But the model also includes two self-focused forms of morality that correspond to the moralization of self-control and of self-advancement, respectively. Notably, even in this very inclusive model, hedonism is absent as a moral motive. Indeed, for the term "morality" to be something more than a synonym of "values" there must be some values that are *not* moral in nature. Hedonism and openness seem like good candidates for exclusion from the moral sphere. When they conflict with other values and concerns, the most moral choice is to forgo enjoyment and excitement—to help others, to advance one's self in a more meaningful way, or to fulfil one's duties and obligations.

What is moral?

This trip around the circle of Schwartz's values has provided some answers about which human concerns can reasonably be put forward as moral end-states. Recall that hedonism seems to be the least moral value, while self-transcendent values are named by most people and cultures as a key part of morality. This suggests that the moral axis has to do in some way with concern for others rather than self. The conservation values, in fact, can be seen as ways of encapsulating large-scale concerns for collective rather than individual others—systems of hierarchy and duty. And when actions that benefit the individual are morally praised, it is because they also represent a transcendence of the short-term individual perspective. The "other" you help with an act of personal self-control is yourself in the future. The most comprehensive definition of morality may in fact be more about what is *not* part of morality: only actions that are taken to benefit one's self in the here and now exist completely outside the moral sphere. They are not necessarily immoral, except when they interfere with other, more morally relevant concerns.

This definition recognizes that the view of morality as just "the most important *mores*" is too broad, and also that the single-concern view of morality leaves out many values that traditional and conservative views tend to moralize. The values it excludes as moral concerns are hedonism and pure self-interest. Like the Sartrean morality of freedom, these values have their moralizers and philosophers, but can we really say that ordinary people who follow unrestrained pleasure and power are practising a moral code? A warlord like Genghis Khan or a crime lord like Al Capone can hardly be said to have acted in line with a morality, even a Nietzschean one. Certainly, such people exercised power and personal interest as if it were their supreme virtue, letting nothing within them stand in the way of plunder and profit. Do criminals' actions fail to count as morality only because they made the mistake of not writing a philosophical justification for them? If "morality" is not going to be equated with just any "most important concern," it needs to have a meaning that excludes such selfish interests categorically. Although this might seem unfair to a few iconoclastic thinkers, it is necessary to avoid a tautology of "morality" and "value."

This definition also fits the functional view of moral emotions from which I will build a theory of emotions in the next chapter. The economist Robert Frank (1988) argues that the irrational and uncontrollable influence of emotion in the short term is actually beneficial in the long term, because it helps the individual make choices more suited to long-term development and social cooperation, and provides earnest signals of these noble intents to others. Being unable to control or fake emotions such as guilt, sympathy, and affection is vital; otherwise we would turn them off at will when we saw an opportunity for short-term profit at the expense of our future or our relationships. On the other hand, pleasure and profit do not need a moral system to impel us to follow them. They contain their own reward systems.

To sum up, I define morality as a concern that is (a) normatively placed above most other concerns and (b) takes as a goal something other than one's own immediate material or sensual self-interest. This view fits well with empirical studies of the contribution of morality to social and group-related attitudes. These find that the involvement of morality in an issue increases the importance, strength, and defensiveness of related attitudes (Skitka & Houston, 2001); that moral concerns are not easily bought off with material compensation (Tetlock, 2003); and that moral traits such as honesty predominate in forming and maintaining beliefs about a group (Leach et al., 2007). This view is also compatible with the moral synthesis proposed by Haidt (2007), in which some moral values such as fairness and care for others can be found universally, while others, such as obedience to family authority or sexual chastity, vary across cultures. Vauclair and Fischer (2011) have supported this view, finding evidence of universality of moral attitudes toward cheating and lawbreaking, but much greater cultural variation in attitudes toward sexual morality. However, neither this research nor Haidt's has dealt with the possibility that self-enhancement values with a long-term payoff—hard work, self-control—might also form part of the moral sphere in some cultures.

Before closing, there is another distinction that can help lead us out of the subjective, Nazi-infested moral swamp with which I started this chapter: the contrast between universal true morality and parochial moralization (e.g. Baron, 2003). A belief based on morality must be upheld equally for everyone. Moralization, though, is a defensive use of morality. It is concerned with arguing, parochially, that one's self, ideas, or allies are morally good and that one's enemies are morally bad. True morality is more interested in drawing universal commonalities among moral agents and objects. In a recent study, for example, political liberals in the US responded to terrorist attacks with universalist moral responses such as perspective taking and greater concern for other nations, while political conservatives responded with strongly moralized group-protective responses such as revenge-taking and calls for increased loyalty (Janoff-Bulman & Sheikh, 2006). Moralization calls upon the importance and inflexibility of moral values, but applies them in a parochial way, taking for granted that "we" are good and "they" are evil.

It is tempting, but wrong, to conclude that morality focuses on the self-transcending values such as fairness and justice, while moralization is rooted in the conservation values, such as loyalty and security. Conservation values need not be limited to mere moralization; they can be universalized as general principles. For example, an American with a strong patriotic morality might still believe it is a moral duty for citizens of other countries to have patriotic feelings toward their country. An ecumenically minded Catholic with strong respect for the Pope can also believe it is moral for adherents of other religions to respect their own religious leaders. And standards of sexual morality that Western university students see as only conventional are seen, in other cultures and social strata, as moral issues (Haidt et al., 1993). Conversely, even values that Schwartz puts into the "universalism" cluster, like fairness and honesty, can be moralized when we apply double standards to other people or groups that we don't apply to ourselves. While the number of people embracing universal patriotism may be few, it is far from clear that any greater number of people truly follow the values of universal fairness or freedom from harm, as we can see from the literature on group bias in morality (chapter 3).

True morality is a very exacting standard to meet. Almost none of us are capable of putting it perfectly into practice, bearing the weight of the world's suffering as if it was that of our neighbour. However, as an ideal, the universal application of a moral law can help us distinguish the Nazis' propagandistic abuse of moral feelings from the true morality that would allow us to righteously condemn their deeds. Schadewaldt's Nazi case for Polish atrocities, in fact, shows no sign of drawing a universal moral lesson from them—honestly, how could it, when the SS was already carrying out much, much worse things in 1941? Its argument ends up attributing the violence to the inferior nature of the Pole, parochial to the end. Jonathan Littell's sprawling and grotesque novel of the Holocaust, *The Kindly Ones* (2009), makes a point about parochial moralization in a noteworthy scene. A dinner-party conversation among Adolf Eichmann and other philosophically minded SS officers raises the difficult point of how their atrocities can be squared with the imperatives of Kant's ethics. In the end, they have to destroy Kant with parochial restrictions in order to save him; Kant's universal imperatives don't apply during wartime, they apply only to the German people, are automatically fulfilled by the will of the Führer, and so on, descending to *ad hominem*—" 'Excuse me,' one of the guests said, 'but wasn't Kant an anti-Semite?' " (p. 567). These evasive self-indulgences of wicked men show Kant's universalistic moral philosophy, and more generally the morality–moralization distinction, to be a powerful compass with which to judge moral feelings as worthy or misguided. All the same, the principles of moral emotions outlined in the rest of this book operate in the same way for the righteous and the damned alike. We must look elsewhere for tools to distinguish the two. The truth is that both myself and a Nazi can feel anger, pride, disgust, or shame, and this is nothing more than part of our common humanity.

Overview

In the remainder of this book, I will first outline a functional conflict theory of moral emotions, which I have briefly described in chapter 2. I will use the analyses of morality and emotions from the first two chapters as a framework to consider three intersections among the concepts at play in this book: emotions as a component of morality; emotions as they relate to groups; and morality as it relates to groups (chapter 3). The next three chapters deal with comparisons and contrasts involving similar clusters of moral emotions, reviewing the literature on these emotions using the structure of the four functions and their potential conflicts. Chapter 4 contrasts the other-condemning emotions of anger and disgust with each other. Chapter 5 treats the self-condemning emotions of shame and guilt in a similar way. After so much negativity, chapter 6 deals with three sets of emotions linked to moral positivity—although the watchword of all three chapters is that each emotion is both good and potentially bad, involving a healthy functionality as well as potential pitfalls. Finally, chapter 7 is built around two topics of research interest to my lab and collaborators in recent years, in which moral emotions play a critical part—the judgment of sexual behaviour, and the effectiveness of apologetic statements made between groups.

2 Emotion: A functional conflict theory

This chapter presents a theory of emotion that integrates four major views of how emotion works and what it is for. My position is that emotion has come to fulfil four major functions for the human mind in society, but in the process of doing so, the different functions can interfere with each other at times. Specifically, functions that:

- demand flexibility in emotional response can conflict with functions that demand rigidity in emotional response;
- help the individual assert his or her interests can conflict with functions that help maintain the larger social context;
- respond in harmony with the world as it exists can conflict with functions that kick against the world as it exists in order to defend valued ideas or bring the self closer to a desired goal.

Here, I will outline the general question of whether emotions are functional or dysfunctional, before showing in detail, through each of the four functions and their conflicts, how emotions' multiple functions can lead to dysfunction.

Emotions and their function

A perennial question in philosophy has been whether emotions are a good thing or a bad thing for us (Solomon, 1993). How should we feel about feelings? Some philosophical writers, like the Stoics, Socratics, and Buddhist scholars, traced human misery or vice to emotion, teaching mastery over emotions. Others, most notably David Hume and Adam Smith, saw emotions as necessary to the highest goals of morality. These eighteenth-century scholars proposed philosophies of moral sentiments that are highly influential in psychology today. A middle ground, exemplified by Aristotle and Descartes, recognizes that passions are sometimes used well, but sometimes used poorly, so that moderation and discernment are required when dealing with the emotions.

Psychology, of course, has the long shadow of Freud over its early history. His well-known view was that emotions often reveal conflicts within a person. Suppressed ideas can lead to inexplicable, displaced emotional outbursts. Affects arise in the deep needs and unrealistic wishes of the organism, the id. Infantile rage, frustration, and desire must be channelled and transformed into more accept-able motivations through the secondary process, with repression and other defence mechanisms arising as responses to this conflict. At first glance this system of conflict looks dysfunctional. But evolutionary interpretations of psychoanalytic theory (e.g., Slavin & Kriegman, 1992) argue that it ultimately reflects the biolog-ical reality of conflicts at the genetic level: between the individual's drives for self-preservation and the social demands of family and society, with which the individual shares some amount of genetic material.

Even if we didn't have an intrinsic functional conflict between serving ourselves and others, the ideal of the perfectly adapted organism would still be a myth, better suited to a creationist theory than to the random, clumsy work of evolution (Gould, 1992). In natural history, we see numerous structures that are less than perfect because they have been *exapted*, to use Stephen Jay Gould's coinage (1991), from another structure with a different function; Gould's well-known example is the panda's thumb, a crude but useful grasping digit that developed from one of its wrist bones. Cultural evolution shares a common process with biological evolution (Dennett, 1996) but is often overlooked by evolutionary psychologists. Here, too, there is no shortage of cultural beliefs and practices that are counterproductive. For example, the QWERTY keyboard was originally developed to slow down the operation of jamming-prone mechanical typewriters by placing frequent letters in inconvenient places. On a digital keyboard or even a well-made typewriter, this arrangement becomes an inconvenience, but one that has persisted over more rational alternatives well into the digital age (Gould, 1987). Cultural dysfunction happens even though we can reflect on culture and change it in a way we can never do with our biological selves. Altogether, it may be too much to expect our feelings to be perfectly adapted to whatever situation confronts us.

This ambiguity in emotions is recognized by most major theories of emotion in psychology: while basically functional, they can lead a person to irrational action. Some, such as appraisal theories, principally blame improper cognitive inputs for faulty operations (e.g., Lazarus, 1991). Others blame the structure of emotion itself as a contributor to dysfunctional effects (e.g., Baumeister, Vohs, DeWall, & Zhang, 2007; Slavin & Kriegman, 1992). However, it is the socio-functional theory of Keltner and Haidt (1999) that gives the best clue to the paradox of emotion. They treat emotions as exapted psychological processes that serve a number of functions, derived from an original reflex or motivation in the species. These have their roots in biological evolution, but also exist in forms that respond to features that are clearly socio-cultural in nature. As a detailed example, Keltner and Haidt (1999) outline the many adaptations of disgust. This emotion initially originated as a motive to expel unhealthy substances from the mouth. It then was extended to any kind of contact with a potentially disease-bearing thing, functioning as an implicit germ theory. A kind of existential disgust at the fallibility of bodies, even one's own, comes next, presumably as a by-product of self-awareness and the existential conflicts mentioned above. Finally, disgust is recruited as a moral emotion that motivates chastisement of people who violate sacred norms, and as a social emotion that labels people as repellent pariahs.

One by-product of this multiple functionality, I believe, is that emotions are almost guaranteed to go wrong sometimes. The flying squirrel can navigate both the tree and the air, its legs connected and restrained by membranes that serve as makeshift wings. However, it does neither job particularly well. Bad information can certainly lead to bad emotions. But often that bad information is generated in the course of fulfilling the other, unrelated functions of the emotion. For example, if another person violates conventional norms through no fault of his or her own—unknowingly having sex with an underage person, perhaps—this triggers moral disgust. Yet the disease-protection functions of disgust generate information that the person is contagious and to be shunned, things that don't sit well with the way we think justice ought to work. In another example, shame lets us give sincere signals that we are not worthy, appeasing a social superior. But in order to be convincing, we have to believe our own self-deprecation to some degree, and the resulting damage to self-esteem can harm us in other situations. Throughout the rest of this book, and in particular in chapters 4 to 6, I will trace out these tragedies of function for each of the major moral emotions: anger, disgust, shame, guilt, and a variety of positive emotions.

Tragedies of function are well known in various psychodynamic theories of psychology. I have already briefly described the internal conflicts proposed by evolutionary interpretations of psychoanalytic theory (Slavin & Kriegman, 1992). Another idea, better known to social psychologists through terror management theory, states that the supreme psychological conflict is found between self-awareness and the instinct to live (Becker, 1973; Pyszczynski, Greenberg, & Solomon, 1999). Self-awareness is functional: it lets us plan for the future and abandon pursuits that we see to be futile. But once we realize that our most basic instinct of self-preservation is doomed to fail eventually, a fundamental existential conflict arises, one that most people solve by ignoring the apparent facts of existence most of the time. Many of the well-known defects of emotion, I believe, are conflicts of this kind—clashes between different systems that draw on emotional force and feelings.

In the previous chapter I confessed my particular interest in those emotions that seem to be instigated by a number of different kinds of stimuli and thoughts. Perhaps not by coincidence, many of these emotions relate to morality: anger, disgust, sympathy, admiration, guilt, and shame. Moral emotions are particularly complex because they are based on emotions that have been adapted to serve a number of different functions for humans over time. Keltner and Haidt (1999) identify four levels of functionality for emotion: to help the individual (individual level), manage social relationships with other individuals (dyadic level), help the individual get by in social groups (group level), and support a culture's adaptive practices (cultural level).

My functional conflict theory also classifies the conflicting functions of emotion, but using a different scheme, one that integrates insights into emotions' function from a number of influential theories. I see emotions as serving four main kinds of function:

1   They are part of a system of motivated *appraisal* of the current environment, leading to appropriate action tendencies.
2   They are an *associative learning* system, more simple and rigid than other types of learning, that forms emotionally based attitudes by associating pleasurable or painful emotions with an object.
3   They are also a *self-regulation* system that responds to feedback about one's own actions.
4   Finally, they are a *social communication* system that provides output and cues to others.

These four functions are common to most kinds of emotions, though not all emotions serve all four of them; for example, as we will see in chapter 4, there is little evidence that disgust works by appraisal. Also, while some correspondence exists between functional conflict theory's functions and socio-functional theory's four levels of adaptation, this correspondence is not exact. For example, associative learning can serve the needs of the individual, but it is also involved in maintaining group and cultural bonds; the communicative system can work within a dyad, a group, or an entire culture.

As outlined in chapter 1, there are multiple systems that make up emotions, and each contributes to at least three of the four functions. Starting with core affect, physiological indicators of arousal and valence form a subjective experience that indicates the self-relevance and valence of the emotion, with important implications for appraisal, regulation, and learning. Facial expressions, posture, and other muscular embodiments of emotion are primarily communicative, but also provide feedback that further reinforces the subjective experience (for a review, see McIntosh, 1996). Cultural scripts and emotion concepts serve social communication, but likewise help the individual organize the world for appraisal and self-regulation. Finally, emotion language lets people communicate emotion to others, and talk to themselves about their own appraisals and regulatory goals. As with the four organizational levels of socio-cultural theory, functional conflict theory's four functions each are expressed through multiple physical or psychological phenomena, each of which serves the function in its own way.

Theories that don't consider all four functions of emotion will encounter problems and inconsistencies. Often, a theory that presents a quite complex view of emotion will still miss out on some of these functions. For example, Leventhal and Tomarken (1986) argue that emotions exist as primitive affect, more elaborated concepts, and fully elaborated language. Apart from being more of a descriptive than a functional model, this view focuses on the appraisal and learning functions rather than regulation or communication. Likewise, the Keltner and Haidt (1999) sociofunctional theory focuses mainly on the role of emotions in preparing the correct responses to a number of threats and opportunities that are relevant to the individual and the social group. Although these responses can involve communication, the internal functions of associative learning and self-regulation are not differentiated from the others. In my view, each of functional conflict theory's functions is worthy of consideration in its own right; only by differentiating them can we gain a systematic view of the ways they conflict with each other within the profile of the specific emotions I will consider later on.

The appraisal function: Acting on situational goals

The idea that emotions and feelings depend on our cognitive appraisals of the environment is an old one. The Stoic philosophers embraced it in their desire to control the emotions, urging their followers to curtail the thoughts that led to extreme emotions. This idea explains at once why people have different emotional reactions to the same event, and why some emotional reactions seem to be more appropriate than others. Starting from the observations of Magda Arnold (1960), and the initial work of Lazarus and colleagues on the appraisal of coping potential in emotional reactions to stress (Lazarus & Folkman, 1984), appraisal theories of emotion have multiplied (Ortony et al., 1990; Roseman, 1984; Scherer, Shorr, & Johnstone, 2001; Smith & Ellsworth, 1985). There are differences in emphasis among these models, in the exact appraisals that are considered important, and in the mapping of those appraisals to emotions. But the basic claim of all appraisal theories is that specific emotions rest upon specific interpretations of a person's surroundings. An appraisal theorist might argue, for instance, that fear comes from an appraisal of the core theme of danger while anger comes from the core theme of injustice. One person, reacting to news of a terrorist attack, might think only of the danger to his or her own person and thus react with fear. Another might dwell on the malicious unfairness of the terrorists, and react with anger.

Appraisal theorists have continually been challenged by the view that cognition is not necessary for emotion, and by examples of emotional processes that seem to arise without cognitive input, or that do not seem to respond to any one appraisal (e.g., Kuppens et al., 2003; Parkinson, 1997; Zajonc, 1980). Indeed, many common-sense examples—the fear felt in situations of great danger, for example—leave no time for a deliberate formation of emotion. In response, appraisal theorists have emphasized that appraisals can themselves be fast and unconscious, getting there in time to account for the rapid appearance of emotional feelings (Lazarus, 1984; Moors & De Houwer, 2001). They point out that from the very beginning, appraisals were thought of as potentially automatic (Arnold, 1960). However, another important feature of cognitive appraisals is that they can be formed and changed through slower and more conscious thought, a key element of Lazarus and Folkman's (1988) studies of appraisals in coping with stress. One way people cope with unpleasant emotions—shades of the Stoics!—is reappraisal of the situation. Maybe it's not so bad after all; maybe he isn't really to blame. Thus, more recently developments in appraisal theory acknowledge that appraisals can be fast and automatic as well as slow and deliberative (Scherer et al., 2001).

The functional completion of the appraisal story can be found in the concept of emotional action tendencies (Frijda, 1986). These are motivational consequences of emotional states that prepare a person to act in a certain way. Thus, love leads to benevolent approach, anger to hostile attack or censure, fear and disgust to withdrawal, guilt to reparations and apologies for the wronged party. It is important to note that action tendencies are only tendencies; humans can strategically inhibit or change the actions that their emotions lead them toward. But I see action tendencies as critical to the larger appraisal function of emotions, because all this processing of goal-relevant input from the environment should guide actual progress toward those goals. We see a threatening silhouette, automatically think of danger, feel fear, and instantly feel the desire to flee. We may reappraise the silhouette as a traffic sign, reducing the fear and stopping our feet. Or, we may instead see it as a bear, and give rein to our action tendencies, running away. Or, we may further note that it is the back rather than the front of the bear, and strategically change our action tendency, choosing to duck down and be quiet instead of running away.

Numerous studies have linked distinct appraisals to reports of distinct emotional feelings. This goes both ways—that is, asking about appraisals and eliciting emotions (Ellsworth & Smith, 1988), or asking about emotions and eliciting characteristic appraisals (Roseman, Spindel, & Jose, 1990; Smith & Ellsworth, 1985). Appraisals have also been manipulated and shown to have a causal influence on emotions (Roseman & Evdokas, 2004). Although appraisal theory is robust and well-established, it has attracted criticism for its claim to phenomena. I believe these criticisms are valid in light of the fact that emotions and emotional phenomena have other functions apart from responding to appraisals. If they are to be a comprehensive explanation of emotions, appraisal theories run the risk of losing what is distinctive and important about the appraisal function.

Challenges to appraisal as a comprehensive theory of emotion

Predominant in recent developments of appraisal theory is Scherer's component process model (2001), which presents an appraisal model of emotion so comprehensive as to cover almost all possible input into the human mind. In a rapidly activated time sequence, early appraisals assess such things as the novelty of a stimulus, and its intrinsic pleasantness or unpleasantness. Later appraisals assess things such as how relevant the stimulus is to our goals, how much it supports or blocks them, and other things like certainty and our ability to cope. While these later appraisals are more cognitively complex, the appraisal of intrinsic pleasantness, for example, doesn't seem to involve much cognitive content. What is pleasant? That which pleases us; or, that which makes us have positive feelings. The unpleasant, likewise, is that which makes us feel bad. There is no cognitive meaning, apart from the feeling itself, that will let us identify an intrinsically pleasant appraisal. Although this kind of connection has been called a "non-constructive appraisal" (Moors, 2010), if that is so, it's hard to see what kind of possible input that had an effect on the system could *not* count as an appraisal. A theory of appraisal that covers all input, while comprehensive, also risks losing any specific or useful meaning of the term "appraisal."

I think that earlier formulations of appraisal theory (e.g., Lazarus, 1991) were on firmer ground when they proposed the support or hindrance of a goal as the primary appraisal separating pleasant from unpleasant emotions. That judgment at least puts a cognition—goal conduciveness—between the stimulus and the feeling. Recent research also shows that current goals can modify evaluation of stimuli and situations automatically (Ferguson & Bargh, 2004; Moors, 2010), so that even quickly arising emotion can be traced back to appraisals that depend on goal conduciveness. But for me, there are profound differences between evocation of feelings through a novel, goal-directed appraisal, and the activation of simple, learned associations.

The elicitors of disgust, in fact, are notoriously problematic for appraisal theory. Although I will discuss this problem in more detail in chapter 4, disgust seems to depend principally on learned associations rather than a necessary cognitive concept. So, while cheating may be disgusting, this association comes about because we hear people using metaphorical language like "slimy," "dirty," and "disgusting" in relation to cheaters, not because we hear people saying that cheaters are "unfair" or "harmful" in a literal sense. Disgust, then, is a good candidate for an emotion that comes about mostly through concrete associations rather than conceptual propositions. It is in fact this concreteness of disgust that has prompted arguments against disgust's status as an emotion (Panksepp, 2007). In this view, disgust is too strongly connected to its sensory input, and too little connected to current self-relevant concerns, to count as an emotion in the same class as, for example, rage or fear. I don't agree with this extreme position; disgust can be treated as an emotion, because it is not inextricably sensory, can be learned from others through their expressive cues (everyone in the room wrinkling their noses when a social pariah walks in), and can be trained to respond to non-sensory concepts such as incest. But it is not far from Panksepp's observations to point out that disgust has very concrete mental representations and antecedents.

However, let's accept for a moment the classification of non-constructive processes as appraisals. What possible challenges to appraisal theory would remain? For one, emotions can be generated by internal biological processes, through the feedback effects of grimacing facial muscles (Strack, Martin, & Stepper, 1988), or through unusual methods like hypnosis (Wheatley & Haidt, 2005). While all of these things have been demonstrated experimentally, it is unlikely that in the real world they play a large part in the generation of emotion. It's also unlikely that facial feedback is a strong cause of emotions in most situations in life (McIntosh, 1996), though it might reinforce emotions that are being felt, in line with research showing that paralysing the facial muscles reduces the intensity of felt emotions (Davis, Senghas, Brandt, & Ochsner, 2010).

It's also possible that some emotional processes can be activated not by appraisals, but by signs: through the mere effects of hearing emotionally laden words in language, or through the example of other people's expressive behaviour. This kind of input would bypass cognitive judgments and can be thought of as a direct contagion of the emotion. Indeed, there is evidence both for the priming of specific emotion concepts (Hansen & Shantz, 1995) and the social contagion and mirroring of emotional expressions (Hatfield, Cacioppo, & Rapson, 1993). Some experiments have gone further and shown that emotion-specific priming by means of emotion words can be unconscious (Zemack-Rugar, Bettman, & Fitzsimons, 2007). These kinds of experiments are a problem for appraisal theory, because the appraisals that lead to a certain emotion are not contained within the mere words or facial expressions that refer to that emotion. Although it could be argued that these cues to emotion create appraisals, which then go on to influence emotional states, such an interpretation lacks parsimony.

Perhaps cues such as internal physiological feelings, emotion words and facial expressions, too, can be labelled as "non-constructive appraisals"—but if so, this term comes even closer to explaining everything and nothing. The input is not any cognitive concept that can be distinguished from the emotion, not even a general "good or bad" evaluation that can be distinguished from the specific emotion, but a concept or sign that denotes the specific emotion itself. This better fits a view of emotions as associative schemas consisting of subjective feelings, labels, and associated concepts, the whole of which can be activated by the activation of any part (Izard, 2007). Conceivably, it is possible to extend the term "appraisal" to the perception of any part of this schema, and say that one "appraises" one's own visceral rumblings, blood pressure changes, the facial expressions of others, and so on. But terms in science are not necessarily more useful the more things they cover.

A question of greater interest is what each possible cause of emotion contributes functionally. Constructive appraisals are able to extract fairly abstract meanings ("danger") from a new object or from a changing environment, process that meaning in light of current or chronic goals ("avoid harm"), and provide an affective response ("fear") that guides and motivates behavioural tendencies ("run away"). They are responsible for reappraisal and cognitively driven control of emotions. Non-constructive "appraisals," that is to say the activation of simple associations, are not so flexible. They serve a different purpose, working in an associative learning system that backs up inflexible lessons with the force of hot, visceral emotions, creating stable emotional attitudes. We will visit this functional system in the next section of this chapter.

There is one remaining limitation of appraisal theories, which is not a problem with the idea that cognitions can call emotions into being, but with the *schemes* of mapping between emotions and appraisals that each appraisal theory has proposed. The various individual appraisal theories don't just claim that cognitions produce emotions. Most of them have offered a scheme in which each emotion is created by a specific set of appraisals. A view of emotion as produced by just one set of appraisals, however, does not square with the evidence, at least when it comes to most of the potentially moral emotions that are the focus of this book. By contrast, a multi-functional view of appraisal is able to solve these problems. Multiple appraisals each can lead to the same emotion, each one representing a separate adaptation of that emotion to confront a biological or social problem.

No two appraisal schemes in the literature are exactly the same, but each one independently finds support for its predictions. However, a number of studies integrating a number of possible appraisals have shown that some basic emotions share no single consistent appraisal. For example, studies by Peter Kuppens and colleagues (e.g., Kuppens et al., 2003) have asked people about what makes them feel angry, and manipulated the presence of various appraisal components. This research has unearthed a large range of possible triggers for anger: for example, obstruction of goals, injustice and unfairness, hostile others. No single one of these seems to be necessary for anger; rather, different people show different patterns of preferred appraisals, some becoming righteously angry at injustice, others selfishly angry at things that threaten them. Cottrell and Neuberg (2005), also, find that multiple kinds of threat predict single emotions in the context of intergroup attitudes; notably, each kind of threat they studied, from physical danger to menaced social values, had something to do with anger.

We can add to this list of appraisals the possibility, discussed by Berkowitz and Harmon-Jones (2004), that even physical irritants such as pain can fuel a primitive form of anger. Parkinson (1999) has also found evidence against single appraisals; asking people why they felt anger and guilt, he stipulated that the instance recalled be either reasonable or unreasonable. The appraisals associated with "reasonable" emotions were quite different from those associated with "unreasonable" ones. Finally, accounts of disgust also call attention to the large number of conceptual stimuli that can evoke this emotion, from the purely sensory, to the existential worries about our own bodies, to moral condemnation of a variety of transgressions (Rozin, Haidt, & McCauley, 1999a; Tybur, Lieberman, & Griskevicius, 2009).

It is not a coincidence, I think, that many of the doubts raised about single-appraisal schemes focus on potentially moral emotions with basic roots: anger, disgust, guilt, shame. These are in fact the kind of emotions that are most likely to show multiple distinct functions. Fear, for instance, distinguished from anxiety, is straightforwardly a response to something threatening, and increases to the extent that we doubt our own ability to deal with it well. So even in a social, intergroup context, fear responds fairly clearly to the threat of physical violence posed by a social group (Cottrell & Neuberg, 2005), increasing to the extent that we see ourselves or our group to be directly threatened (Dumont, Yzerbyt, Wigboldus, & Gordijn, 2003). Other more cognitively distinct emotions, such as gratitude, are specific to the extent that they clearly only have one function and one appraisal. But with the possible exception of guilt, the multi-functional moral emotions involve more primitive reactions as well as complex adaptations relying on more sophisticated cognitive appraisals. The details of these schemes will be worked out more fully in later chapters of this book. For now, if we accept the idea of multiple appraisals for the same emotion, then an important feature of emotions emerges: emotions activated by one appraisal (such as anger from personal frustration) can influence the thoughts and actions taken in another (such as moral outrage at the leaders of another country).

To sum up: If emotions were a system that only allowed us to respond to our environment according to what we believed to be true, we would never experience interference from our own feelings. We might have conflict, but it would only be the conflict of two goals, ultimately quenched in a decision about which one is more important. We might behave irrationally, but it would only be because our facts were wrong. This hypothetical person whose emotions only serve the appraisal function is perhaps a Stoic ideal, but is far from reality. People often feel emotions as an intrusion on their dominant goals and reasonable thoughts. This conflict is fundamental to the nature of emotion, and it happens because emotions serve other functions than our current personal goals. They are influenced by learning in the past; by the success or failure of our own actions; and by the need to make a compelling communication to other people.

The associative learning function: Emotional attitudes

Imagine that you learn the following facts. An accountant named Basil Glepz received a large sum of money up front from a small family business for catching up on their accounts. Basil then walked out from his contract, took the money and went to Fiji, never coming back.

At first, this story takes some amount of processing. We figure out who promised what to whom, whether the promise was kept, where the money went, and where Basil went. Our building up of the hero and villain of the story happens fairly quickly, an example perhaps of the speed that even constructive appraisals can show. At the end, we can sum up the story to a friend with a simple, evaluatively loaded term: "Basil Glepz is a rat" (or worse). This process is entirely constructive. There is not a single word in the story that can transmit the negative connotations of "rat." And yet out of the dry words we build a web of appraisals that lets us come up with a very negative emotional attitude. Attitude has been defined as a persistent evaluation of an object (Eagly & Chaiken, 1993). In this case, the evaluation is implicit in the hostile emotion of anger, and its object is Basil Glepz.

Attitudes, however, exist on more than one level; while we may build them constructively, we also use pre-existing associations in a less rational way. This point is made by research on paradoxical phrases: we might think "casual" is a good thing to be, and so is a "surgeon," but a "casual surgeon" invites doubts rather than doubled approval. Likewise, we may hate a "roach" and think a "killer" is a bad thing, but see a can of "roach killer" as good and useful. However, even in these simple examples, the original meaning of each individual word persists in our mind on some level. This was shown in an experiment on very fast processing of value conducted by Greenwald (1992). The experiment tested implicit understanding of the phrases' value, flashing them at speeds too fast to consciously detect and seeing whether they were more likely to speed up responses to subsequently presented words with a positive or negative meaning. In fact, primed compound phrases like "casual surgeon" tended to speed up positive words and slow down negative words, while phrases like "roach killer" had the opposite effect.

Another experiment (Deutsch, Gawronski, & Strack, 2006) found similar effects with negation phrases, originally in German, such as "not clever"; when presented subliminally, the meaning of "clever" registered and sped up positive words, and the "not" was ignored. The only negative phrases that registered anything like a negative meaning were very familiar ones in German; perhaps in English, "not guilty" would come out as positive rather than negative, because we are so used to hearing it as a reprieve in courtroom dramas and reporting. Our first, automatic take on the goodness or badness of words, then, only relies on their stored meaning.

These experiments reveal basic evaluations that fall a long way from a full-fledged, specific emotion like fear, happiness, or anger. A recent model of evaluation identifies them as part of an associative process, as opposed to a propositional process that is more regulated by logical consistency and other language-like concerns (Gawronski & Bodenhausen, 2006). As we have seen, they may form part of the initial "non-constructive" assessment of an object. Even though they are less than emotions, quick evaluations like this serve to orient people to what is good or bad in the environment (Fazio, 1986), even without thinking them through or being aware of why we feel that way. We just know we love strawberries; we don't like snakes; that man over there gives me a creepy feeling but I can't say what it is. These are simple, merely positive or negative feelings linked to an object. There are no reasons, no intervening concepts, and we don't need to know where we picked up this association between the thing and the feeling. The man who gives you a creepy feeling? It could be because you saw a news report last night of the escaped criminal Basil Glepz, and that's the man. Or, you saw that news report, and the man just looks like him, enough to stir the creepy feelings (Andersen & Glassman, 1996).

Even though appraisal theorists may include them in the same system, these simple associations are functionally different from more complex appraisals. They are more fallible, more primitive, less flexible, and yet more immediate. Appraisals, as I define them, depend on a goal you have activated. Associations don't have to depend on a goal, and sometimes that's good. Imagine all the avoidance goals you would have to have at this moment if only goal relevance explained feelings. It would be less than parsimonious to maintain that we can simultaneously hold the active goals to avoid pigeon droppings, poisonous snakes, angry bears, outrageous political opinions, and everything else we evaluate negatively. And yet each of these things, when we see it, activates a strong negative feeling and a related urge to get away. These kinds of evaluations are good to deal with things that we don't encounter often, but almost always end up bad for us when we do. Also, we can think of things that have supplied our needs so often that a permanent halo of good feelings surrounds them—kittens, perhaps, computer games, or sex. Some of these, like the first or the last, may in fact be biologically primed preferences. Kittens are cute, because they share traits with human babies, which we need to protect. Sex is fun—where do you get the babies from in the first place?

These stored evaluations, or *attitudes* (Eagly & Chaiken, 1993; Fazio, 2007), are focused on an object rather than a situation or a meaning. Although they can be created and changed by fairly complex processes of reasoning, they can also be created irrationally (Nisbett & Wilson, 1977). Merely being exposed repeatedly to a neutral object can create a liking for it, a process that can happen even when the object is presented subliminally (Zajonc, 1968) and exploited by marketing pros who seek the maximum exposure for their product. Research on learning by classical conditioning shows that becoming aware that a neutral object is repeatedly paired with a strong evaluative stimulus—pictures of cute puppies, for example—leads to the improved evaluation of that object (Olson & Fazio, 2001; Staats & Staats, 1958). The new thing becomes a cue for good feelings—warmth by association, if you will. This trick is known to advertisers. Drinking a cola beverage doesn't usually lead to euphoric laughter (especially after they took the cocaine out in 1903), but see enough commercials where the two appear together, and you might start having warm feelings toward the stuff.

Specific emotions can also be associated with objects. These *emotional attitudes* combine evaluations with representations of the emotion category. Although they have often been called "affective attitudes" or "the affective component of attitude" by researchers (e.g., Crites, Fabrigar, & Petty, 1994; Esses, Haddock, & Zanna, 1993; Zanna & Rempel, 1988), my term avoids a confusing use of the term "affect," which can refer to general good or bad feelings as well as specific emotions (cf. Giner-Sorolla, 1999). In an emotional attitude, if Basil Glepz has harmed people important to me, I may develop not just a dislike for him, but his very name may set off a rage in me, with an angry grimace and a feeling of hotness in the face, perhaps even thoughts of his unfair and threatening nature. Given a certain combination of predisposition and experience, I may associate an overwhelming blend of fear and disgust with spiders. And when I hear my country's national anthem, a certain pre-rational patriotism might swell in me, and I feel pride. It's not because I've appraised the song as conducive to my goals. Rather, the song feels right; it's associated with the very foundation of my identity, and makes me feel true and real, beyond any utilitarian concern.

Emotional attitudes can take the form of statements like "Statistics exams make me feel terrified" or "Chocolate torte makes me feel happy." They can be contrasted with cognitive attitudes that have a more instrumental, goal-relevant feel: "Statistics exams are useful for me" or "Chocolate torte is unhealthy." Some objects have a mainly emotional basis of evaluation, and some a mainly cognitive basis. In the above example, a person with those conflicting attitudes toward statistics class, but who liked statistics overall, would have a cognitively based attitude centred on the usefulness of the subject. However, someone who had the same conflict between fear and usefulness, but had an overall negative view of statistics class, would have succumbed to terror and embraced an emotionally based attitude. Functions of attitudes such as persuasion, or the speed of accessing relevant statements, are most effective when the information at hand matches the emotional or cognitive basis of one's attitude (Fabrigar & Petty, 1999; Giner-Sorolla, 2004). But emotional attitudes, across a broad survey of relevant studies, seem to have the upper hand over cognitive ones when it comes to predicting intentions to behave and actual behaviour (Lavine, Thomsen, Zanna, & Borgida, 1998). This should not be surprising given emotion's close connection to motivation.

The appraisal function of emotion, as we have seen, presumes a certain order of events in an emotional episode. First, you become aware of an object, or a setting, or an object in a setting. You extract meaning from that thing, beyond just its identity, something that refers to a property that is relevant to your current motivational goal. And on the basis of that process, which can still be very fast, an emotion springs up, providing a recipe for action. Figure 2.1 illustrates this sequence.

But with an associative emotional attitude, this sequence is out of order. The emotion is something that you begin to feel whenever you think of an object; love if you think of your beloved, anger if you think of Basil Glepz, and so on. And crucially, the emotion that is set off by the object in turn can generate its own meaning, so that everything looks more dangerous when you feel afraid; everything about yourself, your school, or your country is great when you feel proud. Figure 2.2 illustrates this reversal of emotion and meaning in the associative learning function.

Research indeed shows that emotion activated in one setting can influence the meanings that come to mind in another setting. While most research on mood effects on thought is limited to general positive or negative (usually sad) moods, moods can be created by direct cueing of emotion from cultural associations, rather than from specific appraisals. Sad music creates a mood because of the connotations we have learned about the minor keys, slow tempo, and so forth, and this provokes people to think more negative thoughts (e.g., Segal, Kennedy, Gemar, Hood, Pedersen, & Buis, 2006). Comedy films make us happy because

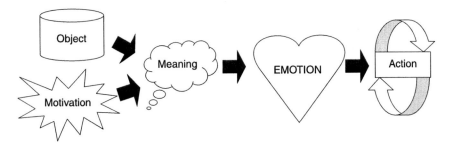

Figure 2.1 Place of emotion in the appraisal function.

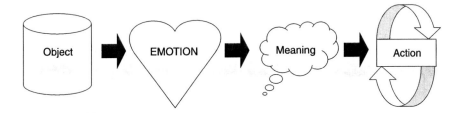

Figure 2.2 Place of emotion in the associative learning function.

they just are funny, not because they represent the achievement of any goals, and this kind of mood induction likewise affects thought; people generally become less critical and see things in a more optimistic light (Schwarz, Bless, & Bohner, 1991).

Specific emotional episodes, too, can carry over to irrelevant contexts, where they influence thought. For example, unresolved anger after injustice makes people more likely to make blaming judgments in a different situation (Goldberg, Lerner, & Tetlock, 1999); and fear primed through thinking about terrorist attacks increases the perception of a dangerous world, even for risks completely unrelated to terrorism such as catching flu (Lerner, Gonzalez, Small, & Fischhoff, 2003). In this way emotions, whether they come from an appraisal or a stored emotional attitude, reinforce themselves. They cue their own appraisals, which then spawn more emotions of the same kind. Anyone who has ever been in a laughing fit, where the giddy mood created by your own mirth makes everything seem hilarious, can testify to these effects. At the other extreme, negative emotions can perpetuate themselves so viciously that they become pathologies of mind as well as heart. Depressed people reinforce their negative mood by ruminating on their hatred for everything and their destiny of failure (Beck, 1967). Socially anxious people see justifications for their fear around every corner (Lucock & Salkovskis, 1988). And narcissistic people not only feel a shallow, rigid pride in themselves, but believe it to be based on truth (Rhodewalt & Eddings, 2002).

There is just one problem with all these demonstrations of the way emotions colour the meaning of our world. They don't seem to make sense in a functional system of appraisal. Leaving aside the mental disorders in which sadness, anxiety, disgust, shame, or pride take over, even mentally healthy people have times when an emotional state bleeds over inappropriately from one context to another. Some jerk of an experimenter insults our performance on a test; we go around angry afterwards, even though the anger won't solve anything (Harmon-Jones & Sigelman, 2001). Why does a fun fair give people a happy, reckless hangover? Why does jealousy manufacture its own evidence, in the real-world situations that give Shakespeare's Othello such resonance for us as a tragic character?

The evolutionary approach to psychology often answers this kind of question with the observation that some human traits, once functional in the ancestral environment, may have been outgrown by our current society, technology, and world of ideas (Cosmides & Tooby, 1990). Emotional associative learning works fine for a rodent, and could have worked fine for us, too, right up until the modern era. To take phobia as an example, if you see a spider in the wild, it is going to be real and potentially a threat. There are no such things out there as spider pictures, spiders under glass, or Spiderman. Although we may strive to appraise things rationally with constructive appraisals that fit the context and the current goals, associative learning persists, tagging along like a slow kid brother.

Or maybe not so slow. Based on research on fear learning in animals, some have argued that a system that reacts to very simple perceptions and superficial sensory stimuli has the advantage of being very fast (LeDoux, 1996). On a battlefield, for example, a soldier learns to fear the sound of gunfire, hitting the ground at any loud report; a split second can make a difference between life and death. The advantage of the fast emotion learning system is literally a few centimetres of neural connections saved in comparison to another system identified in those studies, which is routed through the frontal cortex and allows more discrimination of stimuli and context. In dangerous situations it is also an advantage to hold on to the emotional association once learned.

So, the frontline veteran, coming home, starts at the sound of the fireworks launched in his honour. However, in the original environment of the human species, these irrational vestiges of a traumatic learning experience would not pose a serious obstacle to survival. Also, the ability of emotions to organize and create their own reasons and appraisals out of thin air fits those times when maintaining an emotion gives us an advantage. So, in a contest of wills between two angry people, the one whose anger is sustained the longest wins. In the aftermath of a traumatic terror, letting go of the cautious thoughts that keep the fear alive can be fatal. Associative learning, from this perspective, is just a holdover from our species' adaptation to a simpler and more dangerous environment.

But I see another function of the associative learning of emotions that is far from primitive, and helps sustain us as self-aware human beings. Specifically, simple emotional and evaluative associations form the basis of our networks of values, the end-point concepts that anchor our beliefs about what is good and bad. As research shows, "values are truisms"—that is, value concepts such as obedience, freedom, and equality are strongly positively evaluated but people have trouble coming up with reasons why (Maio and Olson, 1998). Values are reasons that themselves need no reasons. Their strong influence comes not from cognitive reasoning, but from affective association. We can also identify negative concepts that are truisms; actions that are categorically out of bounds such as murder, incest, and cannibalism; ideologies that put one beyond the pale, such as communism and racism in the United States in the early 21st century. Many of these moral prohibitions, too, act like truisms; people cannot generate convincing reasons why acts that violate them but have no negative consequences are nonetheless wrong (Björklund, Haidt, & Murphy, 2000). And it is noteworthy that morally prohibited acts also attract strong emotions of disgust, hatred, anger, or anxiety (Haidt, 2003a).

Next to values in the map of emotional attitudes are the people, countries, or symbols that exemplify those values. Patriotism, of course, depends on unconditional love of country and its symbols, extending to the self so that a patriot feels not just happy but proud. Western liberal culture recognizes moral exemplars such as Winston Churchill, Dr. Martin Luther King Jr., John F. Kennedy, and Mahatma Gandhi. On the opposite side, we have moral nadirs such as Hitler and Stalin, or whole countries and groups of people that play the demonized role: terrorists, child molesters, or the members of the "axis of evil." Just as attitudes toward saints and heroes are characterized by received emotions of admiration, pride, and elevation, so attitudes towards villains and demons are tinged with emotions of condemnation and horror.

Imagine, then, that suddenly all these learned emotional associations go dead in you and you have to evaluate everything all over. In the first place, the judgments you can make lose all motivational force; Hitler had millions killed, did so intentionally, and without provocation, but millions of Germans were also killed, and anyway, where now is your emotional revulsion to the taking of human life that would let you say that all these deaths were a supremely bad thing? Constructing new value judgments is not only time-consuming and effortful, it also brings on uncertainty. Different positions have to be considered with no clear way to choose between them. Uncertainty has been identified as an existentially threatening condition (McGregor, 2006). Although it may be useful at times to question our preconceptions and set aside our biases, most of the time, most of us prefer the kind of certainty that derives from following our emotionally based attitudes. In fact, all kinds of benefits to the individual from strongly held attitudes have been documented, from greater resistance to colds (Fazio & Powell, 1997) to more decisive action (Kraus, 1995).

For a person to know that his or her emotional associations are strong, not contingent on reasoning, and not changeable by the context—all of this gives a sense of confidence, a bedrock on which to build the self. If I believe that, no matter what, I will always be disgusted by racism, be stirred by Beethoven, or love my partner, I gain a certainty about myself and the world; doubting any of these attitudes brings uncertainty, a state most of us can tolerate only in very limited doses. Existential uncertainty, whether brought on by reminders of one's own mortality or by more general ruminations on the transience of things, leads people to more strongly assert their core beliefs and values (McGregor, Zanna, Holmes, & Spencer, 2001) in an attempt to regain meaning. In this way, emotional attitudes have adapted themselves to serve a vital role in the mental life of a self-aware human being, as the very basis of the values and preferences that give a sense of stability to the self.

The self-regulatory function: Calling for corrective behaviour

Whether dealing with appraisals or simple associations, theories based on the first two functions assume that emotion is the source of motivation. That is, emotion instigates a certain kind of action tendency following from the processing of a stimulus, whether that processing is deep or shallow. However, another group of contemporary emotion theories question this assumption. They instead see emotion as a system that checks on the progress of our actions toward fulfilling a motivational goal. Emotions, in this view, give feedback relevant to the question of whether to continue toward the goal, abandon it, or take another approach toward it. However, in this cycle, the action comes first, then the emotion. Figure 2.3 shows this schematically. The same elements as in the appraisal function appear, but the position of action and emotion is reversed. There is a continual checking loop between the two of them. Also, a fifth construct is introduced, a non-emotional motivation that arises from meaning given to an object or situation. This motivation gives rise to action in the first place.

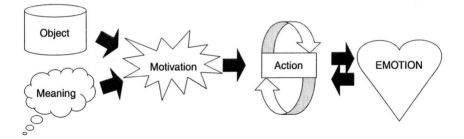

Figure 2.3 Place of emotion in the self-regulation function.

Before surveying the theoretical positions that have given us this very different view of emotion, a short example should make its plausibility clear. Let's go back to the familiar bear-in-the-woods situation. In retelling the tale of their encounter with the grizzly, people use a shorthand for the episode; they say, "I was afraid and I ran." But the ordering in time of the different components of emotion is not so clear-cut (Schachter, 1964).

An alternate reading of the situation would go like this: the first thing that happens is that you start running as fast as you can, pushed on by a strong motivation to put distance between yourself and the bear. Later, you take your action, the situation, and some aspects of your physical arousal as evidence that you were "scared." But the truth is that you were not half as scared as you would have been if you had been caught in a bear trap and unable to move.

An appraisal theorist would say that in the bear trap, your danger would be objectively greater, or your coping potential lower, and these perceptions can explain the greater fear. A feedback theorist would instead say that your fear grows over time as you find your goal to run being thwarted, and your action not succeeding. Because you can run, your lesser degree of fear was due to a positive state of relief at the achievement of your goal, overlaying a good deal of physical excitement. You didn't need emotions to run; your instincts and reflexes did that job for you.

One of the first theories to remark on the feedback function of emotion was self-discrepancy theory (Higgins, 1987). In this account, negative feelings in general come from perceived discrepancies between the actual self and either of two self-standards: an ideal, which is what the self would like to be, or an "ought," which is what the self feels obliged to be. Discrepancy from the ideal self leads to depression and guilt, while discrepancy from the ought self leads to anxiety and shame. In later research, the predictions about depression and anxiety were confirmed more strongly than those about shame and guilt (Higgins, Klein, & Strauman, 1985; Niedenethal, Tangney, & Gavanski, 1994). The original theory also seemed more focused on what could explain emotions of depression and anxiety than on the possible function of such an emotional system, because it took emotion rather than action as its end-point. Still, self-discrepancy theory is a noteworthy early investigation of the self-regulation potential in emotion.

A more fully worked-out account of emotions' role in behavioural feedback came with later developments in motivational theory (Carver & Scheier, 1990, 1998; Carver, Lawrence, & Scheier, 1996; Carver, Sutton, & Scheier, 2000). In this model, the motivational processes driving actions were described as a hierarchy of loops. In each loop, an initial change in the environment leads to input, which is then tested against a goal or standard, possibly leading to action. This action's effect on the environment is then assessed against the goal in a process of feedback. The assessment may lead to continuing, intensifying, or ceasing action, depending on its outcome.

As Carver et al. (2000) acknowledge, however, their model soon drew upon a number of Higgins' insights about approach and avoidance motives, as well as self-discrepancy theory, to incorporate distinct kinds of affect. Four different kinds of goal-relevant emotion were proposed. There was a pair of feelings, elation and sadness, that respectively correspond to success and failure in reducing the distance to a positive goal; but also a different set of positive and negative feelings, namely relief and anxiety, that correspond to success and failure in increasing the distance from a negative goal. In another important advance, the model went beyond the self as a reference standard, opening up to any source of goals. The role of emotion in Carver and Scheier's motivational loop, however, is primarily responsive; it starts with an evaluation of progress toward a goal, and only then directs further action respective to that goal.

The most recently developed feedback theory is an explicit challenge to appraisal theories and their assumption that emotions motivate behaviour (Baumeister et al., 2007). In this view, behaviour is often prompted by quick, automatic, unconscious affective or evaluative responses. However, they see full-blown emotions as experiences that come after behaviour and depend on feedback from it. Emotions' function is to regulate continued behaviour, and ensure future associative learning of evaluative responses. So, in terms of the functions of functional conflict theory, the Baumeister et al. (2007) theory champions the learning and regulation functions, rather than the appraisal function, as an explanation of how emotions work, why they are felt strongly, and why they seem uncontrollable. The strong feelings are necessary for learning; in particular, negative feelings have to be strong and difficult to avoid, or we would lose the valuable learning and behaviour regulation that comes from them. Indeed, some of this argument parallels economist Robert Frank's (1988) analysis of emotions as being uncontrollable for rational reasons, because they can act as commitments, motivating us to make choices with the long term in view.

This theory has its roots in earlier work on misregulation in self-control (Baumeister & Heatherton, 1996) and self-esteem (Baumeister, Campbell, Krueger, & Vohs, 2003), two areas that present problems to an appraisal-function view of emotions as encouraging realistic behaviour. For example, research on self-esteem challenges the idea that positive emotions associated with the self need to be encouraged in order to promote children's good behaviour. Instead, quite the opposite has been found. Although self-esteem is correlated with positive outcomes, this is because self-esteem follows on good behaviour, not the other way around (Baumeister et al., 2003). Bolstering self-esteem alone is as counterproductive as heating up a thermostat in a cold house; the thermostat, "thinking" everything is all right, makes no effort to heat the house. Likewise, in moral behaviour, performing a tokenistic morally positive gesture can make people feel better about their moral selves. But because this appeases the goal to act morally, it reduces people's motivation to act morally in subsequent decisions, rather than increasing it (e.g., Monin & Miller, 2001).

Emotions, then, are hard to change for the same reason that auditors and inspectors—regulators, in a word—should be hard to bribe. But while our emotional regulators are not corrupt, they can be hindered and distracted indirectly. Emotional experiences are ends in and of themselves, as well as means to the ends of self-regulation and learning. As self-conscious beings, we know and anticipate our own emotional states. This function, as Baumeister et al. (2007) acknowledge, is an important part of emotional learning. But if we can consciously feel and anticipate emotions, this also means that we can cheat the regulators. We can achieve relief from negative self-regulating feelings and enjoy the positive ones, not through the hard work of actual behaviour, but by shifting our goals, lowering our standards, or seeking distractions and excuses.

One key example is the failure of emotional self-control. In a syndrome known as restrained eating (Appleton & McGowan, 2006; Polivy & Herman, 1985), self-critical emotions of shame and guilt that come after breaking one's diet with an eating binge do not lead to repentant behaviour, as they should if they were doing their job. Instead, the restrained eater paradoxically eats more after an initial indulgence, even though he or she should eat less according to the normal workings of appetite. Similar effects have been shown with alcohol drinkers. Guilt after a binge drinking episode leads to worse behaviour, not better (Muraven, Collins, Morsheimer, Shiffman, & Paty, 2005).

What can account for this paradox? One answer is that the restrained person has inflexible goals. By these harsh standards, just one failure is taken as a signal that the goal of abstinence is going to fail, leading to a "what the hell" effect and the wholesale abandonment of the goal. But other experiments show the pivotal role of emotions, and in particular emotion regulation, in the loss of self-control after restraint (Tice, Bratslavsky, & Baumeister, 2001). People who indulge after breaking restraint seem to do so because they think the short-term gratification will alleviate the distress from their strong emotional reaction to their initial fault. In these experiments, some participants were told they had been exposed to a treatment that would make their mood unlikely to change. Without this treatment, participants showed greater indulgence in cookies after receiving negative feedback about the self; with it, they failed to do so. Knowing that their mood was frozen, there was no point in eating to improve it.

The irony is rich. Although emotions exist in part to regulate us, we in turn seem to be quite good at regulating our emotions. Outside of the legends of yoga, there is no way to turn off feelings at the source. But shortcuts, such as the self-indulgence of restrained eaters, often work to shield us from the consequences of self-awareness. Even one of the originators of appraisal theory, Richard Lazarus, developed a coping theory with Deborah Folkman (Lazarus & Folkman, 1988) in which there are "secondary" strategies to cope with distress by changing reality, as well as "primary" strategies to cope with distress by reducing it in one's own mind. This harkens back, in turn, to Freud's well-known distinction between a wish-fulfilling primary process and a reality-aware secondary process. These considerations explain why strong emotions can be counterproductive in self-regulation. The mere anticipation of anxiety or guilt sets off psychological defences that can discourage the very good behaviour they are meant to instil. The lure of happiness or pride, conversely, can lead people into a self-generated fool's paradise, in which they can escape the distress of reality.

Baumeister and his colleagues (2007) acknowledge the problem that these kinds of paradoxes cause for a functional view of emotions, but believe that they may only arise when a person starts from a point of very strong negative emotion, and tend to be rare. I want to suggest a further explanation. Paradoxes of emotional defence come up in the course of everyday life because they arise from a conflict between two functional systems of emotion: associative learning and self-regulation. When a person becomes aware of breaking a standard—let's say, a student staying up all night watching television instead of studying—he or she feels remorse, in line with the regulation function of emotion. Assuming there is any further opportunity to act correctly, the remorse should in theory lead the student to switch off the television, and head for bed. This taste of remorse, in the Baumeister et al. (2007) account, becomes a reminder to calmly head off repeating the transgression in the future, when the same situation arises. But is it necessary to feel remorse in order to learn effectively? We should be able to imagine bad feelings ahead of time, without actually having to feel bad. Fear of guilt, not guilt itself, is the emotion best suited to self-regulation, and the mere *concept* of guilt should be the best stimulus of all. Of course, the feelings of guilt need to exist, to back up this anticipated threat. But problems happen when guilt feelings actually come into being, thanks to the associative function of emotions.

Emotions and evaluations, as we have seen, can spread their message by mere association. That is part of their survival value. But associative learning also interferes with the smooth functioning of self-regulation, just as it can interfere with appraisals of novel situations. For our hypothetical student, the thought that appears most closely associated with negative feelings is not the television watching. That indulgence produced pleasure, in and of itself. Instead, the bad feelings become associated with the self-aware standard that says "you should be studying instead of enjoying yourself." Studying started out as just boring and not fun, but now even thinking about it brings on a wave of guilt. The situation of self-control, with all its ideals and oughts, becomes toxic by association. And the even worse threat is that the self, which most of us strive to surround with a strong base of unquestioned positive associations, will also pick up these negative associations.

More generally, the self is why the emotions, as regulators of conscience, so often backfire. Were it not for the self, we would be able to take guilt, pride, and all the other emotions as mere signals that we are closer or farther away from our goals; living and feeling only in the moment. (Buddhist psychology, by the way, takes this as not just a descriptive statement but prescriptive advice; see de Silva, 2000.) The human autobiographical self allows us to construct a long-range model of our being, spanning past, present, and future (Damasio, 1999). This kind of self-awareness is a relatively late arrival in evolutionary terms. While it certainly increases our capacity for long-term problem solving and for thinking about our social relations, it also comes with some drawbacks. Most of the time we are able to regulate our emotions to our benefit. We can even adopt an unpleasant feeling such as anger if the occasion calls for it (Tamir, Mitchell, & Gross, 2008). But negative emotions associated with self-awareness have an added cost. They are particularly painful because they threaten to taint the entire self by association. In fact, this fate is what defensive thought and behaviour try to avoid.

Many well-researched theories in social psychology also document the emotional consequences of acknowledging unpleasant facts about the self or its place in the world. Experiments in terror management theory have shown that the denial of one's own mortality and animal nature underlies many defensive motivations (Goldenberg, Heflick, Vaes, Motyl, & Greenberg, 2009; Solomon, Greenberg, & Pyszczynski, 1991), and identifies anxiety and disgust as the negative feelings that arise when defences falter. We alternatively may be motivated to seek out the comfort of believing that the world is a just place (Hafer & Bègue, 2005), or that we are more certain about things than we really have a right to be (McGregor, 2006). We can be motivated to avoid the guilt that would come from the full acknowledgement of evil deeds committed in the name of our group (Castano & Giner-Sorolla, 2006); or the anxiety that would come from acknowledging our vulnerability to health risks (Ditto & Lopez, 1992). Denial and other defence mechanisms have no place when running from the immediate, concrete threat of a lion, tiger, or bear. But they are terribly tempting when dealing with the multitude of invisible worries, imagined or real, that our highly developed cognitive powers open us up to.

Self-conscious emotions—pride, shame, guilt, regret—specifically respond to the kind of long-term goals that are particularly important in self-regulation (Giner-Sorolla, 2001), and so this function is especially predominant when dealing with them. Although appraisal theories have also acknowledged that self-conscious feelings respond to appraisals of the self and its actions (e.g., Weiner, 1995), I want to point out a difference between the logic of appraisal and that of self-regulation. The appraisal function treats knowledge of self like it treats any other kind of information, forming an evaluation of the self in relation to a goal, and treating the self as a resource or an obstacle. I am doing well at tennis; this evaluation, and the subsequent pride, leads me to approach, eagerly, my goal of winning a tournament. If I am doing badly at tennis, it will be harder to win; I feel ashamed, and I should avoid the tournament. Emotion, in this view, comes before motivation and controls it (cf. Oatley & Johnson-Laird, 1996).

However, the self-regulation function works in the opposite way. It starts with the motivation already in place and works homeostatically to regulate effort, like a thermostat or a self-righting gyroscope. The emotion's evaluation of the self becomes a cue to kick against that evaluation, to restore equilibrium to a desired set point in the opposite direction. If I am doing badly at tennis, and feel ashamed, self-regulation logic says I should try harder, because the goal will take more effort to reach. If I am doing well at tennis, and feel proud, self-regulation logic says I should take it easy, because the goal is within reach. As I will argue in more detail in chapters 5 and 6, the role of emotion in regulating human motivation oscillates between these two functions, one working on a positive feedback loop, the other working on a negative feedback loop. This ultimately allows us to decide whether to pursue or abandon difficult goals in a flexible, but also error-prone, way.

Other emotions, not usually seen as self-conscious, can serve the self-regulation function. For example, the non-self-conscious emotion of anger has a regulatory function. It responds to failure in an important goal with persistence and redoubled effort. In the case of anger, these self-regulatory functions can often interfere with the role of the emotion in dealing with external threats and social situations. Someone who applies the same angry persistence to persuading you as they apply to washing a sink full of dirty dishes can come across as unreasonably abrasive. This is not optimal design, perhaps, but it is the human condition. We use our emotional system for self-regulation, even though this use is prone to interference from its appraisal and associative learning functions. This is what engineers call a "kludge," an adaptation of a system fit for one purpose to serve another. Because of this, perhaps, the best approach to self-regulation is to be aware of your own emotions, but not driven by them.

The communication function: Social good faith

While the three functions of emotions so far benefit the individual feeling them, emotions can't be confined just to the boundaries of any one person. Emotions leak out to others through the muscles of the face, the cracking of the voice, and the

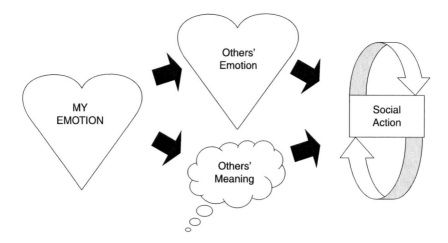

Figure 2.4 Place of emotion in the social communication function.

posture of the body. As I have already noted, these expressive cues play a part in the maintenance and intensification of an individual's emotion. But they are not necessary to the three functions I have discussed so far, which suggests that they primarily serve another function, a social communication function (Parkinson, Fischer, & Manstead, 2005; van Kleef, de Dreu, & Manstead, 2010). People look to the faces, bodies, and voices of others to judge what they are feeling. Sometimes, whether it's the class clown looking for giggles or the class bully looking for tears, people even act to provoke expression of emotion from other people. Communications of emotion are sometimes unintentional, but partly lie under our control.

Cultures teach their members rules of emotional expression, which may eventually become automatic, but serve to suppress or exaggerate displays of feeling. And emotion is also thought about and communicated through language. We confide to others in conversation about our emotions, and gossip about the emotions of third parties. Most languages contain a number of metaphors and specific terms to refer to emotions—English, by one count, has close to 800 emotionally expressive words (Johnson-Laird & Oatley, 1989), and there are many more metaphors for emotion, such as "boiling over" for anger, "bubbling" for happiness, or "blue" for sadness (Kövecses, 2003).

Of course, emotions in a larger sense are social, in that many of the appraisals that set them off originate from other people or from our thoughts and goals about them (Parkinson, 1996). But the communication of emotions to other human beings, the output in addition to the input, deserves to be seen as a function of its own (Parkinson et al., 2005). When we look at the expressive output of emotions, it's possibly only the display of anger that communicates a useful message from humans to members of another species. Resolve, and the potential costliness of any attack, is what's shown by bared teeth, narrowed eyes, and clenched fists. But anger is also a powerful social signal to our own kind, while expressions of sadness, fear, shame, joy, or disgust don't seem to have any purpose in signalling to non-humans, even though we may attempt communication with pets and other animals. Emotions signal our mental states, relationships, and intentions to others, and in turn can evoke emotions and signals from those others (Figure 2.4). The messages we send via emotions can also have incentive value themselves (Keltner & Kring, 1998); think of smiles and frowns, which are such a basic incentive currency that they appear in sticker form on children's school assignments.

But functionally, why do we still hang on to this primitive channel of emotional communication, when humans have a perfectly good, fully developed system of language that lets us say whatever we can imagine? In communication, as in self-regulation, emotion has the advantage that its expression is hard to control (Frank, 1988). Sincerity is an important asset in a social species whose individuals pursue their own interests as well as those of multiple groups, friends, and relationship partners, and have the brains and tongues to come up with lies so they can try to have it all. A person who could cheat on a business deal without remorse is not one to be trusted. Someone who marries for purely pragmatic reasons is likely to abandon that marriage when a better situation presents itself. In this situation, expressions of sincere love, or at the very least the knowledge of impending guilt and shame, are required as a bona fide of sincerity. For these reasons, emotions need to be hard to fake and impossible to turn off at will.

Now, it is in theory possible for one person to look at another person's emotional display and pick up the signal in a cold, emotionless way. Like an "anthropologist on Mars"—neurologist Oliver Sacks' metaphor for autistic engineer Temple Grandin (Sacks, 1995)—even someone with biological difficulties in responding emotionally can, with some effort, use the reasoned learning system to figure out what is being communicated by emotions. In a more sinister way, sociopaths, who themselves suffer a deficit in empathy, also are able to master the pretence of having social feelings in order to deceive others (Mealey, 1995). But these are exceptions. For most people, emotions talk to emotions. There are automatic and unconscious processes at work here, in which one emotion cues another directly, as well as more conscious and articulate processes in which emotions convey meaning—which itself may lead to other emotions (for a similar two-process interpretation see van Kleef et al., 2010). Emotions can trigger each other symmetrically, cueing a similar emotion state in others; or asymmetrically, cueing a different emotion state that nonetheless is functionally relevant to the first.

The most basic symmetric process is emotional contagion (Hatfield, Cacioppo, & Rapson, 1994). It is observed in infants, who cry in maternity wards just because other infants are crying (Simner, 1971), and who as early as 10 weeks old return the angry, sad, and happy expressions of their parent (Haviland & Lelwica, 1987). In adults, mood can be transferred contagiously between people without awareness; for example, through subtle cues in a speaker's voice even reading unemotional text (Neumann & Strack, 2000). A related process is emotional mimicry, in which one person automatically and spontaneously perceives the emotional expression of another, reproducing it in his or her own motor expressions (Lundqvist & Dimberg, 1995). Mimicry does not always lead to actual contagion of emotions, but the two processes can operate side by side (Hess & Blairy, 2001).

Empathy represents a more advanced, conscious channel of symmetric emotional communication. As distinct from sympathy, or concern for others (about which, see chapter 6), empathy follows the perception of an emotion in others by feeling the emotion in one's self. Unlike the automatic influence of contagion, an empathetic person is aware of the link between these feeling states (Hatfield et al., 1994). Empathy is a strong determinant of successful relationships (Cramer & Jowett, 2010), and works to encourage pro-social behaviours toward others (Eisenberg & Miller, 1987). Being able to not only catch others' emotions, but also to be aware of the process and act on it, seems itself to be an important social signal for cooperation.

Studies of the brain, in fact, show that for many emotions, the key structures involved in sensing them in others are the same as the key structures involved in feeling them one's self—for example, the amygdala is involved both in feeling fear and interpreting its facial expression, and likewise for the insula in disgust (Costafreda, Brammer, David, & Fu, 2008; Jabbi, Bastiaansen, & Keysers, 2008). Neurological studies also show that deficits in emotional feeling accompany deficits in responding to others' feelings; for example, in autism (e.g., Blair, 1999).

According to this evidence for an embodied view of emotion, our own emotions are intimately involved in the process of seeing and thinking about emotions in others. Given such a close relationship in the brain itself, emotional contagion and empathy seem almost destined to happen.

Symmetric cueing of emotions in social communication has a complex relationship to other functions of emotion. Often it reproduces their functional logic, but at a social rather than an individual level. For example, if you and I feel the same emotion in response to the same situation, this means our appraisals are coordinated; you and I are likely to have the same goals, interpret the situation the same way, and take the same kind of action. Emotional symmetry here works as a shortcut to achieve faster agreement and coordination among people. Instead of hoping that everyone sees things the same way and therefore feels the same emotion, symmetric emotional coordination puts the emotion first, in the hopes that thought and action will follow from that. This is another important functional reason for the tendency of emotions to bias individual cognitions, which seems illogical from a purely individual appraisal point of view. In the angry mob, joyous party, or fearful pack, success in cooperation follows from having the shared emotion reinforce task-relevant thoughts—injustice, success, danger. The "correct" appraisal is made at the group level, and from that point of view, individuals who see things a different way are just holding back the rest.

A great deal of associative learning of emotions also has to come from social communication. Rather than experience directly all the harmful and disgusting things that the world has in store, it is much easier for a child to learn that stoves are hot and bugs are nasty from the concerned expression and raised voice of a parent. Some emotional associations can't be learned any other way than from other people; a patriot who feels a swelling heart at the sight of the national flag is unlikely to have been directly gratified by that piece of fabric (although one never knows . . .). Rather, we learn these deeply emotional responses to symbols from the emotion-laden communications of others. This is especially likely to be true for feelings that depend on our most self-relevant values and moral standards. As mentioned before, we have little cognitive backing for emotional reactions to the kinds of values that anchor our networks of attitudes—freedom, equality, loyalty (Maio & Olson, 1998). We cannot have direct experience with the nebulous concepts they refer to. Instead, it's more likely that these concepts acquire their emotional charge through direct emotional input from family, leaders, and peers.

Just as our values depend on emotional communication, so ultimately do the standards that drive the self-regulation functions of emotion. After all, there is very little debate in psychology that the motives and feelings of the self ultimately come from reactions to a child's behaviour by parents, teachers, and other important adults. Without society, there is no self (Cooley, 1964/1902). It is the emotion of approval or disapproval in the face and voice of one's elders, more so than any reasoned explanation, that lays down the initial standards for behaviour and achievement. This observation goes back to Freud, and has been highly influential in the fields of psychoanalysis and moral development, as one of the most accurate parts of his error-riddled developmental theory (Emde, Johnson, & Easterbrooks,

1987). Applied to the moral emotions that deal with the self, internalization means that guilt or pride at our own failure or success, which we as adults experience as our own, originates in the child's symmetrical imitation of important others' disappointment or joy.

There is also a meta-message that is communicated by the very fact that two persons' emotional displays are symmetrical and synchronized. This coordination both signals and encourages rapport, which carries a number of implications for the future of a social relation. If our emotional reactions build on each other in a spontaneous way, we like each other, we can trust each other, and we will cooperate. Thus, symmetric emotional communication is important for satisfaction, whether it happens in a casual interaction (Cappella, 1997; Hennig-Thurau, Groth, Paul, & Gremler, 2006), in a friendly or romantic relationship (Anderson, Keltner, & John, 2003), or in a small group (Barsade, 2002). Likewise, observing the reactions of other people to things in the natural or social world can tell us a number of things about them. People who laugh at a funeral, for example, are considered untrustworthy and possibly even mentally ill. Through culture, people set up situations that coordinate and test the emotional reactions of potential comrades. Storytelling, for example, was and often still is a face-to-face activity. In this context, failing to laugh at the stories people find funny, or finding repulsive things enjoyable, likewise sets one apart as strange.

Precisely because symmetric emotions signal a relationship with another person or a social group, we tend to deny emotional symmetry to people who are potential enemies. For example, Bourgeois and Hess (2008) found that people mimicked only positive, not negative, emotional expressions of members of social outgroups (defined as members of another political party, or those that do not share one's own love or indifference to basketball). The conscious process of empathy is even more strongly bounded by group distinctions; empathy is greater for similar others (Batson, Turk, Shaw, & Klein, 1995) and people are less likely to feel symmetric emotions for, or act on their empathy for, members of different social groups (Brown, Bradley, & Lang, 2006; Sturmer, Snyder, Kropp, & Siem, 2006). So, symmetric emotional displays not only build social relationships but to some extent define their boundaries.

Asymmetric patterns of emotion cuing have been less extensively studied, and because each of these patterns is specific to the emotions involved, I will have more to say about them in the coming chapters as I discuss each of the specific emotions. In one well-supported example of asymmetric cuing, angry faces cue responses of fear and anxiety, even when presented subliminally, and even when the fear response is measured subtly through psychophysiological recording (Öhman & Mineka, 2001). However, asymmetric responses can be flexible and differ according to the context. Rather than anger cueing fear, in recent studies from our lab (Giner-Sorolla & Espinosa, 2011), angry faces that were presented as the reactions of peers in a social context provoked feelings of guilt, while disgusted faces provoked shame. Research supporting a model of emotions as social information also shows that the message sent by emotions depends on the pre-existing relationship between people (van Kleef et al., 2010). For example, an expression of guilt from a friend will increase cooperation with that person, but the same expression from an opponent in a contested negotiation can be seen as a sign of weakness, triggering stronger rather than milder demands (van Kleef, de Dreu, & Manstead, 2006).

In general, asymmetric cuing owes its effects to concerns about the imbalance of power, threat, and caring between individuals, rather than to any need to coordinate emotions. A dominant emotional signal seeks appeasement, an aggressive signal seeks flight, a signal of distress seeks attention and sympathy. In the longer term, an emotion sends a message not just about momentary motives but about the personality of the person expressing it; a person who acts angrily when provoked, for example, is sending a message that he or she is tough rather than warm (Hareli & Hess, 2010).

Conclusion

Functional conflict theory attempts to explain why emotions seem to be such a problem for humanity when they do so much for us. First, we saw that one important function of emotions is to help us flexibly appraise and act upon the outside world for our own benefit. However, the other functions of emotions work against flexibility, making a virtue instead of inflexibility. Associative learning is with us because it has been useful in laying down strong, survival-related patterns. As self-aware beings, too, we are comforted by the certainty we find in the unquestioned emotional associations that colour our most strongly held values and attitudes. Furthermore, when emotions help us regulate our actions in line with long-term goals, it is important that it not be easy to switch them off. Self-regulation thus becomes a struggle between the better judgments of our self-conscious emotions, and our own attempts to manipulate the emotional associations that are linked to our self. Social communicative functions of emotions, too, can sometimes require emotions to be inflexible and uncontrollable, so that our signals to others are genuine, even if they cause distress to us individually. It is these conflicts among functions that can explain why, so often, emotions strike us as inappropriate and irrational. They can't help it; by serving one function well, emotions run the risk of serving another function poorly.

3   Emotions, morality, and groups: Intersections

Emotions, morality, and groups intersect with each other in three important ways. For the past 20 years, the role of emotion in the way people think about groups has been a rich and diverse topic of study in psychology. For the past 10 years or so, controversies about the role of emotion have been central to the psychological study of moral judgment. And more recently, research has begun to look at how people evaluate social groups' morality, and how morality depends on the social group's concerns. Each of these two-way intersections deserves its own review. But the interconnection among all three concepts also suggests a synthesis; a three-way intersection that I will sketch out at the end of this chapter. No two of these concepts are complete without considering the third. The way that emotion works within and between groups serves moral concerns. The working of emotions as a part of morality involves the emotional input of other group members around us who belong to the same moral community. And morality at the group level is regulated, reinforced, and communicated by emotions.

Emotions and morality

The role of the feelings and passions in morality is not a new topic in philosophy. Plato in *The Republic*, and later Aristotle in *Ethics*, laid down a two-sided sketch of emotions that Western philosophers have followed ever since. Thus Plato draws a distinction between base feelings and desires that divert attention from moral concerns, which he likens to slaves, and the more noble feelings of honour, which he likens to the warrior class (*The Republic*). Aristotle also sees both vice and virtue as emotional; "the whole concern both of virtue and of political science is with pleasures and pains; for the man who uses these well will be good, he who uses them badly bad" (*Ethics*, book 2, chapter 1). He sees anger and shame, for example, as not being good or bad in themselves. Instead, they are part of a character that can be good or bad. Both these emotions are morally best when felt appropriately and in moderation.

Later philosophers have often departed from these balanced viewpoints of antiquity, taking a dimmer or brighter view of emotion's effect on morality. On the one hand, the Stoics championed reason over emotion as a guide to good action in life, and Kant asserted that the ends and principles of morality could be derived from reasoning alone. On the other hand, the emotionalist school in philosophy, led by Hume, asserted that emotions are indispensable to moral reasoning. Hume argued that a perfectly rational person would also be perfectly self-interested and unswayed by moral ends; only moral sentiments such as sympathy or remorse drive people to move beyond self-interest and consider the interests of other people. This philosophical argument has recently been elaborated on and intensified, with references to the latest psychological research, by Jesse Prinz (2007). In his view, our sense of morality is in fact constituted by emotional reactions. Reasoning can inform these but not completely supplant them.

In psychology, a parallel debate about the role of emotion in morality has been going on over the past decade. Initial psychological investigations into the development of morality were dominated by the study of moral reasoning via Kohlberg's theory (Kohlberg, 1981). This research emphasized the process rather than the outcome of moral reasoning, and valued more abstract reasons (e.g., appeals to values and principles) as developmentally more advanced than more concrete reasons (e.g., appeals to authority or utilitarian consequences). The first criticisms of this theory questioned the necessary superiority of abstract principle-based reasoning (e.g., Bloom, 1986). Notably, Gilligan (1982) argued for the benefits of a style of moral reasoning seen more often in women and girls, in which social consequences are weighed and considered against each other.

Some early research on moral development from the 1960s onward has considered emotions. Martin Hoffman, for one, was an early investigator of empathy in moral development, which he defined as an affective phenomenon dependent on, but not the same as, cognitive perspective-taking (Hoffman, 1975, 1977). His theory and research also recognized the importance of feelings of guilt and remorse in the self-regulation of moral behaviour (e.g., Thompson & Hoffman, 1980). Affect also played an important part in other contemporaneous research on altruism and helping behaviour (e.g., Cialdini & Kenrick, 1976; Krebs, 1970). Kohlberg's main concern was with the complexity and stability of the reasons for moral judgment, which went together with a deliberate methodological indifference as to the outcome of those judgments pro or contra. Hoffman and the altruism researchers, however, saw emotion as an answer to the question of whether a person will make a choice that supports moral norms, helping other people rather than the self. In some ways, then, Kohlberg's choice of a cognitive question defined his cognitive answer, as much as questions about what determines good and bad behaviour have ended up promoting an affective answer.

The emotionalist argument received a major boost in 2001 with the publication of Jonathan Haidt's article, "The emotional dog and its rational tail." The research underlying Haidt's social intuitionist theory of morality is principally concerned with the reasons for moral disapproval, rather than the self-regulation of helping behaviour. For example, one series of studies conducted in the United States and Japan (Rozin, Lowery, Imada, & Haidt, 1999b) showed correspondences between distinct emotional reactions of anger, contempt, and disgust on the one hand, and judgments of different kinds of acts as morally wrong on the other. Emotion also proved a strong predictor of moral judgment, more so than reasons, in a study of judgments of the morality of sexual acts (Haidt & Hersh, 2001). In a compelling demonstration that directly addressed the role of reasoning, a series of "moral dumbfounding" experiments conducted by Haidt, Björklund, and Murphy (2000) presented student participants with descriptions of morally taboo behaviours from which all potential negative consequences and violations of rights had been removed. For example, one scenario described a consensual incestuous fling between a brother and sister on holiday in Paris (there's something about Paris . . .). Multiple forms of contraception are used, nobody finds out, and the siblings suffer no psychological harm and don't make a habit of it. In spite of the act's harmlessness, most participants judged it as wrong. But when probed to explain why, they had trouble. Some referred to harmful consequences that had been explicitly ruled out, others used their emotions as a reason ("It's just disgusting"), and still others relied on more basic judgments ("It's just wrong"). Reasons in this example seemed superfluous. The intuition of wrongness, tinged with the emotion of disgust, was enough to explain reactions to the incestuous pair.

Sometimes, when Haidt's 2001 article is discussed, the "social" part of his theory gets left off in favour of the "intuitionist" (e.g., the replies of Pizarro & Bloom, 2003, and Saltzstein & Kasachkoff, 2004, engage almost exclusively with the primacy of intuition). This may be because Haidt himself has emphasized the primacy of emotions and intuition, both in the article's title, and in the main research examples advanced to support it. But emotion is not just there to let us make individual decisions; it serves as an interface between social groups and morality. And Haidt's social intuitionist model in fact does not ignore moral reasoning, but characterizes the main function of moral reasoning as social. Having stated a moral opinion, a person must often justify it, convincing other people of its rightness. Different intuitions and different arguments come into play. We sometimes do this for ourselves, in a process Haidt terms "private reflection," but this is mainly because we so often have to do it for an audience of others. Communication with other people also explains where our moral intuitions come from in the first place—and how they may be changed.

Ignoring the "social" in "social intuitionism" is a mistake, because this feature adds an important element to emotionalism. Social communication provides a check on intuitive gut reactions, allowing the perspectives of others and their substantive arguments to influence moral judgment. And sometimes we can even internalize these arguments and work things out for ourselves. But, as we have seen in the previous chapter, emotions also play a strong role in social communication. It is likely that this kind of communication is less about the individual's gut-level evaluative intuitions and more about the full expression of emotional feelings, which find an outlet in the face, voice and vocabulary, with a particular persuasive impact. Aristotle did not in vain devote a full book of his Rhetoric to the emotions. Although he had ethical doubts about the power of emotions to cloud the truth, he understood that the social transmission of emotions can be decisive in the kind of moral arguments that Athenians cared about. Contemporary research on psychology, marketing, and communication also puts a strong emphasis on the role of emotion in persuasion, from primitive intuitive feelings to influences of specific, elaborated emotions (Crano & Prislin, 2005; Nabi, 2002).

Nonetheless, Haidt's claim for the primacy of quick, unthinking feelings in morality has received more attention than his elaboration of social corrective processes in morality. As with Zajonc's (1980) claim for the primacy of affect in the area of attitudes, this claim did not go uncontested. Pizarro and Bloom (2003), for example, argue that dilemmas in which reason must be used to decide between two competing intuitions are more common—or if not common, at least important—than Haidt lets on; that decisions arrived at by moral reasoning can become routine and express themselves intuitively and emotionally. Saltzstein and Kasachkoff (2004) make many of the same points, and also note that moral beliefs often change through moral reasoning. Haidt's replies (2003b, 2004) focus on the ability of social intuitionism to explain change, dilemmas, and reasoning in terms of socially rooted processes. But the critical empirical test seems elusive in this exchange, and in a later exchange on similar topics between Narvaez (2010) and Haidt (2010). Examples of intuition and reason in moral judgment can be arranged against each other. But claims about which process is more prevalent, more important, or causally primary, have proceeded more from reviews and interpretations of research than from a decisive, dedicated programme of investigation.

It is likely that the truth lies somewhere between the two claims. I'll go even further and assert, with the history of previous psychological debates as a guide, that it's highly likely that the truth is best served by the contextualist approach (McGuire, 1983): finding out under which circumstances intuition or reason best applies. In fact, Monin et al. (2007) point out that intuitionist and rationalist explanations may be talking past each other because they take different kinds of moral judgments as examples. Intuitionists draw their conclusions from quick condemnations of heinous acts, such as the incest described in moral dumbfounding studies. Rationalists, however, draw theirs from difficult moral dilemmas, where multiple principles conflict. This, broadly speaking, is the kind of resolution that ended the debate between Zajonc's affective primacy perspective (1980) and Lazarus' cognitive primacy perspective (1982) on the relation between cognition and affect. Eventually, it emerged that Zajonc's examples defined affect as very minimal, rapid, and undifferentiated evaluations, while Lazarus' arguments, based on studies of cognitive appraisal of emotions, referred to fuller and more distinct kinds of emotions (Lazarus, 1984; Zajonc, 1984). This observation resulted in an enrichment of emotion theory allowing for multiple modes of processing (e.g., Leventhal & Scherer, 1987), as we have seen in chapter 2, acknowledging that associative learning as well as reflective appraisals can both trigger emotions.

Similar dual-process solutions have been brought up to resolve the intuitive–rational issue in morality (e.g., Craigie, 2011; Fine, 2006). A recent empirical example emerges from studies of moral dilemmas by Greene and his colleagues, in which participants typically judge the morality of killing one person in order to save several others (Greene, Morelli, Lowenberg, Nystrom, & Cohen, 2008). Evidence from behavioural and imaging studies among normal people, and from studies among abnormal populations, suggest that a more deliberative system pulls in favour of the utilitarian act of killing one to save many, while a more intuitive system pulls against it, following an aversion against killing in any circumstance (Greene, 2009a). The intuitive system engages areas of the brain associated with emotion and social thought (Greene, Sommerville, Nystrom, Darley, & Cohen, 2001; Greene, Nystrom, Engell, Darley, & Cohen, 2004). It becomes more influential when moral issues are vivid and personalized (Greene et al., 2001) and when people are mentally busy (Greene et al., 2008). More utilitarian judgments, however, are made when regions of the brain involved in generating social emotions are damaged (Koenigs et al., 2007), and such judgments involve brain regions associated with more abstract cognition (Greene et al., 2001, 2004).

Although emotions get more involved when a moral case is personally involving, it's also important not to confuse emotions with quick and intuitive processes (Giner-Sorolla, 1999). As Hauser (2006) argues, moral intuitions need not be particularly emotional to be quick and unreasoning, although they are strongly evaluative in a simpler sense. This is particularly evident when we hear about a minor offence committed in a far-away country by a person we don't know. When reading the headline "Anonymous Uzbek steals a sheep," we can have a quick and consequential response that the act of stealing is wrong, even if no great emotion accompanies the judgment. But if my neighbour Erica steals my sheep, or I am contemplating stealing hers, the personal involvement in the case strengthens the emotions involved (Batson et al., 2007). As we have seen in chapter 1, it is the self that brings emotions into play as a response to new events. Here, the self also includes the extended self, made up of the people and social groups we care about. While some doubts still linger over evidence that emotions are utterly necessary for moral judgment (Huebner, Dwyer, & Hauser, 2009), emotions undoubtedly play a critical role in breathing motivational life into dry judgments. Their role, in fact, can be analysed using the four functions of functional conflict theory, because each of these functions is relevant to how emotions work—or fail in their attempt—to encourage morality.

Appraisal and associative learning in moral judgment

Moral judgments sometimes come to acquire associated emotional reactions. Some people are disgusted by the mere mention of torture; others are angered by people they have come to associate with unfairness. These associations can contribute to rigid moral rules that prohibit concrete kinds of actions—"thou shalt nots" applied under a zero-tolerance policy—or to the demonization of hated people and peoples. The categorization of immoral acts under the emotionally loaded terms "incest," "murder," "cannibalism" does take place. But by the same token, a theory of morality would be poor indeed if it just caricatured moral emotion as a quick, reflexive, conditioned intuition. This view captures the associative function of emotion, but does not do justice to the other parts emotion plays in our complicated minds.

To begin with, we need emotional appraisal when actions or people lack a pre-existing evaluative tag. When teenagers started using camera phones to send naked pictures of themselves to each other, many of them in the USA were caught on the wrong side of the law. Their electronic exhibitionism was criminalized as "child pornography" with zero tolerance. But existing associations with "child pornography," "sexual harassment," or "phone sex" didn't seem adequate to judge this new development. When a moral judgment needs to be built from scratch, we test the new phenomenon with reference to specific moral goals. Those goals are values. As Moors (2010) argues, situations and objects can be evaluated quickly but flexibly in the light of active goals. We know that a toothbrush is especially good when we have the goal to get the fuzz off our teeth; mightn't we also know that treating people the same way is especially good when we are mindful of the goal to act fairly? Values that are moral are central, and close to the concept of the self. So, actions are likely to engage strong emotions when they are appraised in terms of moral values.

Values can also be contrasted against moral rules. Rules refer to a concrete act; values refer to a concept that can be upheld or violated by many different acts. "Freedom is good" and "Adultery is bad" are both unarguable anchors of moral reasoning. The main difference is that an argument leading to the adultery rule is likely to be about categorization (recall Bill Clinton's famous denial, "I did not have sex with that woman," belabouring a technical point about what exactly sex was). But an argument leading to the freedom value is likely to be about the correct means to achieve it, a potentially much longer-running dialogue. Associative emotions are entirely compatible with a simple moral rule, involving a yes/no categorization and an evaluation: "Requiring identification from hotel guests is fascism; fascism is bad." Appraisal-based moral reasoning and emotions involve a more complex claim. This goes beyond the mere association of the verb "to be." Instead, the *propositional* claim of an appraisal is better expressed through an action word relevant to a goal, such as "promotes" or "reduces": "Requiring ID from hotel guests reduces adultery; adultery is bad." Combining this last pair of statements into an overall judgment has to involve complex, propositional thought. Specifically, resolving two negatives into a positive, following principles of consistency, is an operation that associative thinking cannot perform (Gawronski & Bodenhausen, 2007). However, this exact operation is required to end up with the correct inference, "Requiring ID is good."

We also have to use more complex reasoning when moral values conflict with each other, and with other non-moral values we hold important. To illustrate, Tetlock's studies of British and US legislative speeches (1981, 1984) showed more complex reasoning and argumentation among moderate-left politicians than among either right-wing or hard-left politicians. This was, Tetlock argued, because moderate leftists often have to balance two sets of strongly held values, while socialists and free-market conservatives make a more definite choice between, say, economic liberty and economic equality. This interpretation was later confirmed experimentally; university students, writing about issues that pitted two values against each other, generated more complex reasoning if they held both values in high regard than if they strongly preferred one to the other (Tetlock, 1986). This is really no different from the role of reason in arriving at the best action to fit a number of self-serving goals. When a person I like asks me out to see a film I like, the response is quick, positive, and seemingly intuitive, but when I like the person but hate the film (or vice versa), more complex thinking has to occur before I reach a decision I feel comfortable with.

Moral evaluations can thus be generated either by quick, mindless associations, or by more complex and flexible appraisals. However, strong, "hot" emotions can arise either on the basis of slow or fast thought (Giner-Sorolla, 1999). So, I see it as a mistake to assume that only intuitions activate our emotions. What determines whether they come into play, instead, is the self's involvement. Perhaps the moral decision is directly relevant to my self's own moral image. Perhaps I see the suffering of another person and feel empathy, which turns the other's problems into the self's problems. Perhaps the moral decision is completely vicarious, involving other people, but touches on a centrally important value that I hold close to the self. Or perhaps the people involved are themselves close to me, having a meaningful family, friendship, or group connection.

A final definitional issue, very relevant to the title of this book, is what constitutes a "moral emotion." My perspective, as we've seen, is that any single emotion can serve a number of functions, some of which are relevant to short-term interests, and some of which are more about serving the larger-scale and longer-term interests of morality. Actually, very few emotions intrinsically serve a moral purpose. I'll argue that guilt is one of those, and sympathy, perhaps, another. But anger, disgust, shame, admiration, and pride can all focus on selfish as well as moral concerns, involving evaluations of a person's practical competence or social standing rather than anything morally relevant. My selection of moral emotions for the remaining chapter of the book is based on current opinion about which emotions have the most salient moral usages (e.g., Haidt, 2003a), but is not all-encompassing. In fact, it could be argued that other emotions not on this list can also be applied to moral situations. For example, surely the concept of a "moral panic" involves moral anxiety (McRobbie & Thornton, 1995); displays of sadness and distress may also play a part in morality by drawing attention to others' needs. In sum, when I mention moral emotions in this book, I want to call attention to how specific emotions work in a moral context, not necessarily drawing a thick line between moral and non-moral classes of emotion.

Self-regulation in moral judgment

So far, we have seen that the appraisal function explains the workings of emotions in relatively complex or novel moral dilemmas, while the associative learning function can explain how emotions defend well-learned moral tenets and taboos. But self-regulation as a function of emotion is also highly relevant to moral behaviour (Monin et al., 2007). In a dilemma quite relevant to self-regulation, we are often confronted with *temptations* in which the short-term or personal consequences of an action oppose its long-term or social consequences (cf. Cross

& Guyer, 1980). I have elsewhere labelled these kinds of situations as "guilty pleasures," in which short-term benefits oppose long-term drawbacks—such as eating an enjoyable but fattening slice of torte—and "grim necessities," in which short-term drawbacks oppose long-term benefits—such as burning off the calories from that torte with a long and unpleasant session of exercise (Giner-Sorolla, 2001). In these situations of individual self-control, and similar situations such as the self-regulation of social exchanges (DeSteno, Bartlett, Baumann, Williams, & Dickens, 2010), the Stoic view that emotions are bad for self-control needs to be qualified.

Indeed, different emotions weigh in on different sides of these dilemmas. The short-term view is supported by non-self-conscious emotions, such as happiness in a "guilty pleasure" and frustration in a "grim necessity." These emotions are relatively more accessible as associations to the object of the dilemma for people with low self-control, and bringing them to mind increases impulsive behaviour (Giner-Sorolla, 2001). But self-conscious emotions such as guilt and shame for "guilty pleasures" and pride and confidence for "grim necessities" weigh in on the other side, supporting consideration of the long-term positive and negative consequences that match the valence of those emotions. Associations with self-conscious emotions are more accessible for people with good self-control, and making them more accessible decreases impulsive behaviour (Giner-Sorolla, 2001). Different kinds of emotion, too, may help to resolve inaction in different ways when faced with dilemmas of self-control, pushing a person's decision one way or another depending on the functional meaning of the emotional cue. When we are anxious, this may signal that things are uncertain and it is better to go for the short-term payoff, making more impulsive behaviour preferable (Gray, 1999). But more thoughtful emotions like guilt or gratitude may signal, instead, that the needs of others and the long-term needs of the self should be attended to (DeSteno et al., 2010; Monteith, Ashburn-Nardo, Voils, & Czopp, 2002).

Self-control itself is also seen as a moral virtue (Baumeister & Exline, 1999). For example, it shares variance with morality in predicting whether people will refrain from antisocial behaviour (Antonaccio & Tittle, 2008). In Schwartz' value model, self-control forms part of the conservation values (Schwartz, 1992). But beyond its status as a moral end, we also often need self-control to help us act upon other moral values, such as helping others and seeking justice. When we observe and reflect on our own moral behaviour, an aspect of self-regulation that Monin et al. (2007) label moral self-image comes into play. Here, it is not so much that regulation is moralized, but that morality is regulated. In particular, self-conscious emotions such as pride, guilt, shame, and regret come into play when we assess, not just how competent we have been, but also how moral we have been. Numerous studies, both in the behavioural and neuroimaging literatures, document the arousal of negative feelings when people are told they have violated internalized standards such as anti-prejudice ideals (e.g., Monteith, 1996; Plant & Devine, 1998) or when they imagine themselves violating social norms intentionally (Berthoz, Grezes, Armony, Passingham, & Dolan, 2006). However, because these emotions have intrinsic pleasure and pain attached to them, we are also tempted to look for ways to switch off the painful emotions and turn on the pleasurable ones, without actually having done anything to be proud of.

In moral self-regulation, the most widely studied of these ways to cheat is moral disengagement (Bandura, 1999). Bandura's theory outlines a number of excuses and justifications typically offered by people who have done wrong to others. The underlying motive for these excuses, according to Bandura, is to quiet the emotional disturbance that would happen in a morally sensitive human being who realizes that he or she has harmed another. Some of these excuses include: "the victim is responsible for what happened"; "the victim wasn't really harmed"; "the victim wasn't really human"; "everyone else is doing it"; "I was provoked." Moral disengagement beliefs accompany and predict many different kinds of antisocial behaviour, including crime and delinquency (Hyde, Shaw, & Moilanen, 2010), teenage bullying (Hymel, Rocke-Henderson, & Bonanno, 2005), foul play in sports (Boardley & Kavusannu, 2007), and opposition to apology and restitution for war and colonialism (Castano & Giner-Sorolla, 2006; Leidner, Castano, Zaiser, & Giner-Sorolla, 2010).

If moral disengagement is the easy way to make guilt go away, the recently studied phenomena of moral licensing and moral credentialing seem to show an easy way to attain the positive state of moral pride (Merritt, Effron, & Monin, 2010). This line of research shows that people see morality as a goal that, when reached in one situation, allows a person to rest on his or her laurels and act less morally in other situations. For example, in one study, participants were put in a situation where they could give biased advice to a fellow player in a game with a cash payoff. They had a vested interest to give bad advice—that is, they could make actual money from advice that was less than optimal for their "client." But when participants were forced to act honestly by disclosing their interest to the other participant, they actually gave more biased advice than participants who weren't made to disclose, and their victims did not take into account the conflict of interest as much as they should have (Cain, Loewenstein, & Moore, 2005). The symbolic hand-washing of disclosure looks like an easy way to feel morally righteous. But all it did in that experiment was satisfy the conscience and open the door to morally questionable behaviour.

The role of emotion in moral self-regulation is easy to speculate on but sometimes hard to prove. Of course, if a certain standard of morality is seen as an "ideal" or "ought" characteristic for self-regulation, then anxiety, dejection, and self-critical feelings should follow if we depart from it. The moral nature of an offence, or at least the extent to which it harms other people, may also help determine whether its self-critical emotions are experienced as guilt, as opposed to the non-moral emotion of regret (Berndsen, van der Pligt, Doosje, & Manstead, 2004). However, the prevalence of defensive processes means that it can be difficult to connect them directly to live instances of guilt or shame. People who behave well, after all, have no reason to feel these emotions. But people who behave badly may have deployed their defences well ahead of time, ensuring that there are no second thoughts—or feelings—about their bad behaviour. Or, they may have felt badly immediately after the deed, but rationalized it later, by the time feelings can be measured.

But assume that someone does manage to feel guilt or shame. These emotions, all the same, are not guaranteed to lead to better behaviour. The problems we have already seen with guilt and shame, arising from the conflict between associative learning and self-regulation, are reflected in the mixed research findings on whether they are good or bad for moral behaviour. Although much research has been devoted to showing good outcomes from guilt and bad outcomes from shame (e.g., Tangney & Dearing, 2002), some critics have pointed out that these results rest on a trait measure of guilt that focuses more on behavioural motivation than on measuring the intensity of feelings (e.g., Giner-Sorolla, Piazza & Espinosa, 2011; Luyten, Fontaine, & Corveleyn, 2002). Other, more affective and situational measures of guilt tend to behave like shame and appear together with worse, not better, behavioural outcomes (for a review including the developmental literature, see Eisenberg, 2000). And, as with fear appeals in marketing, guilt-based appeals for products or charities with positive moral implications have to be deployed carefully. Defences against guilt can cause them to backfire (Basil, Ridgway, & Basil, 2008; O'Keefe, 2002).

Communication in moral judgment

Consider for a moment the nightmare scenario of a baby girl raised by beings who lack any way to express or recognize emotions: by aliens, say, or robots, or most plausibly *alien robots* (because it's very likely that any self-aware robots that humans manage to construct will have some form of emotional capacity built in; e.g., Levy, 2006). The robots may punish and reprimand the child for acting in certain ways, but she will have no motivation to treat the robots' rules as anything more than the rules of a game she has to attend to. They may tell her certain things are "wrong" and other things are "right," but without expressive emotional anchors, her understanding of those terms is likely to come from a non-empathetic rather than empathetic theory of mind. So, she learns that "wrong" is "that which displeases the robots" and "right" is "that which pleases the robots." She can't internalize moral standards from non-emotional sources, so she grows into a Machiavellian woman. She is great at understanding what is good and bad from different points of view, but has no sense of morality as values, as objectively true articles of faith.

Now, someone with doubts about the emotionalist explanation of morality could tell an equally plausible story. The robots could read the girl edifying stories, and impress on her that moral rules are always to be followed above all else, turning her into a successful moral individual. But our robot story has resonance because it is backed up by research in child development. Starting in infancy, touch and the sharing of warm feelings between caregiver and infant is critical for creating a sense of attachment, which in turn underlies later moral development (Narvaez & Vaydich, 2008; Zahn-Waxler, 2010). Later on, parents communicate their emotional disapproval of selfish behaviour, and this increases the chances that a child will later develop well-internalized moral standards (Laible & Thompson, 2000).

The emotional expressiveness of parents also is related to the personality development of children. For example, one study found that positive expressions in response to children's pro-social behaviour encourage more pro-social traits among children (Dunsmore, Bradburn, Costanzo, & Fredrickson, 2009). Not just any emotions are good for the moral upbringing of children, though. In fact, much of this research also finds that expressions of angry or controlling emotions by parents create children who show less moral concern for others. Eisenberg (2000) argues that the threat created by hostile displays creates strong negative emotions in children. This leads them to worry about their own safety, instead of feeling secure to care about other people. But emotional responses in the early development of attachment leads to empathy, at first toward the parents and later toward others, that forms the basis of caring moral action.

Adults, too, use emotions to communicate about moral norms. Walking into a room and having every face turn to you with an angry expression can be an unnerving experience. If those faces belong to members of a hostile army unit, then morality never comes into it. The first impulse is self-preservation; fear is the emotional result. But if the faces belong to members of your family, or your friends, it is more likely that you will stick around, because you value those relationships. Then a complicated process of discussion will begin. You may try to find out what is wrong, or explain yourself if you think you know. Whether or not their anger is justified can come under discussion. If you find their reasons overwhelming yours, you offer your own emotional expressions of contrition, as sincere tokens of your submission to their judgment. Further emotional expressions from them, perhaps communicating forgiveness or satisfaction, close the circle, and repair the damage to the social relationship that all this friction has caused.

Research supports this view of emotions as critical to moral communication. In the first place, when people transgress moral and social norms, other people react with emotional feelings and expressions, primarily anger but also sometimes contempt, disgust, or sadness (Rozin et al., 1999b; Stouten, de Cremer, & van Dijk, 2006). If the target of these expressions accepts that the norm is legitimate and that they are correctly chastised for violating it, various emotions of appeasement follow (Chekroun, 2008; Giner-Sorolla & Espinosa, 2011). If the target doesn't think the criticism is fair, though, he or she is likely to snap back with feelings and expressions of anger, defending against social control (Chekroun, 2008; Hopfensitz & Reuben, 2009). Brain imaging studies even show that private responses to personal social transgressions involve areas involved in processing angry faces in others (Berthoz, Armony, Blair, & Dolan, 2002). This is striking evidence of the value of moral–emotional expression in everyday conduct. Even when meditating on their sins in a giant doughnut-shaped electromagnetic scanner, normal people feel the sting of remorse in terms of other people's angry faces.

Emotions and groups

Because emotions deal with concerns that are close to the self, it makes perfect sense that people should get emotional when they tie their sense of self to a social group. A human being can sit watching television with all basic needs provided, and with no particular reason to feel happy or proud as an individual. But just let this being identify strongly as French, as an FC Barcelona supporter, or as a scientist. Then, things on the television have the power to move our hypothetical couch potato, even though they have no implication for his or her personal well-being. So, the French person might shudder when French sailors in the Gulf of Aden fall victim to pirates, even if she has never been there and never will; the supporter will stand up and cheer as if he had scored the winning goal himself when FC Barcelona clinch a trophy, although his only contribution was funding a minute fraction of their star player's salary through the purchase of a licensed shirt; and the scientist may feel vicariously ashamed of a report on unethical conduct of researchers from the same field, even if she had nothing to do with their sins.

The influential intergroup emotion theory (IET; Mackie & Smith, 2004) explains these phenomena by joining theories of social identity and theories of emotional appraisal. In appraisal theory, events are judged according to their relevance for the self and its important goals. In social identity theory, people identify with social groups they belong to, so that events that happen on the group level take on relevance to the individual. This identification in turn predicts how much they will think and act with the group in mind; for example, classifying people readily as inside or outside the group, preferring to associate with group members, or discriminating against non-group members when resources are handed out (for an overview, see Brown, 2000). To social identity theory's "think" and "act," IET adds the possibility that people feel in line with the goals of the group they identify with.

As one consequence of IET, highly group-identified people should feel different specific emotions as a result of different specific appraisals they make on the group level. If I think the Russians are a strong threat toward my country, I will feel not just negativity toward them, but specifically fear. This happens much as I might feel fear towards a bear in the woods who threatens me personally (as understood by the creators of a 1984 political advertisement for Ronald Reagan that alluded to the USSR as, yes, a "bear in the woods"). Another consequence is that a set of characteristic emotions becomes a part of identifying with a social group. The way I feel as an "American" at any given time may be different from the way I feel as myself, and more similar to the way my fellow Americans feel as Americans. But at the same time my "American" feelings can differ from my feelings as a male, as a social psychologist, or as someone of Catalan-speaking parentage. Yet another possibility, raised by Iyer and Leach (2008) in their review of group-based emotion research, is that a person will identify as an individual, but feel emotions toward a group based on an impression of its members—an individual emotional attitude.

A further consequence of group-based emotions is that, just as self-conscious emotions take the self as their object, so self-conscious emotions take the ingroup as their object. Here, the relations among emotion targets can be particularly complex. The research literature has examined in detail two kinds of situation: the self-conscious feelings of the individual in trying to control his or her own prejudiced beliefs and expressions vis-à-vis the outgroup (e.g., Monteith & Mark, 2005), and self-conscious feelings such as collective guilt felt on behalf of the actions of the whole ingroup or its representatives (e.g., Doosje, Branscombe, Spears, & Manstead, 1998; for a review see Wohl, Branscombe, & Klar, 2006). The link between the individual and his or her own group is less extensively studied, but makes sense as yet another source of self-conscious emotions. After all, if I can feel proud for being a good citizen, might I not feel guilty for being a bad one? Indirect evidence that people feel guilt at letting down their group comes from a study by Cohen, Montoya, and Insko (2006) in which only highly guilt-prone people showed a link between having concepts of group loyalty activated and promoting hostile action against other groups. Nonetheless, this potential source of guilt is important, because it may help explain why people don't feel more guilt about the bad behaviour of their own groups in the international arena (Leidner & Castano, 2011).

While these aspects of intergroup emotion theory paint a vivid picture of multiple appraisals, research is just beginning to acknowledge the other three functions of emotions at the group level. But there is evidence that associative learning, self-regulation (and group regulation in this case), and social communication all play their parts in the functions and malfunctions of group-based emotions.

Group-based emotions and associative learning

Most treatments of group-level emotions see them as arising mainly from perceptions of various threats and opportunities that affect one's own group. Certainly, under this view group-level emotions can be irrational or inaccurate, but only as much as the beliefs and perceptions that give birth to them are irrational or inaccurate. This view might explain someone's hatred and fear of gay teachers, for example, as arising from the mistaken belief that they indoctrinate unwilling children in the gay lifestyle; or pride in the Chicago Cubs might be traced to the belief that this baseball team is superior in matters of morality (possibly exaggerated) or competence (definitely exaggerated). But feelings only sometimes follow beliefs. At other times they take on a life of their own, arising from repeated appraisals or from direct social learning. So, if we see emotions arising together with beliefs, it may instead be that the belief arose as a justification of the emotion, not as a cause of it.

Emotion, for example, strongly underpins and upholds the sense of patriotism. This is hard to explain without acknowledging the associative learning of emotions. Children learn to associate their country and its symbols with respect, pride, and celebration. They take these lessons from their family, peers, and social institutions, principally school. The learning is emotional, symbolic, and associative. Somewhere there may be a rationalist country that asks its children to withhold their emotional evaluation of their homeland until they've carefully compared its inventions, heroes, and breathtaking natural wonders with those of its competitors. But that country is probably not where you or I grew up. Hess and Torney

(1967) made similar points in a study of over 12,000 schoolchildren in the New York area. Reporting on the daily pledge to the flag and national anthem singing in school, they observed that "these rituals establish an emotional orientation towards country and flag even though an understanding of the meaning of the words and actions has not been developed" (p. 106). Not only conditioning-like processes, but also a more relational transfer of emotions can be seen in Hess and Torney's finding that children with strong fathers also had developed a more positive and respectful attitude toward the President. The upshot of this intriguing link between *pater* and *patria* can also be seen, for example, in findings of a survey of US students reported by Feshbach (1987); a measure of patriotism, or emotional attachment to the ingroup (but not necessarily at the expense of any outgroups), was correlated with self-reported attachment to one's own father. Children's positive feelings transfer from school and family to country, most likely without much thought required.

Negative feelings towards other groups can also be socially learned without needing to envision a threat, realistic or fantasized, coming from them. The mere pairing of a nationality's name with negatively valenced words, as Staats and Staats (1958) demonstrated very early on, can produce negative attitudes toward that country, even without awareness that something is going on. Conversely, the psychological process of classical conditioning can improve negative group attitudes. Olson and Fazio (2006) demonstrated this across three experiments in which Whites' racial attitudes improved after seeing photos of African-Americans consistently paired with positive words. As with the 1958 experiments, participants were not aware of the link in the experiment between pictures of Blacks and positivity. Beyond specific groups, the general concept of the ingroup can itself go from being a conditioned to an unconditioned stimulus, leading to more positive evaluations of things associated with a completely novel and meaningless ingroup (Ashburn-Nardo, Voils, & Monteith, 2001) or even with the pronoun "we" as opposed to "they" (Perdue, Dovidio, Gurtman, & Tyler, 1990).

These studies involved basic evaluations, rather than specific emotions. But emotions also can create a particular kind of emotional prejudice toward particular groups, beyond mere negativity. DeSteno, Dasgupta, Bartlett, and Cajdric (2004) put participants in an angry, sad, or neutral mood from an incidental manipulation, and then measured attitudes toward a recently described, novel group. This group was further described as one that the participant either belonged to or did not. The hostile emotion of anger created specifically negative attitudes toward the outgroups, even on implicit reaction-time tasks, in a way that the less hostile emotion of sadness did not. If the relationship between groups and emotions is associative, then the group should be able to cue the emotion; a direction of effect that makes no sense if emotions are assumed to just appraise the existing environment. Tapias, Glaser, Keltner, Vasquez, and Wickens (2007) studied pre-existing emotions toward outgroups among White, heterosexual participants. Their experiments found that the specific associations between disgust and gay men, or between anger and African-Americans, had become reciprocal, so that cueing the emotion made the concept of the group more accessible as well as the other way around.

There are some intriguing consequences of emotions becoming associated with a group without much reasoning. Because people are motivated to justify their pre-existing emotions, they may come to express beliefs about the group that are inconsistent with each other; but, if their pedigree is traced back, both beliefs are consistent with the emotion. Allport, in *The Nature of Prejudice* (1954), gives a few choice examples. There was the White Rhodesian colonist who characterized the "natives" as lazy and then, a few hours later when he saw a group of them working, as mindless labouring brutes. Or the anti-Semite who pronounces first that Jews are "clannish"—too "groupy" by half!—and then that they are "rootless cosmopolitans"—not "groupy" at all! The easiest explanation for these conflicting stereotypes is that they're post-hoc elaborations of a single emotion. Contempt, based on two different ideas, seems to explain the paradox of the White colonist. And the contradictions of the anti-Semite both seem to come from a feeling that might be interpreted either as realistic anxiety about a competing social group, or existential anxiety about someone who belongs to no social group at all.

The dual-process nature of emotions can also mean that prejudice itself takes on a two-levelled nature. As Cacioppo and Berntson (2001) argue, conditioning processes can lay down an early aversion, impossible to justify, toward another group. Such a gut-level prejudice can, however, be opposed by other, more thoughtful concerns, such as realizing that the group has been historically oppressed and it is not fair to dislike them (see also Katz & Hass, 1988; Wilson, Lindsey, & Schooler, 2000). Different emotions that support justice, such as guilt, sympathy, or anger, can then oppose the associative prejudice, working through the more appraisal-like route. One poignant illustration of how the same information can have completely different effects on these two systems of feeling comes from studies in which words signifying unjust victimization, such as "oppressed" and "maltreated," were shown to participants who were learning about an entirely new, fictitious social group (Uhlmann, Brescoll, & Paluck, 2006, Studies 2 and 3). These negatively valenced terms created prejudice against the group, as measured by a reaction-time task, the Implicit Association Test (Greenwald, McGhee, & Schwartz, 1998). Implicitly, the negative meaning simply rubbed off, leading to stronger automatic associations of the group with negative concepts. However, when making explicit statements, participants took the context of injustice into account, and showed positive attitudes toward this group that had been described as oppressed.

Group-level attitudes also take part in delivering the existential benefits of strong, certain emotional associations. Both disparagement of outgroups and increased attachment to ingroup symbols have been demonstrated as responses to existential threat brought on by thinking about one's own death (Greenberg, Solomon, & Pyszczynski, 1997). Existential concerns can also bring about more positive reactions to outgroups, as long as this supports central attitudes and values. For example, existential concerns can make attitudes more positive toward a person who validates a stereotype about a group (Schimel et al., 1999); and for someone who holds egalitarian values to be important, existential concerns can motivate calls for fair treatment of other groups (Greenberg, Simon, Pyszczynski, Solomon, & Chatel, 1992). Similar sharpening of group-level evaluation has been found in reaction to increased personal uncertainty (McGregor, 2006; van den Bos, Poortvliet, Maas, Miedema, & van den Ham, 2005), to information that threatens the worth of the core self (Heine, Proulx, & Vohs, 2006; Sherman & Cohen, 2006), and to personal threats that can be addressed by calling on social allies, such as theft (Navarrete, Kurzban, Fessler, & Kirkpatrick, 2004).

A completely pragmatic view of human motivation can explain these findings, up to a certain point. Groups may be valued more in an uncertain situation because they can provide valid advice and resources, while outgroups may seem more threatening because of competition. But it is hard to see how a pragmatic account could explain the effects of merely thinking about one's own death, without bringing up a specific threat to one's life. All the ingroup love and outgroup hate in the world won't help us live forever; only Tinkerbell in *Peter Pan* can be raised from the dead by everyone getting together and clapping their hands. The evidence instead points to outgroup-targeted attitudes serving existential concerns, defending from the awareness of our final limit: mortality.

Likewise, threats to the self-concept, such as poor performance on an intelligence test, often have the side effect of intensifying prejudice against outgroups (Fein & Spencer, 1997; Spencer, Fein, Wolfe, Fong, & Dunn, 1998), especially among those with high self-esteem (Crocker, Thompson, McGraw, & Ingerman, 1987). This kind of effect is not so easily explained by pragmatic concerns either. True, personal incompetence might increase reliance on the ingroup, but why then would people want to be more hostile towards outgroups? If anything, feeling stupid should pragmatically lead people to think more highly of competitor groups, taking a realistic appraisal of who is likely to win a battle of wits. Again, a better explanation is that unwelcome feedback on performance threatens a valued self-image, which is then reinforced by relying more heavily on group-level judgments; if I am bad, "we" are good, or at least "we" are better than "them".

Group-based emotions and self-regulation

As already discussed, emotions can be felt toward a group one identifies with, as well as toward other groups. This raises the possibility that we can apply individual-level insights on the regulatory function of self-conscious emotions to groups. In the latter part of the 20th century, a number of national groups visibly wrestled with collective feelings that could be seen as self-regulatory feedback to the group's previous collective behaviours. Perhaps the most striking example is the drive after the Second World War, both by the part of the occupying powers and the post-war German leadership, to avoid the mistakes made after the First World War. Since then, Germans have been shown the wrongness of their nation's past aggression by a campaign of public justice and remembrance that continues to this day. Displays and feelings of guilt and shame have figured heavily in this process (Barkan, 2000). Collective joy and pride at a group's achievements—in another German example, the celebrations at the fall of the Berlin Wall—can likewise reinforce and reward the finding of a new way forward.

At the same time, the problems of emotions' regulatory role also show themselves on a group level. Guilt and shame are painful, and threaten the precious national self-image with contamination by association. Thus, the period of soul-searching in the United States after its withdrawal from Vietnam lasted only 6 years before Ronald Reagan was elected, with the promise to erase the "Vietnam Syndrome," restoring interventionism to foreign policy. As the Charlie Daniels Band put it in song at the time—"We're walkin' real proud and talkin' real loud again, in America." Indeed, it is more usual to do entirely without self-doubt after a national wrongdoing. The desire to avoid the pain of deserved guilt and shame, and to bask in false pride, leads groups to rewrite history. American visitors to the 51st Regiment's Museum in Dover, England, near where I live, might feel peeved, perhaps amused, but certainly not guilty, to see their Revolutionary War characterized as a revolt by colonists who objected to taxes levied on them for their own protection. I am not saying whether the US or British perspective is the right one here, but clearly, somebody must be wrong!

Empirical studies have only begun to explore the regulatory role of group-based emotions. In a series of studies about students' perceptions of themselves as members of the "student" group, Maitner, Mackie, and Smith (2006) showed that emotions can regulate motivation on a group level, so that they diminish when relevant collective goals are achieved but stay in force when goals fail to be achieved. For example, if students were told that their group's efforts to redress an injustice against them had been successful, they felt less guilty than if they were told that the students' own weak efforts had failed. Guilt, in this context, was felt not because the student group had committed an injustice against another, but because the student group had collectively failed to support its own aims.

The individual level, however, makes group self-regulation even more complex. At the same time that emotions regulate individual action regarding a group's relationships with other groups, the same emotions can also regulate the individual's relationships with both ingroup and outgroups. In practice, this means that we can break the chain of group-level self-regulation at two places, in order to keep bad feelings away from the extended self. Either we maintain our affiliation with the group while morally disengaging from its misdeed (the conservative way—"America would never do something like that, but if we did, we must have our reasons"), or we reduce our affiliation with the group while maintaining consciousness of the misdeed (the liberal way—"That's terrible, and you know, I've never been the typical American that supports that kind of stuff"). Positive acts can be exaggerated just as negative ones are avoided, either by inflating the achievements of the group or by overstating the individual's connection to the group. In chapter 5, I will review research showing why emotions often fail in their job of regulating the moral standing of a group. For now, it is enough to point out that these reasons are similar to the reasons why guilt and shame also often fail at regulating individual conduct.

Group-based emotions and communication

Finally, the role of social communication has also been underestimated in research on group-based emotions. Communication can happen between groups, from the individual to the group, and vice versa. It may seem strange to think of countries and corporations expressing emotions. They don't actually have faces, although their iconic figures can be drawn that way in cartoons—a crying Lady Liberty, a laughing Chinese dragon. But groups have leaders, and their emotions are communicated to other groups, both face-to-face and though the mass media. So, in 2001, George W. Bush announced warm feelings on his first meeting with Russian president Vladimir Putin, saying "I was able to get a sense of his soul." Forty years earlier in New York, it was Soviet premier Khrushchev who gave the United Nations a sense of his sole instead, famously banging his shoe on the desk in a memorable communication of anger and derision toward the US-aligned Philippine speaker.

But emotional communication need not involve heads of state. Average individuals can also express emotions in the public eye, standing in for larger groups. After the Second World War, the discovery of Anne Frank's diary gave a window into the emotional world of the victims of the Holocaust. A decade earlier, Dorothea Lang's photograph of a Dust Bowl refugee mother midway between determination and despair had come to stand for the fragile hope of a whole class of dispossessed in America. There is also some indication from research into group-level apologies that average group members' words communicate more effectively than leaders' statements—for example, when expressing remorse at the group level (Philpot & Hornsey, 2008). A typical group member will usually be seen as more sincere, and less manipulative, than a leader.

The range of feelings that can be communicated from one group to another can thus be very similar to the range of feelings that can pass between people. This also applies to the messages that emotional expressions send from a group to an individual, or vice versa. At a basic level, by accepting the emotional tone of a group and returning it in kind, the individual sends a signal that he or she identifies with the group (Kessler & Hollbach, 2005), sincerely sharing an interpretation of reality (Echterhoff, Higgins, & Levine, 2009) that gives rise to the emotion. Being out of step with a group sends the opposite message. Depending on the larger goals of group and individual, expressing a contrary emotion can set off either measures to reintegrate the individual into the group, or to expel him or her as aberrant (Thoits, 1990). Research on smaller, face-to-face groups also has demonstrated that many channels work to communicate and coordinate the emotions of their individual members—emotional contagion, empathy, explicit discussion of feelings—leading to group-level expressions of emotions coordinated among individuals (Kelly & Barsade, 2001). This emotional coordination in turn improves cohesion and practical performance in group tasks.

Finally, individuals who deal with others across a sensitive group boundary also face challenges to emotional communication, influenced by the larger state of relations between the groups. Anxious feelings make face-to-face interracial encounters less comfortable for both participants, and they also reduce the willingness to seek them out in the first place (Trawalter, Richeson, & Shelton, 2009). Feelings of worry, guilt, and shame sometimes appear as regulatory responses to group-level stereotypes. For example, Whites interacting with Blacks in the US often feel worried that they will be prejudged as racist. Blacks in such interactions have similar feelings, but over concerns that they will not be respected on the basis of their own group's stereotypes (Bergsieker, Shelton, & Richeson, 2010; Shelton & Richeson, 2006; Vorauer, 2006). This anxiety itself can make the quality of the communication worse, leading to a spiral of bad rapport (Gudykunst, 2005). Even the successful regulation of anxiety, however, can also make the interaction worse; it puts a strain on thought, acting as a cognitive load to reduce the amount of attention that can be paid to the other person (Murphy, Richeson, & Molden, 2011).

We have seen here that although intergroup emotion theory has already inspired a rich body of research in the appraisal tradition, it can also embrace three other functions of emotion. Associative learning applies to the social world just as much as to the natural world; we categorize groups of people in much the same way as we categorize plants and rocks, and form emotional attitudes toward them on the basis of previous appraisals, social transmission, or mere association. The axiomatic, unreasoning nature of associative emotional attitudes can also link us to group concerns in a way that gives us additional certainty. Self-regulation has often been studied on a group level as a way to appraise the ingroup's actions. But I think that insights from the self-regulation function can also explain why these emotions are often unsuccessful in regulating behaviour on a group level, when group members deploy psychological defences that short-circuit the unpleasant implications of collective guilt and shame. And finally, groups and group members—singly, collectively, and officially—use emotions to communicate with other groups and their members. For some of the self-conscious emotions, as we will see in chapter 5, the benefits of seemingly irrational self-punitive feelings may only fully emerge when we recognize their ability to communicate within and outside the social group.

Morality and groups

Morality can influence groups on a number of levels. Humans, as we have seen in chapter 1, live in concentric circles of relationships, each with its own interests to defend: individuals, friendships and romances, family groups, coalitions within a group, and yet larger units. Regardless of the size of a group, there is a continual tension at each level between the interests of the smaller unit and those of the larger. This tension shows itself along horizontal lines, when sub-units of roughly equal status decide whether to cooperate or compete with each other. In most societies, there is also vertical tension regarding the relative contribution and entitlement of people at different levels of the social pyramid. The duties of more powerful people to less powerful people create concerns about their abuse of power. The duties of the less powerful to the more powerful also create concerns about their respect for power. All these kinds of concerns can be "moral" if they work against the individual's immediate self-interest for the greater good of the group.

A moral stance can also work to argue against the selfish concerns of a smaller subgroup and for the concerns of the next largest group of which it forms part. Thus, for example, a smaller group can be urged to show respect for a larger group that it is part of from a moral point of view, not because the larger group desires power, but because respecting the larger group identity is seen as good for all society. In this respect, I think that the kind of support for status and power differences that we see in system-justifying beliefs can be part of the moral domain, or at least represent a moralized stance (Jost, Banaji, & Nosek, 2004). System-justifying beliefs take many possible forms; for example, they include the beliefs that those with power achieved it legitimately, that anyone can succeed if they try hard enough, or that the poor are happier and indeed morally better than the rich (Kay, Jost, Mandisodza, Sherman, Petrocelli, & Johnson, 2007). Showing their ability to work against immediate material self-interest, such beliefs are often held even by those who lost out on status and power (Jost, Pelham, Sheldon, & Ni Sullivan, 2003).

Especially in Western cultures, morality is often presented as a solitary concern, the lone individual struggling with his or her conscience. Stories where an individual champions moral concerns against a complacent or corrupt collective, such as the classic films "Twelve Angry Men" or "Serpico," are fascinating to watch. But the appeal of good-person vs. bad-group stories comes precisely because these situations are unusual. It doesn't hurt that such a story also bolsters the assumptions of Western individualism, particularly the rugged variety upheld in the United States. But more commonly, it is the group that is more likely to instil and enforce moral behaviour and feelings upon a self-interested individual or smaller group. Even relatively broad definitions of morality, while they anchor one major cluster of moral concerns on other individuals—Shweder's autonomy, Graham and Haidt's harm and reciprocity foundations—anchor the others on relations between individual and group-defined concepts—Shweder's community, and the authority and loyalty moral foundations. Both these latter moral concern clusters ultimately weigh in favour of the group over the individual. The third area of moral concern, purity or divinity, is just as strongly tied to the cultural level of analysis, which often coincides with group boundaries. It imposes a way of treating the body and soul so that group members have a common experience and recognition sign (for example, the behavioural treatment of the different castes in India, or the North American norm of showering daily). Much of morality, then, promotes group as opposed to individual interests. Functionally, it makes sense that the group should act in its own interest by teaching, promoting, and enforcing morality.

If morality is a concern of the group about the individual, it is also a concern that individuals hold about any larger-order relationship, between two people or among many. Here, the ability to trust other people to behave morally takes on the highest importance. In fact, research on the perceived traits of groups shows the morality of a group, more so than its competence or social warmth, to be the most important factor in choosing to identify with the group, evaluate it positively, and feel good about belonging to it (Leach et al., 2007). These studies characterize morality largely in terms of such traits as trustworthiness and honesty, which are clear prerequisites for cooperation and mutual aid. However, framing these questions in terms of the traits of the group creates an interesting shift. Rather than asking the question "Will this group treat me fairly?" one can ask the broader question "Is this group fair?"

But then the question "Is this group fair?" needs to be qualified with the further question "To whom?" Street gangs, for example, prey on other people but promote the tightest code of loyalty among their members. Even outside the thug life, recent studies show that citizens of a country who are reminded of its war crimes tend to endorse and dwell on moral concepts that are related to loyalty and authority, rather than more universalistic moral concepts, a phenomenon dubbed "morality shifting" (Leidner & Castano, 2011). Recall that even Hitler's war machine felt some need to throw up a moral smokescreen, disguising its aggressive acts as a fair and justified self-defence of the German people. The excuses and rationalizations that accompany inhumane behaviour between groups are not symptoms of a complete withdrawal from the moral sphere, as the phrase "moral disengagement" would imply (Bandura, 1999). Rather, they represent the active maintenance of a concern with morality (Giner-Sorolla, Leidner, & Castano, 2012). A person who did not frame his or her group's cruel behaviour as a moral issue would have no need to distort reality by thinking of its victims as less than human or as incapable of feelings at all, yet our research has shown the need to engage these defences nonetheless (Castano & Giner-Sorolla, 2006; Leidner et al., 2010).

The strength of group-based moral concerns also shows itself when other groups are not just dehumanized, but demonized—portrayed as moral villains whose malicious threat to others puts them outside the pale of civilized society (Giner-Sorolla et al., 2012). Demonizing another group has a number of implications. It turns violent action against them into a virtue. This works to reduce people's uncertainty about military action, the collateral deaths of civilians, and even such extreme expressions as rape and torture. Punishment of demonized enemies can be as severe as desired. Likewise, opposition to the excesses of the punitive crusade, whether in moral or financial terms, can themselves be made to seem immoral. Questions of procedure, too, fall by the wayside in moralized issues (Skitka & Houston, 2001). Indeed, Hollywood films such as "Dirty Harry" that celebrate vigilantism against demonized criminals have made sure to show up the impotence of the criminal justice system. The law, in this narrative, is too caught up with protecting the rights of the accused. It is blind to the need for swift punishment when someone is "obviously" a criminal.

All these justifications become easier when the group's members take it on faith that its doings are morally superior to what other groups do. "Because I trust my group, it must be fair to other people" sums up this kind of moralized group identification that has been studied under the label of "glorification" (Roccas,

Klar, & Liviatan, 2006), while earlier work has explored the similar notions of blind patriotism (Schatz & Staub, 1997), nationalism as opposed to patriotism (Kosterman & Feshbach, 1989; Orwell, 1945), or pseudo-patriotism (Adorno, Frenkel-Brunswik, Levinson, & Sanford, 1950). A person who glorifies a group believes from the start in its superiority and rightness of its conduct and leaders, as measured by items such as "Relative to other nations, we are a very moral nation." This collective stance resembles the defensive entitlement seen in individual narcissism. Indeed, measures of collective narcissism directly based on concepts from psychopathology seem to play a similar role to that of glorification (Golec de Zavala, Cichocka, Eidelson, & Jayawickreme, 2009). Because glorifiers start out believing in their nation's morality as an axiom, they tend to endorse beliefs of moral disengagement—"they brought it on themselves," "this is nothing compared with what the other side has done," "those people don't really have feelings to hurt"—in response to information that their nation has behaved immorally (Leidner et al., 2010; Roccas et al., 2006).

Other researchers have often found that ideas of morality are applied differently to ingroup and outgroup members. In competition between nations, the lives of innocent members of the enemy group are valued less than the lives of fellow nationals (Pratto & Glasford, 2008). Judgments of fairness, too, tend to be group-biased. A study of members of the Italian Communist Party found that the aggressive acts of non-Communists were seen as more unprovoked and less justified than the same acts attributed to Communists (Schruijer, Blanz, Mummendey, & Tedeschi, 1994). Likewise, in another study of North American university students randomly assigned to ad hoc social groups, the acts of outgroup members were seen as being more exploitative and less easily forgiven (Wohl & Reeder, 2004). And when wronged victims look to justice from the group that has harmed them, it is not clear that they will find it. People judge fellow ingroup members leniently for their moral transgressions, and outgroup members more harshly, as shown by experiments with samples ranging from American university students (Valdesolo & DeSteno, 2007) to Papua New Guinea highlanders (Bernhard, Fehr, & Fischbacher, 2006).

Sometimes, though, people can take a more objective perspective, answering the question "Is my group fair?" by judging it according to higher and more objective moral standards, and seeing its moral goodness as an evidence-based question rather than an article of faith. In the research of Roccas et al. (2006), this is the profile that characterizes people who are low in glorification while still being strongly attached to their nation, showing love and concern for it. These people feel more guilt, not less, when reminded of their nation's moral shortcomings. Likewise, people with a universalistic moral identity show a wider circle of moral concern for people in other groups (Aquino & Reed, 2003).

Even in these circumstances, though, I would argue that people are moved to criticize their ingroup not so much from a sense of individualism, as from a perspective that sees their group as one "individual" that forms part of a larger community. So, a national glorifier might see an anti-war protest group as immoral because they undermine the interests of the national group, which are presumed to be good in and of themselves. But a person with a universalistic moral attachment to the nation might instead see the anti-war group as acting morally because they have in mind the larger international community. The interest of humanity as a whole is a greater good than that of the group, representing a universalized, rather than parochial, version of ingroup morality. Roccas et al.'s idea of attachment involves loyalty to and respect for one's own group and its leaders. But attachment is also compatible with a belief that members of other groups also have something to love and feel respect for. However, in the eyes of the person with a glorifying national identity, a foreigner who loves and honours his or her own country must be deluded or mistaken. Because these two modes of national identification exist side by side in any country, it makes sense to think of love for the ingroup and dislike for outgroups as separate things, even though one tends to rise as the other falls (Brewer, 1999; Mummendey, Klink, & Brown, 2001).

Intersection of the intersections: Joining emotion, morality, and groups

I have argued in this chapter for the strong involvement of emotions in morality. In particular, elaborated, socially communicated emotions can modify the rapid intuitions often equated with moral emotion. Even intuitions, though, ultimately have to be taught and reinforced in society. Because of this, social groups are vital to the expression, regulation, and enactment of moral behaviour through emotions. It is perhaps not surprising that much of recent research into group-relevant emotions has emphasized characteristically moral emotions such as anger, disgust, guilt, shame, and pride. These emotions follow from the crucial role that moral concerns play in relations between individuals and the group, among the individuals within a group, and among groups themselves.

Of course, it is possible for a person to view relations between groups in purely pragmatic terms, and to feel only emotions relevant to his or her group's own interest: fear when the group is threatened, relief when it escapes a threat, frustration when the group fails, pleasure when it succeeds. But there is something special about the moral emotions where groups are involved. They emerge specifically when we think of the situation in a way that involves *more than one level* of social organization. They advocate the needs of the village when we weigh these against the needs of the self; but they also can advocate for the needs of our nation when weighed against the needs of our village, or for the needs of humanity at large when weighed against the needs of our nation. If moral emotions lead different people to different conclusions, it is because they place different emphases on different levels of group organization. This is why a pacifist can feel shame in the eyes of the world if his country goes to war, while a militarist can feel shame in the eyes of her country if it doesn't go to war.

At the extreme level, a society can refuse to acknowledge any more inclusive social category than that defined by its borders, as happened in states such as ancient China and Rome, where anyone outside the Empire was seen as a barely-human barbarian. Someone who thinks in this way is capable of great moral concern toward the people within the borders, but acknowledges few if any rights for people outside. This bias, as we have seen from research, continues even among supposedly more enlightened societies today. They simply think less of people outside their cultural sphere.

However, to be morally angry with another group, while a hostile feeling, is at least the beginning of moral consideration. Such an emotion implies that the others are not just beasts or bricks who lie in the way of superior people and their goals. That thought might spark off anger, true, but it would be non-moral anger: frustration at an obstacle. Moral anger, as we shall examine in greater detail in the next chapter, specifically responds to concepts of unfairness. This implies that the target of the anger is violating a greater norm observed at a higher level of organization. The higher level can be as concrete as a world assembly in a tall glass skyscraper or as nebulous as an egalitarian view of the human race. To be morally angry at a country for invading another country is impossible without seeing both countries as part of a moral community. Even more so, to feel guilty or ashamed for your own country's aggression implies that you see your country as violating standards set at a higher level.

This explanation can explain why moral emotions sometimes collide. To the person whose primary allegiance is to the nation, the primary moral tension is between the organizational levels of individual and nation. So guilt and shame should be felt by individuals for not supporting the nation; anger, or even contempt and disgust, should be directed at those who fail to support the nation; pride and admiration, conversely, go to those who do uphold the nation. People outside the nation may attract some moral concern. But this is undermined either in the old-fashioned way, by denying foreigners full human status, or in a way that became popular in the 20th century, disabling the moral thermostat by taking national morality for granted. "We have the most moral army in the world," goes another item from Roccas et al.'s (2006) glorification scale. So, of course, they cannot be treating people in a morally bad way.

However, for the universalist whose primary allegiance is truly to humanity at large, the moral tension is between the nation and the larger world community. Guilt and anger therefore are felt towards crimes toward humanity, even and perhaps especially when committed by one's own country. Pride and admiration are felt on the basis of national contributions to humanity. By contrast, while the holder of group-centred morality will gladly feel national pride at great inventions, discoveries, and feats of engineering, things are different when it comes to assigning blame. A nationalist or racist sees the human-race level of emphasis as misguided, naïve, and possibly even immoral, because it draws false equivalences between the real good guys and bad guys.

The universalist and nationalist perspectives both build upon our common human heritage as a social species. Each of them draws on the important species skill of balancing the needs of respected factions within a larger and more exclusive community. What is different is the scale at which the factions and the community are projected onto the scale of a world now grown populous and interconnected beyond any of our ancestors' experience. The universalist thinks in terms of billions of people, the nationalist in terms of millions; but both these moral imaginations are far removed from the couple of hundred known individuals that have characterized the human social sphere for most of history.

Morality, emotions, and groups are mutually bound together in a network of multiple functions at many levels of social organization. In this network, however, emotions are due special scrutiny because of their paradoxical nature. A single emotion can serve four functions, and can be felt in response to events from individual to global; but it remains the same emotion, a central processor overburdened with competing and conflicting demands. The tendency of emotional states to persist over time means that emotions bleed between contexts. The way in which emotions bias thought, as well as respond to it, means that they can take on a life of their own, a perpetual-motion machine generating and feeding on reasons. The need for emotions to be spontaneous, to aid self-regulation and social communication, can work against their flexibility in helping the individual deal with the world.

It may be that all these drawbacks are amply compensated in the grand scheme of things. After all, emotions generally function, day to day, conserving space in our brain's architecture by delegating multiple functions to the same processes. But psychologists are traditionally motivated to explain people's departures from rationality and functionality, and I agree that tragedy makes for better reading than utopia. The focus of the next three chapters, then, will be an explanation of the more mysterious aspects of the moral emotions as they relate to social groups. In doing this, I will draw primarily on the inherent conflict between each emotion's functions, but also the often interesting clashes that occur when the same emotion has acquired multiple purposes within a single function such as appraisal. For each emotion, I review research in my lab and those of others, relating the emotion to morality, groups, and each of the four functions of functional conflict theory.

4 Disgust and anger

In the English language we often hear the emotions anger and disgust spoken of in the same breath. Thus, topmost among the nearly half a million matches in the Google search engine for the phrases "disgusted and angry" or "angry and disgusted", as of 26 September 2010, we find:

- the British Minister of Defence expressing disgust and anger about a computer game that he feels trivializes the conflict in Afghanistan;
- a blog poster expressing disgust and anger about the conservative commentator Glenn Beck; and
- a Twitter user called the "F_U KID" who takes "Disgusted and Angry" as a motto with which to defy the entire world.

In fact, with regard to two other common negative emotions, relative to each word's overall frequency on Google, "disgusted" appeared in conjunction with "angry" about 10 times more often than "sad" did, and about 16 times more often than "afraid".

More systematic analyses have also shown the near-synonymous nature of anger and disgust in English. A statistical analysis of the meaning relationships among 135 English emotion words by Shaver, Schwartz, Kirson, and O'Connor (1987), as well as the more specific analysis of anger words by Russell and Fehr (1994), both bear this out. "Disgusted" and its synonyms appear as close to "angry" as some other words that are considered dictionary synonyms of "angry" (e.g., "irritated"); indeed, some 67% of respondents in Russell and Fehr's study said that "disgusted" is a synonym of "angry." Analyses of other languages' emotion words that include a form of "disgusted" as a common term likewise tend to show that speakers of, for example, Basque and Tagalog see disgust and anger terms as closely related (Alonso-Arbiol, Shaver, Fraley, Oronoz, Unzurrunzaga, & Urizar, 2006; Church, Katigbak, Reyes, & Jensen, 1998). Even preschool-age children in one study confused "anger" and "disgust" more often than any other basic emotion terms, when labelling facial expressions (Widen & Russell, 2003).

At the same time, approaching emotions from the biological rather than language end, anger and disgust seem more distinct. Their facial expressions are different enough for them to be classified by Ekman as two of the basic emotions

(Ekman, 1992), a result confirmed by electromyographical measurement of the facial muscles during facial expression (Vrana, 1993). Although anger and disgust expressions in moral contexts do both involve raising the upper lip (Rozin, Lowery, & Ebert, 1994), and are more often confused with each other than with other emotions, there are enough differences in the two facial expressions to make them reliably different (e.g., Ekman, 1994). Likewise, vocal expressions of anger and disgust are well differentiated (Maurage, Joassin, Philippot, & Campanella, 2007); the emotions show different patterns of activation in the brain, with some overlap (Vytal & Hamann, 2010); and they also show different physiological patterns, with anger speeding up heart rate and disgust slowing it (Levenson, 1992; Levenson & Ekman, 2002). Anger and disgust also show different, in fact opposing, action tendencies, with anger provoking hostile approach and disgust provoking withdrawal (Roseman, Wiest, & Swartz, 1994).

Why does language tend to lump anger and disgust together? A short thought experiment may convince you that these emotions are most like each other in social situations. Imagine a desert island with yourself as sole inhabitant. You might get angry when something blocks one of your goals; that coconut is too far out of reach, perhaps, or a storm destroys the raft you were building. You may get disgusted at some of the kinds of things researchers have identified as core aspects of disgust, tied up with biological concerns about infection (Curtis & Biran, 2001; Oaten, Stevenson, & Case, 2009); a rotten seagull, the guts of the pig you are butchering. When it comes to the individual's survival, anger and disgust each stick to their separate jobs. Anger helps you approach a task aggressively even in the face of obstacles, or frighten off an animal from another species. Disgust in the natural environment keeps you away from things that might make you ill, like rotten or uncooked flesh.

But introduce a human being whose behaviour is being judged, and disgust and anger take on socio-moral dimensions (Haidt, 2003a). If that other human steals from you, you might be angry, but you might also make the judgment: "You are a disgusting person." What's more, a third person will understand your negative moral judgment whether you say "She makes me angry" or "I'm disgusted with her." When a person's behaviour is the target, anger and disgust both lead to an attitude of condemnation, which other people are likely to talk about using the same words. And the same things that a person can be judged for, an entire social group can be judged for as well.

Because of this closeness in language, if we want to consider anger and disgust as separate moral emotions, it's important to seek out contexts in which they can be meaningfully spoken of as separate. Research in our lab and others has investigated the moral contexts in which the use of "disgust" and its synonyms refers to a distinct emotion from anger—the "yuck" feeling signified by raised lip and stuck-out tongue. Reporting their own emotions by endorsing pictures of prototypical anger and disgust faces, as well as by endorsing "angry," "disgusted," and their synonyms, our research participants show a tendency to report anger and disgust together. This is not surprising; both are negative emotions of moral disapproval. But when statistically controlling for the overlap between anger and disgust, our experiments consistently find that what is unique about moral anger responds to violations that involve harm and rights, while what is unique about moral disgust responds to violations of norms about the use of the body—in other words, sexual or eating taboos. Indeed, other studies have also shown a tendency for moral anger and disgust to respond in this way, using vignettes judged to involve harm- and justice-based violations as opposed to (mostly sexual or eating-related) "purity" violations (Horberg, Oveis, Keltner, & Cohen, 2009; Rozin et al., 1999b). Our studies have confirmed these results, but with several improvements. We presented participants instead with stories identical in setting that varied only in what kind of violation they involved, and we confirmed the role of a number of more specific judgments in emotional appraisal through mediation analyses.

For example, in one early set of experiments, anger responded primarily to whether we described a scientist as feeding her friends a foodstuff with or without their consent, violating their rights. Disgust, however, responded to whether we described the foodstuff as an artificially cloned steak made with cells from the scientist's arm, versus a memory-enhancing powder (Gutierrez & Giner-Sorolla, 2007). Extending these findings, in an additional experiment we varied a third factor: whether the scientist had fed the substance to her friends intentionally, or as an accident resulting from someone else's mix-up. This manipulation of intent increased only anger once disgust was controlled for; the manipulation of (harmless) cannibalism, violating a norm about the body, again increased only disgust once anger was controlled for. Further analyses showed that inferences of rights violation and intent explained these effects on anger, while inferences of abnormality and unnaturalness explained the effects on disgust. We have also found similar reactions to stories varying the more or less normal nature of a sexual act, which affected disgust, and whether or not the act was a betrayal, which affected anger (Giner-Sorolla, Caswell, Bosson, & Hettinger, 2011a). In all these studies, both anger and disgust showed that they were morally relevant emotions by being independently associated with how wrong an act was judged to be.

It seems, then, that contexts where a bodily norm is violated are most likely to lead to emotions of disgust that can stand separately from anger. Indeed, there is already evidence that the social-moral disgust evoked by cheating or stealing behaves differently than the bodily-moral disgust evoked by incest or eating dog meat. Socio-moral disgust is much more highly correlated with anger and decays less rapidly (Simpson, Carter, Anthony, & Overton, 2006), and shows different patterns of brain activation that are less similar to non-moral, core disgust (Schaich Borg, Lieberman, & Kiehl, 2008). Another of our studies once again used scenarios that were varied slightly to constitute either a violation of rights (a man has his girlfriend tattooed while she is drunk) or a consensual transgression of bodily norms (a woman gets an ornamental scar on her body). We found that the endorsement of disgust terms in rights violation scenarios was predicted overwhelmingly by anger terms, with only a small contribution from endorsement of disgust faces. However, in bodily norms scenarios, disgust terms showed less overlap with anger language, and were predicted more strongly by the endorsement of disgust faces (Gutierrez, Giner-Sorolla, & Vasiljevic, in press). Therefore, existing studies that support the involvement of disgust in non-bodily moral judgments need to be examined more closely. Often, these studies do not account for the possibility that anger, co-activated with disgust, might account for those morality effects.

Disgust and groups

Even if we are careful to exclude uses of disgust language that are indistinguishable from anger, a visceral, physical disgust still lurks behind the most vicious and persistent examples of hostility between social groups. When a group is set apart by its bodies or what they do with them, disgust becomes directly relevant to prejudice. For example, high levels of disgust have been shown to characterize attitudes towards gay people (Cottrell & Neuberg, 2005), and conversely, people with high levels of disgust sensitivity toward physically repulsive things also tend to show more anti-gay attitudes (Inbar, Pizarro, Knobe, & Bloom, 2009; Terrizzi, Shook, & Ventis, 2010). Two recent studies from our lab have also identified disgust as a reaction to brief sexual scenarios involving, for example, sex between men or sex with a transsexual person. We found that disgust was related to how abnormal or unnatural the act was judged, when analysed controlling for anger. Also, disgust increased as the same relationship was described as heterosexual as opposed to non-sexual, and as the relationship was described as homosexual as opposed to heterosexual (Giner-Sorolla et al., 2011a). The role of disgust is so prevalent in sexual prejudice that one widely-used questionnaire measuring anti-gay attitudes includes a direct question about disgust (Herek, 1984).

Eating and drug use are also uses of the body that can create prejudicial disgust. One recent study (Vartanian, 2010) found that US respondents ranked drug addicts, smokers, and obese or fat people as the three most "disgusting" out of a list of 20 social groups. Groups of stigmatized people associated with disgusting kinds of medical treatment can also take on disgust by contagion, as Smith, Loewenstein, Rozin, Sherriff, and Ubel (2007) showed in a study of attitudes toward colostomy patients. Avoidance of the patients was predicted by a person's general sensitivity to disgust. Likewise, in an earlier study involving real-time measurement of approach and avoidance reactions by means of a dial, more disgust-sensitive people showed a faster and stronger avoidance reaction once they learned that a person they had been learning about had been diagnosed as HIV-positive (Pryor, Reeder, Yeadon, & Hesson-McInnis, 2004). Even non-contagious physical disability can be irrationally associated with disease, and by extension with disgust (Park, Faulkner, & Schaller, 2003).

Some societies use disgust to control and exclude people at the very bottom of the social ladder. Bodily differences, as well as fears of contagion, can be exaggerated to reinforce disgust towards pariahs and scapegoats. The best-known such scheme is the caste system in India, whose boundaries are policed by concerns about contagion through physical contact. Lower castes do work that is seen to be contaminating to higher castes, and this contamination is passed on through the bodies of the caste members themselves. But disgust has been recruited into other caste-like schemes of social hierarchy. As historian Mark M. Smith relates (2006), in the segregated US South, some Whites argued that an unpleasant smell attributed to African-Americans, and fears of physical contagion from too-close contact, stood as valid gut-level reasons why public transport, toilets, and drinking fountains should be segregated. Although segregation based itself on overt racial differences, the cultural adaptability of disgust is shown by the persistence of discrimination and contamination fears toward the Burakumin caste in modern-day Japan. Historically viewed with disgust and given a name literally meaning "filth" because of their occupation working with dead bodies and waste, today's Burakumin are distinguished from other Japanese only by reputation and genealogy (De Vos & Wagatsuma, 1966).

Disgust is thus certainly a powerful feeling, readily applied to anyone at the bottom of a social totem pole. If no bodily difference or physical contagion exists in fact, one can be easily invented or exaggerated. Among children, disgust-driven beliefs about contamination are applied on social as well as hygienic grounds. One folklore scholar, reporting on the imaginary contagion known to children in the United States as "cooties," writes: "In its most extreme manifestations, the game functions as a form of ostracism. A dirty or disagreeable child, or a new boy or girl who has problems adjusting, will become a target for cooties" (Samuelson, 1980, p. 209). Disgust as an engine of social prejudice, then, may well be as ingrained as child's play.

Some writers and researchers have linked disgust toward social groups with the tendency to dehumanize them in various ways (see, for example, Nussbaum, 2004). In one extensively-studied model of group stereotypes and emotions, disgust is felt toward social groups and persons completely without social utility, providing neither competence nor warmth (Fiske, Cuddy, & Glick, 2007). This connection has been reinforced by a neuroimaging study in which pictures of homeless people, standing for a group seen as low in warmth and competence, evoked disgust, and also failed to activate brain regions normally associated with thinking about other people (Harris & Fiske, 2006). This suggests that the homeless, for Harris and Fiske's student participants, did not register as social objects.

The connection between low social status, the felt emotion of disgust, and dehumanization is an interesting one that deserves more investigation. It stands to reason that college-student participants most likely see the homeless as being unwashed and not picky in their eating habits, therefore disgusting. But people judged as low on both social dimensions might also provoke other emotions; anger if they are seen as unfair spongers, fear if they are seen as threatening. A recent study in our lab also calls into question the exclusive relationship between disgust and dehumanization (Giner-Sorolla & Hewitson, 2011). In a pretest, we identified three pairs of social groups that attracted negative attitudes of equal intensity within each pair. The difference was that one group in each pair (e.g., the "morbidly obese") attracted disgust more so than anger, whereas the other group (e.g., "crooked politicians") attracted more anger than disgust. Using a measure of explicit dehumanization (Viki, Winchester, Titshall, Chisango, Pina, & Russell, 2006), we found no differences between dehumanization of the angering and disgusting groups. What's more, dehumanization in each individual case was predicted independently not only by the participant's disgust, but also by anger, contempt, and fear.

Disgust and the functions of emotion

Appraisal

At first glance, disgust seems to follow the functional outline sketched by appraisal theories of emotion. It responds to the perception that something is contaminating. This in turn triggers action tendencies: avoidance, or possibly cleansing. This straightforward function was proposed, in the group context, by Kurzban and Leary (2001) in an evolutionarily-based explanation of the role of stigma. Strange individuals and groups, in this scheme, are likely to pose a threat by carrying germs or parasites to which one's own pack has no resistance; also, as we have seen, stigmatizing conditions such as physical abnormalities are taken as cues to disease. Shunning such people was therefore selected for in the ancestral environment, and carries on today in manifestations of prejudice toward strangers and outcasts. Naturally, Kurzban and Leary argue, disease-responsive stigma's predominant emotion should be disgust.

But the parasite-avoidance explanation, while it may explain the application of cooties to the "dirty" and "new" children mentioned above by Samuelson, doesn't explain why "disagreeable" children are targeted by disgust, or why it's only new children "who have trouble adjusting" who are said to have cooties. An appraisal theory that looks for the one defining perception that triggers disgust is going to be in trouble. Disgust, as Keltner and Haidt (1999) explain in detail for that specific emotion, can be triggered by many different things due to its evolutionary history. Even physical disgust can be separated into oral, contamination, and animal-reminder elicitors (Olatunji, Haidt, McKay, & David, 2008). Cultural concerns can also trigger disgust; in one study of emotional reactions to threats posed by different social groups, perception of disease in a group was associated with disgust; but so was perception of a threat to values (Cottrell & Neuberg, 2005). Another study examining prejudice against gay men found that the role of disgust in such prejudice could not be explained just by the threat of disease, but involved conservative sexual attitudes and religious beliefs (Olatunji, 2008).

Even focusing on its biological functions, while disgust does seem to do many useful things to keep us away from contamination, it is not so clear that it does those things through appraisals. Here again, I use the term "appraisal" in the sense of a judgment based on a match between a situation and a goal. One of the key elements of an appraisal, to me, is that it can be reappraised by changing the goal or the perception of a situation. But research in my lab finds that the kinds of things that lead to disgust are not easily reappraised. This leads us to believe that they are also not appraised in the first place; associative learning, rather than appraisal, is a better model to account for the origin of disgust experiences.

There are several thought experiments to illustrate this point that are always a hit in lectures and professional talks, not to mention the dinner table. In Taiwan there is a novelty restaurant with a bathroom theme to its décor called Modern Toilet (Tso, 2009). Diners sit on closed toilet seats. They are served drinks in little plastic urinals and eat food out of ceramic bowls shaped like toilets. The prevalent mood is a blend of amusement and disgust. Meanwhile, in the United States, a widely-circulated Halloween recipe also packages food in an amusing way. The "Kitty litter cake" is served in a clean cat litter box, with a clean cat litter trowel, but is topped with half-melted Tootsie Roll chocolate candies and crumbled cookies for a realistic simulacrum of feline droppings. What would an appraisal view of disgust have to say about our reactions to these culinary practical jokes? The goal to avoid disease and germs is fulfilled, because everyone knows the situation: the dishes are scrupulously clean and the food is delicious. But still disgust appears, because of a mere superficial resemblance between what's about to be eaten and other objects that everyone has learned to keep as far from their mouth as possible.

In their cognitive model of emotions, Ortony et al. (1990) recognize the special nature of disgust, placing it among the object-related emotions such as love and hate, rather than those emotions that correspond to persons, situations, or the self. This is a good insight, from my point of view; it can explain the link between disgust and dehumanization, seeing a person as a socially worthless "thing." However, this categorization also points out the limits of appraisal models in defining an abstract quality that creates disgust. Ortony and colleagues (1990) try to distinguish disgust from other emotions by associating it with "distasteful" things—in other words, defining disgust with a near-synonym for disgust. A similar metaphorical vagueness is apparent in Lazarus' (1991) aetiology of disgust as coming from a "poisonous idea." These schemes of appraisal classify disgust as a negative emotion, toward some object . . . but then, what abstract cognition would distinguish disgust from, for example, hatred or simple dislike? This is not so clear, given the large variety of things that can create disgust.

Royzman and Sabini (2001) argue that what causes disgust cannot be summed up in any single abstract concept. One by one, they demolish numerous writers' contenders for the "disgust appraisal" (such "matter out of place," "abjectness," "teeming with life," or animal-nature reminders) by pointing out cases in which each concept does not lead to disgust. To give but one example, the proposal of "contamination" as a key cognitive element of disgust (Rozin & Fallon, 1987) still does not seem quite right. Something registers as disgusting first, then contagious second. We shy from touching it because it is repugnant, rather than the other way around. Contagiousness and uncleanness are traits we infer from our disgust. This becomes clear from a recent developmental study in which children who did not yet understand the contagiousness of disgusting objects still felt disgust as strongly as those who did (Stevenson, Oaten, Case, Repacholi, & Wagland, 2010).

Another candidate for the disgust appraisal, not considered by Royzman and Sabini, turns up in the bodily-moral context that is relevant to judging social stigmas: "abnormal" or "unnatural" acts. But these, again, seem like explanations that might be given after the fact of disgust. In the mighty Royzman and Sabini manner, I can point to any number of abnormal acts (how normal is writing a book on moral emotions?) and unnatural acts (how natural is eating with a fork?) that are not disgusting. Additional evidence that these appraisals might not be the whole story when it comes to disgust comes from a recent study of ours (Russell & Giner-Sorolla, 2011a). There, appraisals of intent and harm completely accounted for differences between different stories' evocation of moral anger. However, appraisals of unnaturalness and other concepts associated with disgust such as impurity, even taken all together, only partially accounted for differences in disgust. Moreover, another set of studies (Russell & Giner-Sorolla, 2011b) found that people did not come up with "unnaturalness" or other complex concepts spontaneously when justifying their own moral disgust at paedophiles and other stigmatized groups. Instead, our participants preferred to justify their disgust with broad evaluative judgments ("they are evil") or even with the word "disgust" itself and its synonyms, creating tautologies such as "I feel disgust because they are disgusting."

But it is when we try to reappraise our disgust that the clearest evidence comes out: disgust is inflexible, doesn't respond to reason, and can't be eradicated just by cognitively knowing it's wrong. In the spirit of the Modern Toilet restaurant and the cat litter cake, Rozin, Millman, and Nemeroff (1986) conducted a number of studies showing that our reactions to disgusting objects follow two irrational magical principles: the law of similarity, by which appearance signals reality, and the law of contagion, by which essences can be transmitted by contact. Pieces of chocolate shaped like dog faeces, for example, were much less likely to be chosen than disc-shaped ones. Touching juice with a sterilized dead cockroach led to a decrease in preference for the juice, which might be rationally understandable (after all, how thoroughly can you sterilize a cockroach?). But the cockroach demonstration also made people less interested even in a different glass of the same kind of juice, a clearly irrational reaction.

A recent study in our lab also shows the stubbornness of disgust in the face of evidence, but in the moral domain (Russell & Giner-Sorolla, 2011c). Among four scenarios chosen to arouse moral anger and disgust, such as a man eating his pet dog after it dies of natural causes, we asked participants to imagine circumstances that would change their initial moral evaluations of each scenario. Across scenarios, anger changed much more so than disgust as a result of thinking over different circumstances. Also, when participants were asked to imagine that the changes had actually occurred, any actual change in moral evaluation of the scenario was predicted by the change in angry reactions rather than the change in disgusted reactions—not that disgust changed much in the first place. This result is particularly striking because participants were allowed to come up with the circumstances that they thought would change their mind the most. However, even personalized mitigating factors couldn't change the effect of disgust on moral judgment.

Associative learning

As we have seen, associative learning and retrieval in association with specific, concrete cues appears to be a more accurate account of how disgust comes about, relative to appraisal. Disgust's contagious nature helps these processes along. So does the superficial nature of cues that trigger disgust, as shown by disgust's sensitivity to appearances, and insensitivity to realizations about the actual nature of chocolate dog-doo. But just because disgust seems oblivious to abstract cognitive knowledge, this doesn't mean it's a dysfunctional emotion, at least in the big picture. Disgust's learning functions work with the long wisdom of evolution and culture, not the quick intelligence of the individual human mind. This is why disgust seems, on the level of an individual human being, to respond less to abstract thought about an object, and more to concrete cues that identify that object. Those cues have been learned from other people and from experience.

This associative learning of disgust starts at the age when a child starts to roam far away from caretakers and, in pre-modern traditions, to become weaned from breast milk. At this age, it makes sense to be choosy about where you step and what you eat. Developmental studies show that disgust reactions to even the most primary and useful objects of repugnance, like faeces, do not fully develop until between 2 and 5 years of age (Rozin & Fallon, 1987; Stevenson et al., 2010); toddlers, much to the dismay of their parents, will happily smear and play with their own mess if they are allowed to reach it. Less directly disease-relevant objects, such as a glass eye, are even slower to acquire disgustingness in the eyes of children (Stevenson et al., 2010).

This is the paradox of the associative learning of disgust. What disgusts us seems primal, natural, inevitable, and biological. At the same time, what disgusts us is learned from our parents, peers, and culture, and through associative ways, such as contagion and similarity to existing objects of disgust. We may be biologically prepared to learn disgust, but the sheer variety of cultural taboos worldwide that evoke disgust show that, like language, disgust has had its Tower of Babel. If some things, like dung and vomit, seem universally disgusting, this may just represent a trait that all cultures find it adaptive to pass on, just as it is biologically always adaptive to have an anus at the other end of the body from one's mouth. But when it comes to social groups, the associative nature of disgust presents a number of problems. While disgust-based social attitudes may have once helped structure many traditional societies, in the light of modern concepts of fairness and justice, they appear less acceptable.

Disgust is associatively sticky, and hard to wash away. In one study, neutral objects that had been shown in association with a disturbing and disgusting film of an injury showed reductions in participants' fear and anxiety reactions to them over time when they were no longer paired with the gruesome images. Disgust, however, did not fade away as readily (Olatunji, Forsyth, & Cherian, 2007). Small wonder, then, that rhetoric that tries to conjure up prejudice often commandeers the full-strength imagery of disgust—from the imagery of scatology on both sides in the religious battles between followers of Martin Luther and the Pope, to the modern use of disease metaphors against immigrants, dissidents, and minorities

(Sontag, 1977). In fact, one set of studies found that raising concerns about disease using disgusting pictures, as opposed to activating other threatening concerns with pictures of accidents, raised opposition to culturally unfamiliar immigrants (Nigerians, in Canada) relative to more familiar ones (Scots; Faulkner, Schaller, Park, & Duncan, 2004). While the authors propose evolutionary origins to this disease-primed prejudice, it is also possible that participants may have learned ugly cultural metaphors already. Indeed, concerns about disease, immigration, sexuality, and values may evoke disgust because they each represent symbolic threats to the extended self, more generally than just a literal biological anxiety (Burris & Rempel, 2004). The common point, though, is that these threats are symbolic and imaginary, formed by association rather than reasoning.

Knowledge about disgusting things also spreads readily. One set of studies (Heath, Bell, & Sternberg, 2001) found that stories manipulated to contain highly disgusting elements were more likely to be passed on, and that sites collecting "urban legend" stories on the Web display a disproportionately high element of disgust—although today, the revelation that disgusting things can be found on the Internet may have lost some of its newsworthiness. The irrationality of contamination fear, and our studies on the less reasoned nature of justification for moral disgust (Russell & Giner-Sorolla, 2011b), also suggest that, once smeared by disgust, it is hard for a group to argue its way free. Disgust feels so subjectively self-evident and correct that to oppose its conclusions seems downright unnatural, recalling Mark M. Smith's (2006) arguments that "sensory evidence" helped maintain the segregationist US South against pressures towards justice and equality.

It is this unreasoned nature of disgust that leads Nussbaum (2000, 2004) to oppose proposals to enlist it as a progressive force in law, such as by confronting racist or greedy social groups with revulsion and exclusion (a policy argued for by Kahan, 2000). Because disgust is a private, subjective reaction that is hard to articulate, Nussbaum argues, it also resists generally accepted standards of justice. To put it most concisely, visceral disgust is about what someone is, while anger is about what someone does and why. Because disgust's concerns ignore the concerns that liberal jurisprudence has about an accused person's motivation and the act's consequences, Nussbaum argues that it is not an appropriate influence in modern courtrooms. Our research has shown, however, that the "disgust" aimed at racist skinheads or greedy politicians, because it's not rooted in their bodily peculiarities, is likely to have a strong affinity with anger and with the appraisals that cause it: unfairness, harm, and injustice. In this sense Nussbaum's concerns may apply more to the kind of disgust aroused by violations of bodily norms, as opposed to other norms. Our research bears out this point, showing that considerations of harm and intentionality don't influence disgust separately from anger (Gutierrez & Giner-Sorolla, 2007; Russell & Giner-Sorolla, 2011a).

Self-regulation

Our bodies are full of disgusting products, but oddly enough, they don't become disgusting until they leave the body. We mostly manage to get by every day with a mouth full of spittle, for example. But thinking about spitting into a fresh plate of soup and then eating the mixture, some people get disgusted (Rozin et al., 1986). It's highly unlikely that infection could find its way back into you from your personal plate of spit soup. So, more generally, why can people be disgusted by themselves and the appearance of their own body? Practices that cleanse and modify the body, such as washing, shaving, circumcision, and body piercing, vary greatly across cultures. Disgust at obese people, elderly people, and drug use is also often accompanied by disgust at the thought of one's own obesity, aging, or drug use. Finally, disgust at specific sexual practices is also very selective and culturally variable (Blechner, 2005). The term "animal-nature disgust" (Rozin & Fallon, 1987) seems inadequate to cover all these concerns; it's not just being animal-like that disgusts us, but being unwieldy, unattractive, and subject to bodily need and frailty.

In the literature of psychoanalysis, and especially among psychoanalytic explanations of intergroup prejudice, self-regarding disgust plays a critical part. Freud (1905/1962) saw disgust as a defensive emotion, regulating the self's unacceptable desires. Without completely blocking out the thoughts of unacceptable activity, disgust nonetheless reacts to it, preserving psychological balance by painting forbidden thoughts as repellent. Goldenberg, Pyszczynski, Greenberg, and Solomon (2000) have drawn on existential perspectives in clinical and social psychology (Becker, 1973; Pyszczynski et al., 1999) to argue that disgust with one's own body and that of others is a defensive way of regulating anxieties about mortality. For example, an earlier study by Goldenberg, Pyszczynski, Greenberg, Solomon, Kluck, and Cornwell (2001) found that making people think about their own death also made them selectively more disgusted at bodily waste and animals. Since then, research has demonstrated links between death thoughts, the similarly threatening contemplation of similarities between people and animals, and disgust at a variety of reminders of our bodily nature including breastfeeding (Cox, Goldenberg, Arndt, & Pyszczynski, 2007) and pregnancy (Goldenberg, Goplen, Cox, & Arndt, 2007).

These links suggest a deep connection among people's ideas about death, the body, disgust, animals, and disliked outgroups, as Nussbaum (2004) observes (see also Goldenberg et al., 2009). Our awareness of being mortal, physical animals is intolerable, so the observation "humans are animals" becomes "those humans over there, not myself or anyone I care about, are animals." Disgust-based prejudice, whether based on real or imagined bodily differences, then arises to police this sharp distinction.

While this story is compelling, however, research has not yet completely confirmed it. Some of its links are well established. For example, insecurity about the self increases prejudice (Fein & Spencer, 1997), and reminders of mortality can sharpen hostile attitudes toward the outgroup (for a review, see Greenberg & Kosloff, 2008). However, in a recent study of attitudes toward immigrants, reminders of humans being like animals did not lead to any defensive reaction against the outgroup, while the opposite framing—"animals are like humans"—led to more tolerant attitudes (Costello & Hodson, 2010). And when a more direct manipulation of mortality salience was used (Vaes, Heflick, & Goldenberg, 2010), this did not lead to dehumanization of outgroups, so much as increased humanization of the ingroup. These findings are hard to reconcile with the specific existential prediction that people will react defensively against animal–human similarities and take it out on outsiders.

It seems hard to find evidence for the zero-sum equation of outgroup disgust proposed by Nussbaum (2004): that by painting outsiders as disgusting animals, we thereby elevate our own group, if only relatively speaking. Of course, the studies mentioned relied exclusively on undergraduates as a population, who may have more liberal attitudes, such that their existential defences are built around universalistic values rather than outgroup hatred (as shown by Greenberg et al., 1992). Given the role of disgust in anti-gay attitudes among young men, these hypotheses may be better tested in the domain of sexual prejudice. Glick, Gangl, Gibb, Klumpner, and Weinberg (2007), for example, used masculinity threat to increase men's prejudice against gay men who were seen as "effeminate." For the moment, though, the defensive role of disgust in regulating unpleasant truths about the self is not yet well-established as an explanation for group-based prejudice.

Social communication

As we have seen, language often leaves unclear whether a person is feeling disgust or anger. To some extent, this confusion also exists in facial expressions and voice intonation (Johnstone & Scherer, 2000). Any ambiguity in distinguishing people's expressions of these two emotions may have to be resolved, in the end, by integrating multiple channels of communication or taking into account the situation, and in particular by paying attention to the person's further behaviour toward the target of the expression. The greatest difference in the social communication of disgust and anger lies in what each emotion proposes we do with its target. Anger is fundamentally an emotion of hostile approach (Carver & Harmon-Jones, 2009). As we will see in the next section, its social message is a demand that something about the self be valued more (Sell, Tooby, & Cosmides, 2009), be it one's own ability, one's own moral interest, or a moral principle one holds. Disgust, however, is an emotion of withdrawal. Its social message is that something about the target has lowered value, not that something about the expresser needs to be valued more.

These social purposes of anger and disgust underpin a more visible difference in the verbal support typically given to the two emotions. As we have seen, disgust seems to be taught by social learning and associative learning, responds to superficial aspects of things, and often lacks supporting reasons. Because of this, disgust often makes sense on a cultural level, but is hard to argue about in explicit terms on an individual level. Unlike anger, we communicate *that* something is disgusting, rather than *why* it is disgusting (Russell & Giner-Sorolla, 2011b). Evidence for the inherently social transmission of disgust is strongest in developmental studies of children learning from their mothers. But schoolyard experience suggests that consensus on whether a new thing is disgusting also passes from peer to peer. In findings relevant to taste and distaste, too, facial expressions both positive and negative have been shown to condition responses to a novel food item (Baeyens, Vansteenwegen, De Houwer, & Crombez, 1996).

Everyone's personal map of disgusts and pleasures is constructed using a template of cultural norms. For example, if I know that a stranger was raised in suburban North America, I can be pretty confident that the stranger will find foods like horse, goat, or deep-fried guinea pig at least somewhat disgusting. By the same token, failing to connect on the topic of what is or isn't disgusting can be a social deal-breaker, compared with differences in other communicated emotions. On a first date, if you are worried about a new invention in the news and your date sees it as a great opportunity, he or she might reassure you. If you are angry about something that your dinner companion supports, you might discuss the issue in the hope of convincing him or her at least halfway. But if you are disgusted about a moral violation, and your companion thinks it is delightful and fun, the prognosis for a goodnight kiss is not looking good. Sharing common disgusts is one of the materials that holds any culture together. Indeed, a meta-analysis of studies of cross-cultural emotion recognition found disgust (along with fear) to be the emotion that showed most bias in recognition, so that it was recognized in own-group members' faces more than those of others. Anger and happiness, on the other hand, showed the weakest ingroup recognition bias (Elfenbein & Ambady, 2002).

Recent evidence from our lab also points to the role of disgust in social communication (Giner-Sorolla & Espinosa, 2011). University student participants in the UK and Spain were randomly assigned to look at an array of three photographs either of angry people's faces, or of disgusted people's faces. They were told to imagine a social context: they had just walked into a public area in student housing and people there were looking at them with those faces. The results of this study neatly tie together a social communication picture of the four moral emotions covered in this chapter and the next. People who saw the angry expressions felt more guilty, in comparison with people who saw the disgusted ones. This effect was explained, statistically, by a further set of questions we asked: people who saw the angry faces thought they were being reprimanded for a harm- or rights-related transgression (such as being disrespectful or harming someone), and this made them feel guilty. People who saw the disgusted expressions, on the other hand, felt more ashamed, and inferred that they had attracted disgust for a bodily fault, such as violating rules of hygiene or what should be eaten.

Although I will have more to say about anger, guilt, and shame in turn, the connection of disgust to social norms about the body suggests a social, rather than Freudian or existential, explanation to the riddle of why we can be disgusted by our own bodies. Each culture has its own rules about how the body is treated, and because these rules are policed by disgust, there is no arguing back when you are caught violating them. When we are working out the manners of our bodies in childhood, and the new demands of presentation they make in adolescence, a constant worry is the disgust of our peers. It is this reaction, perhaps, that drives repulsion at the unwanted smell or sight of our bodies, even into adulthood. So, the disgust of others can be a mirror that reflects self-disgust and shame back, and these emotions in turn drive us to either make ourselves presentable or hide away from the eyes of the world. In this way, the social communication and self-regulation functions of disgust can interact.

Disgust and its functional conflicts

Analysing disgust through the four functions of functional conflict theory is a different, but rewarding perspective compared with other ways this diverse emotion has been carved up: for example, analysing its functions by magnitude, from the individual to the cultural level (Keltner & Haidt, 1999), or dividing disgust according to nine different types of elicitor (Rozin, Haidt, & McCauley, 2008). My theoretical perspective is different from these. The "conflict" in functional conflict theory explains the irrational side of disgust in terms of clashes between two different functions.

The conflict between the appraisal and associative-learning functions of disgust is not an even battle. Disgust is not an emotion that allows for much reappraisal or even for flexible appraisal in the first place. It is learned primarily by social example, contagion, and association. Our surprise at disgust is especially great when it bursts in on a judgment we think *should* be flexible. As adaptive as associative learning is on the species and cultural scale, its overgeneralizations on the individual scale present problems. People should learn how disease spreads, and not treat HIV-positive people as if they were smallpox carriers. We should judge a criminal case on its own merits, not on whether the accused is a social pariah.

Disgust is also particularly unwelcome when we need to unlearn it in the face of new realities. If a White person is raised by a racist culture to see Blacks as repulsive, then he or she will still feel like needing to wash after shaking a Black person's hand, even intellectually acknowledging racial equality. The way to unlearn disgust seems difficult, and has not been extensively studied. Perhaps we just need to get used to the disgusting object, as medical students can eventually lose their feelings of disgust when working with cadavers (Rozin, 2008). Or perhaps counter-conditioning could be enlisted; for example, viewers could come to associate gay men with witty comedy characters on television, rather than moral disgust. But to be open to contact or conditioning, as with any first experience with sex, beer, or Limburger cheese, there probably has to be something stronger than disgust overcoming its impulse toward avoidance. For medical students and cadavers, this is the pull of personal advancement; for attitudes toward shunned social groups, it may have to be social pressure, or the realization of common humanity.

Enlisted into self-regulation, disgust also struggles against its own learning and appraisal functions. We learn early and inescapably that poop, pee, and rotting meat are disgusting and should be fled from. So, how do we live without fleeing from ourselves, in the face of the undeniable fact that we produce the first two substances daily and are destined to become the third? It may be that the viciousness of disgust directed at the other is, at least in part, fuelled by the need to be distracted from unmentionable disgust at the self.

Perhaps, too, disgust has driven us to invent and embrace the irrational rituals of bodily culture, showing mastery of mind over matter. Meat is fine, if you only eat these animals and only these parts. Your body is okay, if you wash it like this, wear your hair like that, and cut this part off. The regulatory demands of culture, which constantly challenge us to show that we are not like animals, can even tempt us into activities that defy all known cues to disease. Millions of people around the world, every day, eat curdled milk rich with the smell of putrefaction (some of us know it as "cheese"). Self-disgust, whether or not derived from other people's disgust at the self, is a strong regulator of the boundary between mind and body, even if its demands may seem unreasonable by the appraisal logic of disease avoidance.

Anger and groups

Anger is one of social psychology's most studied emotions in the group context, perhaps because anger itself constitutes a social problem. A community where people are disgusted by or afraid of each other is cold, maybe, but can stay peaceful. A community where people are angry at each other is a riot waiting to happen. At the same time, anger can also be directed at social problems. People can get angry at all those angry people fighting, but can also catch themselves in time and refuse to join the fight, using their anger to support collective efforts to stop the violence (as shown experimentally by Tagar, Federico, & Halperin, 2010). Anger is the emotion of aggression, but also of seeking justice. Keeping its two meanings separate is a challenge for any person or group.

This paradox rests on a more basic contradiction within anger. Anger is classified, both by scholars and by lay people, as a negative emotion (e.g., Shaver et al., 1987). At the same time, it involves the motivation to approach (although with hostile intent), and this tendency shares neurobiological features with positive emotional motivations (Carver & Harmon-Jones, 2009). It's also been proposed that anger can actually feel pleasurable under some circumstances (Lerner & Tiedens, 2006), though little research has yet addressed this question. With this ambivalent background, it makes sense that anger is connected to feelings of power and certainty (e.g., Tiedens & Linton, 2001). Power and certainty can motivate people either to fight injustice, or to commit it.

Members of a group can use anger against individuals as a way to reassert the priorities of the group, such as moral norms of sharing. In studies using economic resource games and scenarios, anger emerges as instrumental in motivating punishment against violators of norms such as fairness, reciprocity, and equality (Fehr & Gächter, 2002; Nelissen & Zeelenberg, 2009a; Ohbuchi et al., 2004; Vitaglione & Barnett, 2003). Angry feelings, too, can be directed at groups of people seen as responsible for their own unfortunate status, such as the poor (Zucker & Weiner, 1993), the obese (Crandall & Martinez, 1996; Menec & Perry, 1998), and people with AIDS (Graham, Weiner, Giuliano, & Williams, 1993;

Steins & Weiner, 1999). When a subgroup within society attracts anger, it is seen as unfairly failing to contribute to the overall well-being of the larger group; by not working hard in the case of the poor, or by intentionally risking their health in the case of the obese and HIV-positive. With similar examples in mind, Kurzban and Leary (2001), in their evolutionary analysis of stigma, characterized anger as an emotion aimed at individuals and groups who fail to reciprocate benefits given them.

More generally, moral anger responds to judgments that other people are violating justice norms: harming others, violating their rights, or being unfair. These angry moral judgments usually require some interpretation and depend on the context, unlike disgust, which responds to behaviours that are taboo no matter what (Gutierrez & Giner-Sorolla, 2007; Rozin et al., 1999b). Moral anger, unlike disgust, also responds to such factors as whether anyone was harmed by the norm violation and whether it occurred intentionally, as shown by studies in our lab that systematically varied these things (Gutierrez & Giner-Sorolla, 2007; Russell & Giner-Sorolla, 2011a). Anger in these situations rests upon appraisals of blame (Quigley & Tedeschi, 1996), which itself is a complex construct: blame can take into account causality, effect, state of mind, and justifications (Shaver, 1985). The number of possible ways to excuse and mitigate anger-provoking behaviour makes functional sense. Justice considerations help societies to avoid the destructive spiral that happens when two opposing people or subgroups each get angry at the accusations of the other. Anger tempered by justice can reach a consensus that one party is in the right and the other in the wrong.

Showing the importance of justice to social anger, Nugier, Niedenthal, Brauer, and Chekroun (2007) studied when and why people feel angry in reaction to informal social sanctions from others, such as disapproving gazes or remarks. Anger only arises if those sanctions are seen as illegitimate—for example, the person doesn't agree with the law against walking on the grass, or doesn't acknowledge the authority of the old woman giving the dirty looks. Anger, thus, can be an individual's way of reacting against the group. At the same time, group membership is likely to be a crucial determinant of whether sanctions and punishment are met with meek remorse or angry defiance. If a gang member has stopped thinking in terms of larger society, and feels allegiance only to the gang, even the most severe sanctions from outside will cause only anger rather than shame.

Anger is not just involved in the struggle between the individual and the group. It can also be felt from within a unanimous group moving to action. Aggregating data across many studies of collective action, a recent meta-analysis shows that anger and other emotions of outrage play a key role in reactions to injustice that motivate support for collective action (van Zomeren, Postmes, & Spears, 2008). Perceptions of injustice without the emotion to back them up did not result in action. What is clear from the nature of the actions studied in this literature— strikes, petitions, demonstrations—is that collective anger does not just result in a blind lashing out. When fuelled by a shared sense of injustice, it can bind the angry person together with other angry people in coordinated action. In fact, anger appears as a better explanation of collective action than even the positive feelings that arise from doing something in a group (Becker, Tausch, & Wagner, 2011).

Although injustice appraisals clearly explain anger in the collective action context, research finds a profusion of explanations for anger in the more general context when one group feels anger toward another. Anger does not appear to respond to any one type of threatened resource. Cottrell and Neuberg (2005) found that fear of other social groups was fairly uniquely predicted by their threat of physical harm, and disgust, as we have already mentioned, corresponded to "infections" of disease and unwanted values. But anger was related to nearly every source of threat they studied—physical, economic, values, social cohesion, and so on. Their explanation, in line with appraisal theories such as Lazarus' (1991), is that anger in each of these instances represents "goal blockage" (e.g., goals of safety, morality, and so forth). What determines anger is not the specific nature of the threat, but the more abstract pattern of threat.

On the other hand, Mackie, Devos, and Smith (2000) found support for the idea that anger comes from having a sense of power relative to an opposing group; anger at people who did not share participants' values was greater when this outgroup was presented as a minority rather than a majority. Still another line of research has shown that anger relates to perceiving a group's actions as intentional and unfair, in contexts such as international aggression and academic politics (e.g., Gordijn, Wigboldus, & Yzerbyt, 2001; Yzerbyt, Dumont, Mathieu, Gordijn, & Wigboldus, 2006). One theoretical explanation of emotionally driven inter-group aggression, in fact, has invoked a wide combination of proposed provocations and moderating factors—harm, blame, intent, power, threat to valued things—but as yet, research has not conclusively determined whether each element is necessary or sufficient to trigger aggressive feelings (Lickel, Miller, Stenstrom, Denson, & Schmader, 2006).

Further complicating these myriad explanations for anger, it can sometimes seem to arise for no good reason at all. People are able to report on "unreasonable" episodes of anger, which aren't connected to the standard appraisals such as goal blockage or other-blame (Parkinson, 1999; Parkinson, Roper, & Simons, 2009). Prejudice, in fact, can arise from a mere association between the concept of anger and a group, as shown by DeSteno and colleagues (2004). Recalling an angry incident, but not a sad one, created negative attitudes toward a novel social group. Once established, this association can work both ways. Recall the study I mentioned in chapter 2 (Tapias et al., 2007); when incidentally exposed to words describing Black men, a group stereotypically associated with anger, White, heterosexual participants increased their angry reactions to a later, unrelated story. Irrational anger from threatened sexuality (e.g., after being made to watch a gay erotic film) has also been shown as a feature of sexual prejudice in heterosexual men, following through into aggressive behaviour (Parrott & Zeichner, 2005; Parrott, Zeichner, & Hoover, 2006).

Anger thus plays many roles. One part is that of a disinterested moral emotion (as argued by Haidt, 2003a), and another part is anything but disinterested, a feeling that defends and promotes our own personal interests. But even anger on behalf of another person ultimately responds to our collective interests, based on the evidence (chapter 3) that people care more about those in their group than in others. Seeing a common group membership, for example, increases anger at injustices perpetrated against that group. Selective outrage at victims of outgroup atrocities is, of course, nothing new, as we saw with the example of Germans in Poland at the start of this book. But even an experimental manipulation of subjective group membership can influence anger; for example, by presenting an injustice against students at another university and asking participants to either identify on the common basis of being students, or on the separate basis of their own university. In those studies and similar ones, anger was stronger and more likely to lead to action when the harmed people were thought of as "one of us" rather than "one of them" (Gordijn et al., 2001; Yzerbyt et al., 2002, 2006).

Interestingly, another line of research has manipulated levels of empathy, via instructions to either empathize or be objective when reading about a victim of injustice. It found that only empathetic participants showed moral anger on behalf of the victim (Batson et al., 2007, Study 2). This result was interpreted as evidence against the notion that truly disinterested moral anger might respond to the mere violation of a moral norm. However, it also supports the view that we might get angry on behalf of a random stranger, if we empathize with such an unknown person on a basic, human level. Indeed, that study did not include a no-instructions control condition, so we can't know whether its effects came about because being objective took away this basic empathy, or because special instructions were needed to create it. Ultimately, what makes the emotion of anger truly moral and universal may be the ability to empathize with a person halfway around the world as if he or she were a next-door neighbour. For most people, however, the moral circle is graded like a bull's eye. Victims outside our group are less worthy of sympathetic outrage, seen as emotionally less human, even if our intellectual selves classify them as *Homo sapiens*.

Anger and the functions of emotion

Appraisal

As we have seen, disgust lacks complex conceptual appraisals, responding instead to learned associations with superficial features of an object. Anger, though, has the opposite problem. It has too many appraisals, at least for those who see the job of emotion theory as finding the One True Appraisal for each emotion. We have already glimpsed some of these appraisals in looking at what makes people angry in a group context. Goal blockage, intentional injustice, or a relatively weak antagonistic group were just three of the cognitive elements found to predict angry reactions. What's more, research on the individual level has shown that different people get angry about different things; in other words, there is no single master appraisal that completely accounts for anger across people (Kuppens, 2010; Kuppens & van Mechelen, 2007; Kuppens et al., 2003). The list of different appraisals is long: the existence of a goal obstacle (or frustration); threat to self-esteem; and another person being held blameworthy for an unwanted event, which itself can be unpacked into a greater number of potential influences, such as the other person being responsible, having acted intentionally, controllably, and in an unjustified way (Smith, Haynes, Lazarus, & Pope, 1993). This variety plays out not just in individual differences in appraisal, but also in situational ones, and in interactive effects where individuals show different anger profiles across situations (Kuppens & van Mechelen, 2007; Kuppens, van Mechelen, & Rijmen, 2008).

This variety in anger appraisals, like the variety in more concrete disgust elicitors, is characteristic of a very diverse emotion that serves many different social and non-social purposes. Additionally, some of the "appraisals" of anger, such as threatened self-esteem, actually seem to correspond more to a uniquely self-regulatory function of anger distinct from appraisals. For now, we can focus on three main groups of anger-related appraisals that seem to have different functions within the larger function of appraising the environment.

Appraisal 1: Threat from an aware being

This is the broadest way to characterize what triggers anger-like states among non-human animals, with the primary function of deterring attack and encroachment (Adams, 2001). To work effectively, this trigger needs to be sensitive to three things: a threat to one's own valued resources; a creature that can perform this threat; and the creature being able to heed your angry display. This is not to say that each animal forms each of these ideas explicitly. It's more likely that, over evolutionary time, cues to these distinctions have proven valuable in determining when to set off a hostile reaction ("unknown moving thing facing you in personal space," for example). Interestingly, if this perception is indeed the original trigger of anger, the resulting angry display is a kind of communication, linking to functions we will consider later on in this chapter. The value of an emotionally aggressive reaction has been extensively analysed and studied in the area of animal behaviour. It works to deter encroachment on an individual's food, mates, alliances, or territory. The individual takes a risk and incurs costs to display a commitment to fight. In the short term, this looks like irrational brinksmanship. But in the long term, it is rational, if other rational agents make their own calculations and stop encroaching (Blanchard & Blanchard, 2003; Fessler, 2010; Nesse, 2001).

In humans, this set of appraisals appears most related to the "threat to the self" and "other blame" causes of anger proposed by Lazarus (1991) and studied by Kuppens and colleagues (2003). Beyond food and reproduction, humans care about many self-related concerns that depend on higher-order cognition. With the ability to track, individually or collectively, what other individuals think about you, comes a concern for your reputation. One facet of reputation, in humans and in other animals, is how aggressive one is (McElreath, 2003). Other facets of reputation don't themselves involve aggression, but can be defended by it; for example, a moral reputation based on one's likelihood of cooperation or keeping promises (de Cremer & Tyler, 2005; Nowak, 2006).

Applying the concerns of the extended self in humans to group-level issues, we see that any kind of threat to the group that is attributed to another agent can lead to anger—from the threat to life and limb of a terror attack, to the threat to resources of economic competition, to provocative insults that threaten reputation if not avenged (such as burning the national flag), and even the most abstract kind of moral threat, such as threat to values. The only kind of threat that wouldn't provoke anger, under this analysis, is a threat from one's self (provoking guilt or shame) or from an agent seen as impersonal, such as a tsunami or epidemic (provoking fear and sadness). This ties in well with the wide range of group-level threats related to anger in Cottrell and Neuberg's (2005) studies.

Contrary to Lazarus (1991) and the findings of Mackie et al. (2000), however, I do not believe that having high coping potential, power, or control is needed to feel angry in situations of threat. Impotent rage and the resentment of powerless groups are well-known phenomena. Power and control are not always found to be associated with anger (Roseman et al., 1990). What is different about the anger of the powerless is not the feeling, so much as how they act on it. Individual behaviour encouraged by anger varies according to its target. People are more willing to react aggressively toward people of lower social standing and people they know well. But the more typical behaviour following anger toward a social superior is to avoid that person and to seek out consolation from one's peers (Kuppens, van Mechelen, & Meulders, 2004). Anger may be indulged in by the powerful in order to maintain their power (Tiedens & Linton, 2001), but by the same token, it can also be used by people who feel powerless to reclaim a sense of power.

Appraisal 2: Injustice and unfairness

If people in a society always expressed anger toward a social threat, there would be nothing to stop the escalation of feuds. The aggressive action of one would threaten another, who in turn would act angrily and threaten the first person right back. This is where justice steps in, as a way to resolve competing claims after, or even before, conflict starts. In humans, moral norms about justice coexist with and regulate pure self-interest. The exact components of justice norms have been studied extensively by sociologists and social psychologists. In particular, the distributive principles of equality (everyone gets the same), need-based distribution (to each according to their needs), and equity (to each according to their ability to provide) often conflict in deciding who is entitled to what (Cook & Hegtvedt, 1983; Fiske, 1992). Other norms themselves govern the adjudication and enforcement of these resource norms, such as rules about the proper treatment of social roles and positions (e.g., Sunstein, 1996), and rules about proper procedures (Lind & Tyler, 1988; Tyler & Blader, 2003). Finally, unlike self-interested aggression that cares only about "teaching a lesson" to anyone who steps close, justice and fairness concerns need to take into account the responsibility and state of mind of a norm violator (Shaver, 1985; Weiner, 1995). When judging and punishing, it is only fair to take into account whether the transgression was accidental, uncontrollable, or motivated by strong and justified passion.

The benefits to society if everyone accepts justice norms mean that it's also beneficial in the long term for people to care about justice even if they have no direct personal interest. So, as we have seen, people can get angry at and punish third parties for violating justice norms. There are two differences between justice and mere threat in eliciting anger. First, moral anger inspired by violations of justice can work on behalf of another person (Haidt, 2003a). This anger may depend on empathizing with the other (Batson et al., 2007), but it can take place without any direct personal interest in the matter. Second, moral anger also responds to rules of blame and fairness, taking into account the legitimacy of claims, intentionality of action, whether or not someone is harmed, and generally working with the concept of rights. The responsiveness of anger to these concerns in situations of moral judgment has been shown numerous times, in particular when compared with disgust (Gutierrez & Giner-Sorolla, 2007; Rozin et al., 1999b; Russell & Giner-Sorolla, 2011a).

Appraisal 3: Personal goal frustration

Anyone who has had a computer error destroy ten minutes of work on a data illustration—as happened to me earlier today—knows that anger can sometimes flare up from the mere blockage of a goal, without needing to blame an intelligent agent. Anger created by this kind of frustration forms a distinctive part of the cognitive-neoassociationistic theory of anger (Berkowitz, 1990). According to this two-level model, anger can arise from the kind of appraisals mentioned previously—threat, unfairness, and so on. But it can also arise from sensory irritation, or the frustration of a goal for any reason. Starting with research on the frustration–aggression hypothesis (Dollard, Miller, Doob, Mowrer, & Sears, 1939), the mere frustration route to anger has been verified in numerous experiments (Berkowitz & Harmon-Jones, 2004). Even in the absence of blame or unfairness, obstructions to a goal can lead to angry expressions and aggressive reactions.

One gap in this theory, at least in its latest available statement, is that it's not clear what function the frustration–aggression process serves. The answer, I think, lies in the cognitive and behavioural effects of anger. Anger makes people more certain and more willing to take risks (Lerner & Keltner, 2001; Tiedens & Linton, 2001). Anger also makes people approach and attack, activating brain regions linked to those behaviours and to appetitive rewards (Carver & Harmon-Jones, 2009). The emotion originally developed to scare off predators and competitors, then, also has uses even in front of a computer screen that has just made away with your data and turned your bar graph into a flat line. Obviously, expressions of rage are not going to frighten the computer. However, cognitive certainty, supporting the desire to approach and attack, is going to motivate the same kind of determination as when facing a predator. This is a useful exaptation of anger. Angry resolve opposes the impulse to curl up and mourn the lost data, and helps me to finish the graphic.

The power of angry feelings to give a short-term push in the face of setbacks was shown in a study by Mikulincer (1988), who varied the intensity of a failure experience by giving participants four puzzles in an initial test session. Either four, one, or none of them were unsolvable. Anger and frustration were highest in the moderate failure condition (one unsolvable puzzle). However, those who felt these emotions most strongly went on to do the best in solving later puzzles. Also, greater anger in that condition was related to attributing failure to internal rather than external causes. This shows that appraisals of other-blame did not account for anger in this particular context. Now, looking at those who were given a truly impossible task with four unsolvable puzzles, depression was a more common response, and these feelings of dejection predicted poorer performance later on. Anger may eventually burn out faced with strong and persistent frustrations, which itself is adaptive; people need to see when a task is impossible, and let go. But in less trying circumstances, anger's short-term burst of certainty and approach motivation helps get the job done.

Of these three appraisals, threat, injustice, and frustration, most research so far on intergroup anger has focused on threat and injustice. The perception of a social threat to a variety of resources can explain the diverse elicitors of anger at groups found by Cottrell and Neuberg (2005). The perception of unfairness, in particular intentional unfairness, has also been implicated in anger, as both intergroup and collective action research show. Maybe the strongest social anger happens when unfairness and threat to one's own group combine, so that a self-interested moral claim can be made. Research has been less diligent in investigating the possibility that a group's mere obstruction of a collective goal triggers anger. But the associative nature of the anger schema, as we will shortly discuss, means that any anger felt in a situation of frustration can transfer to other groups, and can bias thought toward perceiving threat and blame from the frustrating group. This makes it difficult to track down any one appraisal as the culprit of intergroup anger.

Additionally, more research is needed to clarify the exact way in which power and perceived coping potential relate to collective anger. Van Zomeren et al.'s (2008) meta-analysis shows that anger influences collective action independently of perceptions of the realistic ability to create change. The findings of Mackie et al. (2000), too, are open to an alternate explanation for the anger felt by high-power participants. By manipulating group power in terms of the majority or minority status of participants' social values within the United States population, they may have also unwittingly manipulated the legitimacy of such values. In a democracy, the majority has a greater claim to legitimacy than the minority, and so a minority claim may seem less fair.

Indeed, in studies manipulating and measuring the nature of perceived threats from an outgroup, our lab has found that fear, but not anger, was affected by power independently of intentionality and injustice (Giner-Sorolla & Maitner, 2011). For example, we manipulated a fictitious UK Home Office description of a terrorist group; we described it as either acting intentionally to harm British interests or not, and either presented a strong or weak threat to British interests. The anger of British participants in both studies, controlling for fear, was only affected by the intentionality manipulation, and their perceptions of the outgroup's unfairness explained most of this effect. The group's power, however, increased only fear, and did not influence anger. While the literature shows that anger leads to appraisals of power, it is not clear whether appraisals of existing power are needed to produce anger.

Associative learning

Unlike disgust or fear, whose associative properties have been studied extensively in the context of phobia (Cisler, Olatunji, & Lohr, 2009), there is not much research on anger's ability to become directly associated with an object. Early experiments showed that the mere presence in the room of a rifle or shotgun, as opposed to a badminton racquet, increased participants' tendency to retaliate when giving out electrical shocks (for review see Turner, Simons, Berkowitz, & Frodi, 1977). However, a later study that separated out emotional from cognitive effects found that weapon priming only made aggressive thoughts more accessible; it did not actually increase anger (Anderson, Anderson, & Deuser, 1996).

What did increase anger in that study, though, was another manipulated factor: extremes of hot or cold temperature in the room. Indeed, there is ample evidence for the related idea that anger felt as a result of one source can carry over to another, irrelevant object of judgment (Berkowitz & Heimer, 1989). Having to stay in an uncomfortable situation represents a continual thwarting of the goal to escape it. Being aggressive to another person by means of electrical shocks will not realistically help you escape. But the fact that the victim just happened to be there, in the cloud of lingering frustration, is enough. A meta-analysis of 82 studies of displaced aggression confirms that an initial annoyance reliably provokes aggression toward an innocent target (Marcus-Newhall, Pedersen, Carlson, & Miller, 2000). This transfer of emotions offers one way to understand the often irrational nature of anger.

But, unlike the relatively simple associative effects of disgust, most theories of displaced anger give a crucial role to the elaborated, ruminative thoughts that anger produces (e.g., Berkowitz, 1990; Miller, Pedersen, Earlywine, & Pollock, 2003; Wilkowski & Robinson, 2007), and research supports this claim. Reappraisal or self-distracting thoughts reduce anger and blame, but rumination on anger dwells on blame, intent, and injustice, keeping the anger alive (Bushman, Bonacci, Pedersen, Vasquez, & Miller, 2005; Kross, Ayduk, & Mischel, 2005; Ray, Wilhelm, & Gross, 2008; Sukhodolsky, Golub, & Cromwell, 2001). Other research also supports the ability of angry feelings to persist in a new context and generate thoughts that support anger. The culpable control model of blame presents research showing that people attribute greater intentionality to wrongs that end up having more severe outcomes, even if that severity is based on chance factors, such as whether a car happened to be downhill from another car whose owner left the parking brake off (Alicke, 2000). This culpable control model proposes that judgments of the severity of harm and intentionality of the act are bound up with negative feelings in a schema of blame, where any one of these elements can activate the others. Lerner, Goldberg, and Tetlock (1998) manipulated anger by showing participants video clips of a bully beating up a teenager, versus neutral videos, and found that this anger carried over to create greater blame in unrelated legal cases. Other studies find that incidentally aroused anger reduces consideration of legal mitigating circumstances (Ask & Granhag, 2007), increases judgments of criminal intent (Ask & Pina, 2011), and increases attributions of interpersonal responsibility for a fault (Keltner, Ellsworth, & Edwards, 1993). No wonder that ruminating in an angry mood can be dangerous. Anger generates thoughts and explanations that are precisely the kind that feed further anger.

Early social psychologists developed influential "scapegoating" theories of prejudice and intergroup violence, attributing these phenomena to frustrations arising from economic disadvantage (Hovland & Sears, 1940). But more sophisticated archival analyses show little connection between economic circumstances and intergroup violence (Green, Glaser, & Rich, 1998). On the level of individual attitudes, though, there is evidence that carry-over associations from irrelevant sources of anger can create more hostile judgments of other groups. Kenworthy, Canales, Weaver, and Miller (2003) created angry and sad moods in the lab. Angry moods made participants more rejecting of an outgroup member compared with an ingroup one, as well as more aggressive toward the outgroup member. DeSteno et al. (2004), as we have seen, also showed that causing participants to recall angry feelings in their life, but not sad ones, created more negative attitudes toward a novel group. In subsequent research, this effect on novel groups was replicated for both anger and disgust inductions (Dasgupta, DeSteno, Williams, & Hunsinger, 2009). But when it came to specific groups that already suffered prejudicial emotional attitudes—disgust for gay men, and anger for Arabs—only the priming of the relevant emotion increased prejudice. This shows two ways emotional associations can reinforce prejudice. A group can become stigmatized for just being associated with bad feelings; later, when those feelings become more strongly associated with the group, they serve as a cue to reinforce prejudice (see also Halperin & Gross, 2011; Tapias et al., 2007). Not only does anger in particular incidentally activate thoughts of blame and prejudice, but it makes people more certain in their stereotypes than sad or neutral moods do, paving an additional way for prejudice to be reinforced (Bodenhausen, Sheppard, & Kramer, 1994).

Self-regulation

Because feedback about a moderate amount of failure activates anger and the desire to press on (Mikulincer, 1988), anger can serve a basic self-regulatory function that is not necessarily social. However, other experiments have demonstrated how anger can also react to the success or failure of social behaviour, in addressing goals related to justice and threat. For example, in Goldberg et al.'s study (1999), anger was aroused by a brutal crime. If participants were then told that the criminals had been punished appropriately, the carry-over effect of the anger, inspiring harsher judgments of different moral situations, was eliminated. A similar effect was shown on a group level by Maitner et al. (2006). In two studies, descriptions of a group-level retaliation or collective response to a group-level insult successfully reduced anger. If the response was not present or it was ineffective, anger rose instead. Both these examples show that anger can spur persistence toward a social goal if progress is not forthcoming, but shuts down once that goal is seen as achieved. In this capacity, angry moods have also been found to increase support for peaceful solutions presented in the context of long-running conflicts, further showing anger's power to fuel persistence in constructive as well as destructive outcomes (Tagar et al., 2010).

The ancient Greeks, however, also recognized that anger can be turned on the self. Leontius, an Athenian mentioned in Plato's *Republic*, reproaches himself for being morbidly fascinated by the sight of corpses lying outside the city walls. Although it is difficult to translate emotion words from Plato's language, the emotion *thumos* attributed to Leontius has been interpreted as anger or indignation. The role anger can play in self-chastisement has been illustrated by Ellsworth and Tong (2006) in a pair of studies exploring the phenomenon of self-directed anger. Anger aimed at the self showed some characteristics of guilt, an emotion more usually defined as self-regulatory. For example, it was associated with blame of the self rather than others. At the same time, it showed some unique properties. Unlike guilt or shame, self-anger did not imply moral unworthiness, and led to action tendencies of withdrawal rather than attack or restitution.

Ingroup-directed moral anger, by contrast, has more things in common with the other-directed form of the emotion, at least when the ingroup's moral character and image are threatened; for example, when Americans or British people learn of Iraqi discontent with the recent invasion and occupation of their country. In this situation, anger at the ingroup was shown to motivate protest, compensation, and support for ending the occupation (Iyer, Schmader, & Lickel, 2007). While ingroup-directed anger effectively regulates the actions of the group, there are reasons to believe it may require a rethinking of the relationships between the angry individual and the group. Either the individual identifies less with the group ("I'm not one of you") or holds a subgroup responsible for the deed ("They're not one of us").

Evidence for lowered identification comes from a study by Kessler and Hollbach (2005). After East Germans were asked to think of an example of anger they felt toward their own group (versus happiness, or versus anger toward another group), participants then identified less strongly as East Germans. Likewise, in research on reactions to discrimination (Hansen & Sassenberg, 2006), women showed less self-directed anger the more strongly they identified with women as a group. Evidence for subgroup splitting comes from data in the Iyer et al. (2007, Study 2), in which British participants rated their anger at the British people, at the UK leadership, and at an allied government involved in Iraq (the US). Anger at the British people was near zero, much lower than anger at either government, and only predicted the guilt-like action tendency of compensation for Iraqis. However, anger at the UK government additionally predicted the action tendencies of confronting those responsible and withdrawing from Iraq. Research still awaits a direct test of whether ingroup anger always involves these re-definitions of group identity, ensuring that an "other" is blamed, in conformity with the typical appraisals of anger.

Finally, anger is an emotion that can itself be regulated, as well as playing a part in self-regulation. Most research on this topic has studied how people try to defuse their own anger (Berkowitz, 1990; Novaco, 2007). But some findings show that people can also take steps to ensure they feel anger in the right context; for example, when trying to use anger as a tool to achieve social aims (Tamir et al., 2008). On a group level, however, the intentional pacification or stirring-up of anger has been unduly neglected in social psychology, probably because our survey and experimental methods focus more on group citizens than on group leaders. In an analysis of civil violence, political scholar Ted Gurr (1968) applied psychological theories of anger and aggression prevalent at the time, primarily the frustration–aggression hypothesis, but also noted how interpretations of events can either calm down or, more likely, incite further protests and riots. On the individual level, Novaco (2007) labels this spiralling of rage as "misregulation." This implies an uncontrolled process. However, leaders who want to stoke national anger for their own ends also know all too well which buttons to push. Although the collective management of anger may be difficult for social psychologists to study, it is still vital to understanding how violence, aggression, and non-violent action wither or thrive in real-life political contexts.

Social communication

Anger has communicative roots that apparently go back to the dawn of our species. Many non-human animals use anger-like displays to deter attack from predator species. In social primates, anger additionally sends signals about willingness to defend resources to other species members, avoiding a costly skirmish. The message of anger in both contexts, as summed up by Sell et al. (2009), is "formidability." Anger makes people seem more dominant and certain, supporting their claims to greater consideration in things material or moral (Hareli, Shomrat, & Hess, 2009). Indeed, while the facial expression of disgust is largely self-protective in function— the extruded tongue to clear the mouth of distasteful things, the wrinkled nose and raised lip to guard against noxious smells (Rozin et al., 1994)—the facial expression of anger increases the appearance of features associated with social dominance and maturity, lowering the brow and increasing the prominence of the jaw (Marsh, Adams, & Kleck, 2005). This speaks to anger's communicative mission.

Angry communications can be directed to our closest friends as well as to complete strangers. Unlike disgust or the related expressions of contempt, which push people away, anger expressions can start a process of reconciliation with another person, if he or she recognizes the justice of the anger. Ideally, the person will respond with guilt and appeasement, making reparations and promising a change in ways; and ideally, this in turn would lead the angry person to forgive and to restore the relationship. Anger's role in relationships is hinted at by studies showing that anger, as opposed to contempt, is more likely to be felt toward people with whom one has an existing relationship (Fischer & Roseman, 2007).

Fischer and Roseman (2007) also speculate that if anger is met by repeated refusals to mend one's transgressions, it can turn over time into contempt, as the relationship is abandoned. This feature of anger has yet to be studied on an intergroup level, maybe because alliances between groups are seen as less interesting objects of study than intractable conflicts.

Pulling in evidence from various studies, the challenge in an expression of anger seems to be met in three main ways: with fear, guilt, or anger itself. The automatic and unconscious effect of an unknown angry face, as demonstrated in numerous studies presenting faces both above and below the threshold of awareness, is to provoke anxiety (Öhman & Mineka, 2001). But we have seen how both angry and guilty feelings can arise from social reprimands (Nugier et al., 2007). This depends on whether or not the anger is justified—that is, whether or not the anger is taken as showing one's own fault. If anger is unjustified, it creates more anger (see also Wubben, de Cremer, & van Dijk, 2009), whereas otherwise it leads to guilt. To access anger and guilt instead of simple fear, though, may require recognizing that relevant social norms apply. Indeed, a recent set of experiments showing that others' angry faces evoked guilt used a context of peers in a common social space (Giner-Sorolla & Espinosa, 2011).

Figure 4.1 shows a model of emotional and behavioural responses to anger in others, based on existing literature on emotional communication and appraisal. An expression of anger is evaluated in two ways: whether or not the angry person can be confronted with some hope of success, either verbally, socially, or physically; and whether or not that person's anger is justified. The second evaluation depends on consideration of abstract norms, and so probably follows the first. All the same, it may have its own heuristic routes for a "quick and dirty" response. For

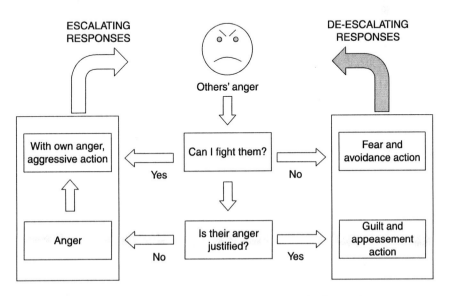

Figure 4.1 A model of emotional responses to anger communication.

example, people from one's own social group may be more likely to be seen as justified than strangers would. It's also important to note that the two appraisals are separate and can coexist. This means, for example, that if a person unjustly expressing anger is also judged too powerful to fight, then anger can coexist with fear and avoidance. Guilt can also coexist with fear, if the other person's anger is seen as justifiable as well as overwhelming to deal with.

Behavioural responses also may vary depending on the emotion felt in response to anger. Research into action tendencies provides some clues toward the likely response from each emotion (e.g., Fontaine, Scherer, Roesch, & Ellsworth, 2007; Roseman et al., 1994). If unjust anger begets more anger, this will most likely provoke further aggression, escalating the conflict. Conversely, fear and guilt's respective responses of avoidance and appeasement tend to de-escalate the conflict. Fear de-escalates by escaping the angered person, who is seen to pose a threat. Guilt de-escalates in a more risky but ultimately conclusive manner. It promotes approach and reparation behaviours aimed at mollifying the angry attitude (see, for example, Tangney & Dearing, 2002). This, at least, is how guilt works best in theory; but as we will see in the next section, other aspects of guilt and the related emotion shame may interfere to yield less than satisfactory responses.

In this model, guilt is the response the angry person should rationally prefer. While an angry reply leads to a costly struggle, and fear's avoidance brings no benefits, guilt moves the target of the anger feeling it to give up resources, attention, concessions, and status. But to create guilt, the angry person also needs to communicate the anger's reasonable nature, its justification. This communication is not just for the target of anger. Because justice claims can be evaluated without a personal interest in the matter, it is critical to get other group members' sense of moral outrage on your side. Anger without social support is impotent rage; worse, it is a social problem. The self-justification of anger with reasons has been shown on an interpersonal level (Baumeister, Stillwell, & Wotman, 1990). And, when whole groups of people are stigmatized, reasons painting them as willingly and actively taking on the stigma—similar to the judgments of intent and responsibility that characterize moral anger—are often recruited in support of negative attitudes (Crandall, 2000). As research in our lab has shown, people tend to justify their moral anger at a social group with more elaborated reasons, compared with disgust (e.g., "they harm people"; Russell & Giner-Sorolla, 2011b).

But are the reasons for anger always reasonable? From what we have seen, anger's associative schema can short-circuit the appraisal process, creating perceptions that others are to blame or that the situation is unfair, even when they are weak or non-existent in reality. A fully justified social-moral anger is a schema that people tend to fill in (especially when defending their own judgments), even if all the elements of the schema are not initially there (Alicke, 2000). The inference of factors such as harm or rights violation from the mere presence of anger can supply reasons even for unreasonably generated anger. Demonstrating this requires showing that anger precedes the inference of harm, rather than the other way around.

Research in our lab took this challenge on. We varied whether moral scenarios were read and judged under conditions of cognitive load (keeping a long number in mind) or no load (remembering a single digit; Gutierrez & Giner-Sorolla, 2007, Studies 2 and 3). We described for participants a situation where people tended to feel anger even though nobody could justly be blamed: the scientist eating a steak cloned from her own cells in the privacy of her own lab, whom I've already introduced to you in the section on disgust. Although disgust was the predominant response to this moral affront, there was also an increase in anger compared with a control condition, even when levels of disgust were statistically controlled for. In addition, participants also judged more harm to others' rights in that condition versus the control group, and this harm judgment was predicted more so by anger than disgust. A similar presumption of harm from apparently harmless acts had been shown before, regarding various sexual and moral taboos (Haidt & Hersh, 2001; Horvath & Giner-Sorolla, 2007). But our studies found that people judged the victimless cannibalism to harm others only when they weren't under cognitive load, while load did not affect anger or moral judgments. So, the harmfulness judgments required more cognitive effort than angry responses, and must have been arrived at after the fact, rather than coming before anger. In this way, we showed that reasonless anger still has the capacity to generate its own reasons after the fact.

Anger and its functional conflicts

Even if appraisal were anger's only function, its three distinct appraisals would make it complex. But would it be conflicted and contradictory? Probably not. If all three appraisals just led to the same emotional results without any further consequences, it would be fairly easy to deal with them. It would be easy to see when someone had anger without a personal target (frustration appraisal), anger with a personal target but no arguments about justice (threat), or anger with a personal target supported by arguments about fairness (injustice). But things are not so simple. Anger also generates thoughts, appraisals, expressions, and communications that fit all three purposes indiscriminately, thanks to the other three functions of the emotion. If the problem of disgust is that it lacks meaningful reasons, the problem with anger is that it's hard to trust its reasons, because they can be generated by the mere fact of anger just as readily as by anything objective.

The associative nature of anger binds feelings and reasons into a schema without regard for which came first. This means that anger brings up thoughts of blame, unfairness, and evil intent no matter whether it came from a real injustice or from a tree down over the road on the way to work. Indeed, feelings of anger aroused by mere association in the first place can be transformed into righteous crusades. The undermining of rational appraisal is helped along by the communicative function. The desire to exert power and formidability through angry expressions, and to justify them socially, pushes people to twist reality in defence of their aggrieved feelings, rather than backing down. Adding to the toxic cocktail is the self-regulatory function. Anger can create a pleasing certainty in the place of doubt, and motivate persistence in a campaign of social attack that (like the Iraq war of 2003) might have been launched on a dubious basis of evidence, fed by anger from an unrelated source (like the September 11 attacks). As we will further explore in the next chapter, anger's certainty often makes it the preferred defensive response when the more painful feelings of self-regulatory guilt, and especially shame, threaten the good feelings we like to associate with our self and our favoured groups.

On a collective level, anger can bring many benefits. It is a spur to social change, and promotes the seeking of justice even for others. It allows the airing of legitimate grievances, and opens the door to reconciliation between social groups. But a keen eye needs to watch how anger is used. Anger between groups can start off because one group is just seen as posing a threat—or worse yet, because of frustrations and displaced anger that have nothing to do with the other group at all. Once anger gets rolling, its strength becomes its danger. Anger is a self-justifying and self-reinforcing emotion, not just within people and groups, but between them. Communications of anger across group boundaries can lead, not to guilt and capitulation, but to further insecurity and anxiety. This, in turn, can motivate further anger aimed back at the angry group, in a bid to regain lost certainty and show resolve. These emotional dynamics may underlie the basic flaw inherent in terrorist strategies identified by Abrahms (2006). Although violent acts are often intended to send a specific message to the target group and so force concessions, they are interpreted by the targets as threatening their very existence or values, and met with escalated expressions of angry violence.

Anger can be just as dangerous when the group confronts the individual. Internet vigilante justice, while existing in Western countries, has reached the level of a social phenomenon in China (Cheung, 2009). Some Chinese Internet communities, known collectively as the "human flesh search engine," have responded to reports of adultery, animal cruelty, or dissident opinions by seeking all personal details about the accused and harassing them without mercy. This can lead to loss of relationships, jobs, and in some cases life. Zhou Chunmei, a 20-year-old student, was targeted by the "search engine" after her ex-boyfriend painted her online as a cruel person who had abandoned him on finding he had (a non-existent) cancer. Spurred on by moral outrage, the Internet mob found out her location, and the jilted lover tracked her down and murdered her with a knife. If we are to avoid the tragic outcome of anger when it strays far away from its goal of justice, we must recognize that anger needs to serve reason, not rule it.

5   Shame and guilt

Like anger and disgust, shame and guilt form a pair of related negative moral emotions. They each involve the condemnation of the self, or something identified with the self, rather than the condemnation of others. Both guilt and shame are also often triggered by violations of moral norms. While disgust's status as an emotion has been subjected to doubt because it seems too concrete and sensory a reaction (Royzman & Sabini, 2001), guilt has been doubted for the opposite reason: it seems too cognitive, a metaphor or judgment rather than a true emotion (Sabini & Silver, 1997). These authors, on the other hand, propose that shame is the true emotion behind feelings of guilt. In keeping with shame's more solid status, it has been proposed as a basic emotion (Elison, 2005), has stronger characteristic bodily sensations (Roseman et al., 1994), and has its own facial and full-body expressions (Keltner & Buswell, 1996; Tracy, Robins, & Schriber, 2009b). Shame, too, has a name that only refers to a feeling, while "guilt" or "guilty" can refer to an emotionless judgment about responsibility for a bad act. At the same time, terms for the two emotions are semantically very close (Shaver et al., 1987). "Guilt" and "shame" are often mentioned in the same phrase, or confused with each other.

Nonetheless, scholars have spent much effort distinguishing guilt from shame. Many of them have proposed very different distinctions, and most of these distinctions have some intuitive truth.

- In the *internal/external* distinction, guilt is an internalized system of moral conscience, while shame is not fully internalized, caring about whether you look bad to other people rather than whether you have been bad.
- In the *act/person* distinction, guilt comes from a negative evaluation of your own actions, while shame is a more painful condemnation of your whole self.
- In the *horizontal/vertical* distinction, guilt regulates reciprocal relationships between peers, while shame regulates a person's own position in a social hierarchy.

These three definitions appear incompatible. But the multi-functional nature of emotions allows each of the guilt/shame distinctions its own degree of truth. The complexities of guilt and shame come about because each emotion serves two different functions within social self-regulation. Adding complexity to shame's function, it can take into account a number of different dimensions of social value. What's more, the associative learning and social communication functions add further complications to guilt and shame. The threat of associating the self with bad feelings and the self contributes to the problem first discussed in chapter 2: when unpleasant emotions such as guilt and shame come up in the course of self-regulation, we seek to regulate them instead. And communication adds a social element to self-regulation. Guilt and shame are not just markers of our misdeeds for ourselves, but signals of our attempts to correct them for others.

Three theories of guilt and shame

Internal guilt, external shame

The notion that guilt enforces moral standards that don't depend on others, while shame enforces standards that do, was most famously articulated by the anthropologist Ruth Benedict in *The Chrysanthemum and the Sword* (1946). Like many other influential ideas in social sciences, Benedict's grew out of the needs of the Allied effort in the Second World War, having been commissioned by the US Office of War Information to write on Japanese culture to guide operations during wartime and the occupation. Benedict argued that the US represented a "guilt culture" driven by internalized individual standards, while Japan represented a "shame culture" driven by the need to answer social pressure and keep up appearances. As influential as this distinction was, it has later come under attack as an unfair representation of cultural difference (Ausubel, 1955; Creighton, 1990). As Dalal (2001, p. 47) observes about a Benedict-inspired psychotherapeutic writer: "The implication of this formulation is that people in the East would try to get away with as much as is possible—as long as they are not found out". This implies that shame is the weaker emotion, arising only if other people express actual disapproval. Guilt is stronger and more consistent, based on an inner conscience that is "always on." But is this entirely true?

Shame undoubtedly has many features of a social emotion. Its expression is fundamentally an interpersonal one, signalling submission and avoidance: lowered gaze, stooped posture, sometimes even covering the face (Keltner & Buswell, 1996; Tracy & Matsumoto, 2008). Shame is also associated with public exposure. Unlike guilt, it's felt more intensely when one's failings are openly shown, as demonstrated in a series of studies that varied scenarios of exposure and analysed literary mentions of shame and guilt (Smith, Webster, Parrott, & Eyre, 2002), But crucially, Smith et al.'s studies also found that a strong amount of shame could be felt in private conditions. It was enough to just imagine exposure to others to feel shame. To claim that shame is only felt under actual public exposure is as absurd as to claim that guilt is only felt in the exact moment after wrongdoing. The difference between the two emotions diminishes even further when we look at diary studies in which participants record their daily experience. One such study found find that nearly all guilt episodes have another person as their target (Baumeister,

Reis, & Delespaul, 1995). If shame feels more social than guilt, it's just a feeling; guilt is objectively just as socially evoked as shame is, and both emotions can be internalized.

Shame for the person, guilt for the act

H. B. Lewis (1971) first proposed that shame involves a negative judgment of the whole self while guilt involves a negative judgment of one's acts. While this original insight came from clinical observations, it later received empirical support in great depth from research by Tangney and colleagues (Tangney & Dearing, 2002). Research by Tracy and Robins (2006) expands this idea. In shame, the person interprets negative self-relevant events as caused by internal, stable, and uncontrollable factors. In guilt, the perceived causes of negative events are still internal, but seen as unstable and controllable; that is, more about the situation than the person.

Whatever its exact form, this person/act distinction has consequences for behaviour. If there's nothing to be done about the global, stable flaws in the self that cause shame, the appropriate thing to do is withdraw and hide. But if the crucial fault rests only in a single act that you had control over, it is easier to approach and repair the fault. These opposite tendencies of approach and avoidance, first proposed by Lewis and demonstrated by Tangney as separate outcomes of guilt and shame, have themselves been studied as a basic distinction between guilt and shame (Sheikh & Janoff-Bulman, 2010).

At first, it looks as if the act- versus person-based distinction contradicts the internal/external distinction. After all, shame involves condemning the whole person, so it appears as the more powerful emotion. But the internal/external distinction promotes guilt as the stronger emotion, because guilt is based on more consistent internal standards. The behavioural tendencies of withdrawal from shame and approach from guilt also seem to contradict the social implications of the internal/external scheme. If shame creates withdrawal and hiding, rather than apology and reparation, after harming another person, then shame is the emotion that involves less—not more—concern for others.

Different researchers in social and personality psychology have noted this duality of definitions, and resolved it in various ways. One way is to raise questions about whether guilt always leads to proactive behaviour and whether shame always leads to counterproductive, avoidant behaviour. A closer analysis of the scale often used to measure dispositional guilt and shame, the TOSCA (Tangney & Dearing, 2002), shows that its items measure "guilt proneness" largely through pro-social action tendencies, rather than through emotional responses (Luyten, Fontaine, & Corveleyn, 2002). In fact, while guilt-proneness according to the TOSCA correlates with pro-social and adaptive actions and outcomes, it does not seem to have much to do with the strength of guilt or any other kind of feelings, either on a chronic level (Fontaine, Luyten, De Boeck, & Corveleyn, 2001) or when the person is made aware of a failing (Giner-Sorolla, Piazza, & Espinosa, 2011b; see also Ferguson, Brugman, White, & Eyre, 2007). Shame-proneness, though, was related to the strength of shame and other self-critical emotions in those situations. Also, a number of studies have shown that shame, as distinct from guilt, can motivate pro-social action, both in situations of individual wrong-doing (de Hooge, Zeelenberg, & Breugelmans, 2007) and collective wrongdoing (Brown, González, Zagefka, Manzi, & Ćehajić, 2008; Iyer et al., 2007). For example, shame can inspire ordinarily selfish people to pro-social action, when that action has the potential to undo the shame in another's eyes (de Hooge, Breugelmans, & Zeelenberg, 2008). These results question the necessity of strong guilt feelings for approach-related action, and show that shame can also lead to reparative action. Shame is not always too painful to deal with by interacting with the social world.

Some recent research has decided to fuse the previous two definitions of shame empirically, finding similarities between shame conceived of as a threat to one's image, and as a threat to one's moral essence, on an individual or group level. For example, Brown et al. (2008) found that threats to the image and to the essence of the non-indigenous Chilean ingroup both formed a single, statistically coherent scale that predicted self-reports of shame felt toward indigenous Chileans. More recent work from that lab did find a distinction between image and essence shame, though even so the two constructs were highly related and both predicted reparative tendencies (Allpress, Barlow, Brown, & Louis, 2010). Recently, in creating a measure of personal guilt- and shame-proneness, Wolf, Cohen, Panter, and Insko (2010) also chose to assess guilt and shame following multiple definitions. Shame was measured as negative self-evaluations and withdrawal tendencies following public transgressions, and guilt as negative behaviour-evaluations and reparative tendencies following private transgressions. This measure intentionally confounded the act/person object of the emotion with the public/private setting and withdrawal/approach behaviour, because the authors' prior research found that this gave the maximum differentiation between guilt and shame. But while these combined approaches have strong empirical grounds, they don't yet give a strong reason why feelings of exposure and global self-condemnation should go together in shame.

Alternatively, researchers can try to identify subspecies of shame, separating its public exposure aspect from its globally self-condemning aspect. This move has been suggested as a resolution by Castelfranchi and Poggi (1990) and Smith et al. (2002), among others. One insight on shame from Crozier (1998) is especially relevant: "shame is experienced when an individual recognizes that an action can give rise to a negative interpretation by others of core aspects of the self, even if he or she does not share that interpretation" (pp. 273–286). This offers a clue to where the self-condemnation in private shame comes from: *accepting* the judgment of others about the unworthiness of the core self. But what is functional about seeing yourself as unworthy, and withdrawing from a situation that you might be better off facing? This response is too common to be completely pathological. For example, means on the shame subscale of the TOSCA in university women typically hover around the midpoint of 3 (Tangney & Dearing, 2002). The answer to the function of internal shame, I believe, lies in its social nature.

Shame as hierarchical, guilt as reciprocal

Theorists who take an evolutionary approach to shame in humans point out its similarity to displays of submission in animals with a social hierarchy (Fessler, 2007; Gilbert, 1998, 2003). In particular, the physical signals of shame are much like the gaze aversion and reduced stature by which one animal acknowledges another's dominance. Having a hierarchy is good for a group because it reduces conflict and increases coordination, but as part of this deal, some individuals have to accept a less privileged position. In this light, internalized, self-lowering shame doesn't work to help the individual cope, but to help the whole hierarchical system cope. A sense of low self-worth, after all, is adaptive if one really does rank low in society. Shame, and related expressions like embarrassment, take on an appeasement function (Keltner, 1995), smoothing over relations by boosting the relative worth of another at the individual's own expense.

In an individualist culture with egalitarian norms, the idea that people should feel shame on the basis of their position seems repellent. It smacks of the social hierarchies in unenlightened times and places—British servants running upstairs and downstairs in the 19th century, or the traditional castes in India. Both liberal and conservative ideologies in the United States, for example, urge poor and marginalized people to reject low self-esteem, although liberals and conservatives then have different suggestions on what to do once shame has been conquered. But there is more than one hierarchy of worth possible in a society. Internal shame still persists as an emotion in the West because it has adapted itself to the hierarchies of social value that are acceptable in that society.

Social value has many possible definitions. Of course, status can be defined by parentage, as with caste systems, cultures that value one race over others, and traditional aristocracies. But an alternative system of social worth is competence, defined variously as intelligence, hard work, physical prowess, or whatever other personal abilities and skills are valued. Another such system takes morality as its criterion, valuing concerns that have little to do with social status, such as honesty and helpfulness. Shame thus can be experienced on both moral and non-moral grounds. Even a society that thinks it wrong to shame someone about an uncontrollable trait can keep shame as a reserve weapon to be levelled at the immoral and the underachieving. And, if a person accepts and internalizes the hierarchy of worth, then evidence of his or her low worth can trigger shame and self-negating behaviour even if nobody is around.

If shame regulates hierarchical social relations, what does guilt do in evolutionary social terms? Trivers (1971) proposed that guilt feelings work to enforce mutual altruism, by levying an additional cost of unpleasant emotions on someone who fails to provide mutual aid; this interpretation is also taken by Gilbert (2003) in a comparison with shame. Guilt, in this view, regulates reciprocal relations between peers. It smoothes out inequalities: accidental harm, unevenly distributed resources, failure to cooperate, and unfair treatment. Indeed, priming of guilt motivates greater cooperation with others in an economic situation (Ketelaar & Au, 2003; Nelissen, Dijker, & de Vries, 2007). Compare this with shame, which reinforces and perpetuates inequalities.

But an important source of confusion is that moral judgments can also lead to concern about a moral hierarchy of good and bad actors. So, guilt and shame can be felt in the same situation, and motivate the same action, but for different reasons. For example, if I accidentally frighten a child, guilt leads me to see the child as an equal, and offer her a toy to restore good relations. Shame, however, is equally plausible, and makes me doubt my moral worth ("What kind of monster am I?") and moral image ("I'll look like a real ogre to her parents"). The toy I offer her will not primarily be meant to make her happy, but to improve my standing in the moral hierarchy. This outcome of shame is fully in line with the predictions of another bio-behavioural model (Gruenewald, Kemeny, Aziz, & Fahey, 2004), which sees shame as motivating actions that help to protect one's social value. Just as anger and disgust overlap in socio-moral situations, shame and guilt have a reason to overlap in situations of moral violation, leading to high correlations between reports of these two emotions.

Unworthiness shame and defensive shame

I want to bring together the three main strands of theory on shame and guilt with some new ideas (as far as I know) that resolve apparent discrepancies between them. The overall basis of the scheme is the last idea I covered: shame regulates relationships that are seen as hierarchical, and guilt regulates relationships that are seen as reciprocal. But within this major division, there are two types of shame that respond to different concerns within a hierarchy: unworthiness shame and defensive shame.

Unworthiness shame

This is the shame of rising too high. It happens when a person becomes conscious of the threat of being granted higher social worth than he or she deserves. The feeling is like being a plumber invited to tea with the Queen of England; like being profoundly out of shape and asked to compare athletic competence with a marathon runner; like Oedipus upon realizing that the enormity of his crimes makes him a moral outcast even in his own eyes—which he must then pluck out as unworthy to see the sun. The experience of this kind of shame is highly painful, and it's unpleasant even to anticipate. Its most important feature is the acceptance of low social worth for the self. This is the kind of shame that the self/action distinction has captured. It leads to avoidant actions, self-abnegating displays. True, these are not immediately adaptive for a modern, Western, middle-class individual who is pushed constantly to engage in self-promotion. However, unworthiness shame's displays are socially adaptive when the feeling of inferiority has social reality: the plumber accepts that a gulf of social rank separates her from the Queen; the criminal bows his head before a public who wants to see admission of moral inferiority; the incompetent CEO withdraws from the scene and retires to play golf, rather than wrecking the company even further.

Defensive shame

The external/internal distinction, by contrast, has captured a different context of shame: shame of falling too low. It happens when a person becomes threatened by the possibility of being given lower social worth than he or she deserves. This is the shame that might be felt by a Queen when asked to fix a leaky pipe; by a profoundly out-of-shape desk worker looking at pictures of his formerly athletic self; by Oedipus when accused of monstrous crimes, in the moments before he knows that he himself committed them. The most important feature of defensive shame is the urge to defend or restore one's own social worth. Such defensive actions can happen as a pre-emptive strike if the shame is anticipated, or a rear-guard action if the shame is already felt. Although looking worthy is an important goal in these restoration efforts, if the shame is internalized, then the person must also actually become more worthy. A criminal who states an intent to reform so that "I can hold my head up again" is showing an adaptive response to humiliation based on the shame of falling too low. While accepting the loss of social value, this kind of response recognizes that it's right to try to regain it, and acknowledges the validity of the moral hierarchy. This should be distinguished from an angry response to humiliation, which rejects the validity of the loss of social value altogether.

In the larger theoretical model of functional conflict theory, unworthiness shame corresponds to the logic of the appraisal function. Although its object of appraisal is the self, unworthiness shame does not react against a threat to the self's status in an attempt to regulate it. Instead, it accepts low status as a fact of the environment, and sets in motion steps to live with that fact. However, defensive shame corresponds more clearly to the logic of the self-regulation function. Seeing status sinking, it sets in motion thoughts and actions that swim against the undertow, seeking to restore a desired social standing. By contrast, guilt also has two main perceptions that set it off; but these perceptions are more clearly self-regulatory, seeking to restore balance in a damaged relationship.

Inequality guilt and injustice guilt

Both types of shame are concerned with the global worthiness of the self in society. Guilt, however, is concerned with the maintenance of a social relationship between peers, making it more inherently moral than shame, which can respond to low social rank or competence. Guilt also motivates a more consistent behavioural tendency to approach the wronged party with offers of apology, restitution, and future attention, in hopes of restoring reciprocal relations. The appeasement from unworthiness shame establishes a person as being below the target in status, while the actions taken to restore status in defensive shame return a person to a desired level of status. But the appeasement that comes from guilt works to undo a temporary inequity, re-establishing the equal and close status of the two parties.

Phenomena variously called survivor guilt, inequity guilt, irrational guilt, or existential guilt (Baumeister, Stillwell, & Heatherton, 1994; Hoffman, 1989;

O'Connor, Berry, Lewis, Mulherin, & Yi, 2007; Parkinson, 1999) show that guilt can arise on the mere perception of inequality between self and other—for example, that I belong to a more privileged social class, or that I have survived arbitrarily where another has died. This promotes the smoothing-out of inequalities in a very basic way (O'Connor, Berry, Weiss, & Gilbert, 2002). However, inequality alone cannot be the basis of guilt-based compensation. A society that follows the simple rule "help those with the least" is at the mercy of free-riders, resource hoarders, and other scoundrels. Because of this, two additional considerations help determine whether guilt is felt.

First, seeing inequality as justified can decrease guilt (Miron, Branscombe, & Schmitt, 2006). This way out protects society against freeloaders and allows even the best-off people to live guilt-free. If a less fortunate person is also less competent, less moral, or just ignobly born (depending on what kind of society you live in), it's only fair they should receive fewer resources. Second, seeing the self as not responsible for the inequality can also turn off guilt (e.g., Weiner, 1995). This reinforces a more specific and limited function of guilt: helping a wrongdoer to restore equality within a specific relationship. These three appraisals of inequality, responsibility, and lack of justification appear to come together in a justice-based schema for guilt. For example, Mallett and Swim (2007) found that guilt depended on independent effects of all three appraisals, rather than on their presence together. This implies that even when responsibility is lacking or excuses are available, evidence of inequality might still lead to mild feelings of guilt among some people.

These considerations give guilt an appraisal structure similar to that of anger. Like anger's injustice appraisal, guilt's most complex appraisal also involves notions of justice, responsibility, and fairness. Like anger's simpler appraisal of threat, guilt sometimes just responds to the fact of inequality. The difference is that guilt judges the self as wrong and the other as right, while for anger it is the other way around. Guilt, like anger, sometimes departs from "reasonable" norms of fairness and justice. This has been used to challenge appraisal theory (Parkinson, 1999). But functionally, the two guilt appraisals serve two social needs, neither of which should completely win out. It makes sense that guilt responds to concerns of injustice, not just inequality. Otherwise guilt would sour the fruits of hard work, because such rewards create inequality between the hard worker and the slacker. But the more sophisticated ways to turn a blind eye to injustice, helped along by self-serving interpretations, can quickly become excuses for an unbalanced resource distribution that harms the group as a whole. Sometimes guilt needs to cut through all the privileged excuses and fight for equality in real terms.

Seeing morality as a kind of hierarchy can also help us see why the same phenomena can be labelled by some "guilt" and by others as "shame"—in both the lay and the psychologists' use of language. Some examples of shame are clearly not guilt—for example, shame at being laughed at due to a poor fashion choice. But most examples of guilt can be thought of in a way that leads to shame. Feeling guilty because you failed or harmed someone can easily turn into feeling defensive shame about falling too low in a hierarchy of morals based on caring.

This can go further into unworthiness shame, if you see the moral failure as evidence that you are a basically unworthy person. In these differences between emotions, the key factors may not be so much whether the term "guilt" or "shame" is applied, but (1) whether the focus of the emotion is the self's moral relationship with the harmed person versus the self's moral standing more generally, and (2) how intense and thoroughgoing the self-condemnation is. Thus one psychologist might label the less intense end "functional guilt" and the other "dysfunctional guilt" (e.g., Parsons, 1989); another might likewise describe more and less painful forms of "shame" (e.g., the "reintegrative" and "stigmatizing" shame of Braithwaite, 2000); while the Lewis/Tangney tradition labels the less intense emotion "guilt" and the more intense one "shame." To get past these traps of language, we need to look instead at the underlying characteristics of each emotion experience.

There is confusion not just about how to label the relative intensities of guilt and shame, but also about whether guilt is self- or other-focused. Some researchers studying moral development (Thompson & Hoffman, 1980) and individual differ-ences (e.g., Leith & Baumeister, 1998) have found a connection between guilt and perspective-taking or empathy. They conclude that understanding a harmed person's pain is what leads to guilty feelings. Theory and research on intergroup guilt, however, tells a different story. Iyer, Leach, and Pedersen (2004) argue that guilt is a self-focused emotion, contrasting it against the processes of sympathy and empathy, which are more other-focused. Supporting this are findings that intergroup guilt promotes a more limited range of actions to redress inequality than intergroup sympathy does (Iyer, Leach, & Crosby, 2003). The conclusion is that guilt is not the best emotion for dominant groups to feel in order to restore good intergroup relations. In support of this view, experiments have shown that illegitimate advantage enjoyed by an artificially created ingroup led to guilt when participants focused on their own group, but sympathy when they focused on the outgroup (Harth, Kessler, & Leach, 2008). Miron et al. (2006) also found that perceptions of unjustified inequality led to greater guilt in a group context (men and women) because they increased self-focused distress, not because they increased empathy.

While these perspectives conflict, they are each partially validated by the overarching insight that guilt—like shame—focuses on the self, but in relation to others (Baumeister et al., 1995). It is not a purely sympathetic emotion of concern for others, nor is it a purely selfish emotion. Iyer et al. (2003) found that the influence of guilt was restricted to the explicitly relational measure of reparations from ingroup to outgroup, stopping short of support for wider policies improving opportunities for the outgroup, which don't specifically involve the ingroup. Like-wise, McGarty, Pedersen, Leach, Mansell, Waller, & Bliuc (2005) found that group-based guilt among non-Aboriginal Australians did predict support for the relational action of an apology to Aboriginal Australians. Nonetheless, it also appears that the experience of moral self-criticism might vary in how much emphasis is placed on the concerns of self versus other. An experience closer to moral shame might involve the concern, "I have harmed you; what does this say about me?" But an experience closer to guilt would involve the concern, "I have harmed you; what do you need from me?" And sympathy might just say, "You are hurt; what do you need from me?"

Unlike sympathy, the range of guilt can be limited by the responsibility of the self, so that the appropriate help consists only of undoing the harm caused by the self. Ironically, this narrow focus can lead to "robbing Peter to pay Paul" as a way to address guilt feelings, as shown by studies in which participants who had wronged another chose to compensate the wronged person by taking from a third person's resources rather than their own (de Hooge, Nelissen, Breugelmans, & Zeelenberg, 2011). But existential guilt aroused by the mere fact of inequality would not bring with it any sense of responsibility to draw this boundary. Existential guilt may thus have effects closer to sympathy, which focuses on the need of the other without regard to one's own obligations.

Because shame and guilt are self-conscious emotions, they also suffer the conflict between associative learning and self-regulation I outlined in chapter 2. To recapitulate: Self-regulation of behaviour through feelings of guilt and shame can backfire, if those emotions become associated with the whole self or group concept instead of just the undesired act. In that case, people may choose to regulate their guilt and shame feelings out of existence by defensive means, instead of letting those feelings regulate their own behaviour.

Guilt, shame, and self-regulation in groups

My previous analysis of the many ways in which groups direct anger and disgust at moral violators can also be applied to the ways moral violators within groups themselves feel guilt and shame. Because shame presumes a social order and guilt presumes social relationships, they are relevant both to an individual's place within a group and to a group's place within a larger unit—nations within humanity, for example.

Feeling bad about one's personal behaviour in a small group may come closest to the original social function of guilt and shame. However, these emotions take on other roles today in relations between large-scale national, ethnic, and religious groups (Iyer & Leach, 2008; Lickel, Steele, & Schmader, 2011). People sometimes feel bad if they violate standards about how people from other groups should be treated (Monteith & Mark, 2005). They can feel collective guilt and shame about their own group's injustices toward other groups (Doosje et al., 1998). Finally, they can feel vicarious guilt and shame about the actions and standing of other individual group members (Lickel, Schmader, Curtis, Scarnier, & Ames, 2005). Overall, this body of research mostly deals with guilt and shame felt by members of a more privileged ingroup toward a less privileged outgroup. Guilt and, in particular, shame have also been studied as a part of stigma: that is, when a group confronts its own disadvantaged standing relative to other groups. A final context for these emotions, though one less well studied, is the situation of a self-critical individual who feels guilt or shame in reference to his or her own individual standing within the ingroup (e.g., Cohen et al., 2006).

The guilt and shame of the powerful

Figure 5.1 arranges, in a two-dimensional space, a number of feelings that have the potential to reduce inequality when a socially dominant group considers a less dominant one. These include the two subtypes each of guilt and shame, as well as the relevant emotion of sympathy (chapter 6). The emotions are arranged along two dimensions. The vertical axis shows the intensity of threat that an emotion poses to the identity of the person feeling it, including the individual in the extended self. Low locations equal low threat and less painful feeling, while high locations equal high threat and intense negative feelings. The horizontal axis

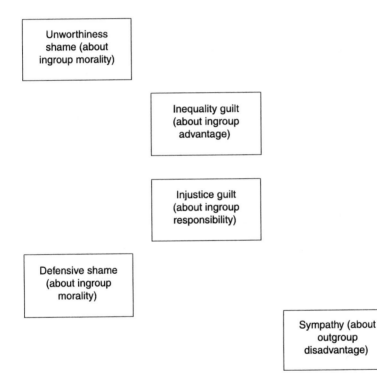

Figure 5.1 Guilt, shame and sympathy as felt by powerful groups.

shows how much each emotion tends to focus on the self as opposed to the other as the object of moral concern.

This graph recognizes that shame, while concerned with input from others, tends to be a more self-focused emotion. Sympathy, as we have seen, is other-focused, while guilt takes into account the relationship between self and other, and so lies in between. The different varieties of emotions also present different amounts of threat to the self. Defensive shame involves accepting a relatively positive self-view and fighting to defend it, which is less threatening than the utter capitulation of unworthiness shame. Guilt about one's own responsibility limits its scope to a single action, and so should be somewhat less severe than existential guilt about a whole system of unfair privilege. Injustice guilt is also possibly less severe than defensive shame, which concerns the entire self's essence and reputation. Sympathy, while still involving some distress about the plight of the other, is low in threat to the self because of its tight focus on the other. On this dimension in particular, the relative positions of each emotion are based on guesswork based on the existing literature; this model is one I hope to inspire research, rather than perfectly reflecting it.

One advantage of this scheme, in all its complexity, is that it liberates us from the confusing lack of consensus in terms among lay people and academics. The real operational outcomes do not depend on the labels "shame" and "guilt" but on the position of any given set of feelings and thoughts on these axes. If a White French person feels a painfully strong negative feeling about her group's relative affluence compared with the marginalization of French people of colour, we do not need to argue over whether this is "existential guilt" or "unworthiness shame"; we merely note the feeling's position in the middle of the horizontal axis, being about the relation between the two groups, and near the bottom of the vertical axis, being highly uncomfortable. This position in itself gives some hints as to the kind of action that is likely to ensue. My scheme calls that feeling "guilt," but the exact terminology is not as important as the feeling's intensity and degree of self vs. other focus.

The vertical, threat dimension is related to the kind of self-regulation or misregulation that the feeling is likely to encourage. Threat can involve both the personal and the extended self. If the self is already fragile or insecure, or if circumstances challenge national worth, this will increase the intensity of bad feelings about the threat. The more intense the feeling, the more the associative learning function ensures that the feeling becomes generalized to the whole question of the ingroup's worth. Faced with this powerful pain, there are two choices. Either accept the group's moral unworthiness and its seemingly low place in the moral hierarchy or regulate the feeling pre-emptively, so that it won't undermine the positive view of the ingroup. This latter route can lead, for example, to denying or avoiding the painful topic. On the other hand, with low levels of threat, the bad feelings are manageable, and they perform as intended within the regulatory function. They mark problems with specific outcomes of the ingroup's behaviour or identity that can then be dealt with through specific steps.

The feeling's horizontal dimension in this scheme decides whether action taken as a result of the feeling will be oriented toward the ingroup, the relationship between ingroup or outgroup, or the outgroup. The more self-oriented the feeling, the more ingroup-centred the action. Of course, some actions can serve all three purposes. A package of aid sent from a conquering nation to the country it has just defeated in war has the potential to demonstrate the morality of the conqueror, to assist the vanquished, and to repair the relations between the two countries. Shnabel and Nadler (2008) analyse relations between stronger and weaker groups in terms of a needs-based model, in which the stronger group is interested in reclaiming its moral standing while the weaker group is interested in reclaiming power. Effective acts of reconciliation satisfy both sets of needs, implying that each group has to take an other-focused perspective in order to make sure that their solution meets the needs of the other group as well as their own.

The danger of a self-focused need is that partial, symbolic gestures can satisfy it. Consider a patriot who criticizes his or her country's brutal foreign wars, but only in terms of the country's own wounded honour and image. Here, helping the war's foreign victims is only one (and probably not the cheapest) of the measures that can reaffirm the country's morality in its own eyes and those of the world. However, other-focused actions are not always going to lead to reconciliation either. While some studies initially showed that taking the perspective of an outgroup member can foster more sympathetic attitudes toward that group (Galinsky & Moskowitz, 2000), later research qualifies this finding. If knowledge of the outgroup depends on stereotypes, an other-focused approach tends only to reinforce those stereotypes. For example, a recent study of interracial interaction showed that Whites who empa-thized with an Aboriginal Canadian during an interaction showed less prejudice reduction, because they imagined (inaccurately) that they were being thought of in hostile terms (Vorauer & Sasaki, 2009). In other words, Whites' empathy was ultimately undercut by their stereotypes about how Aboriginals view Whites.

Moreover, even sympathy can become demeaning, as we will explore in chapter 6. Offers of material aid can backfire and be interpreted as ways to exercise even more control if trust and hope are lacking (Nadler & Liviatan, 2006). And offers of material aid that ignore their recipients' need to preserve their own honour and moral standing are also doomed to failure. Barkan (2000) relates the impres-sive solidarity shown by Philippine women who had been forced into prostitution by the Japanese army during World War II. Offered a considerable sum in settle-ment after the war, they refused the payment until a public official apology had been made. While other- and self-focused perspectives each have their pitfalls, the impulse of different moral emotions toward one perspective or another should help predict which course of action ultimately prevails.

The shame and anger of the wronged

In Figure 5.2, I present a somewhat different two-dimensional graph for some of the negative emotions that might be felt by the victims of ongoing inequality and historical wrongs: shame, anger, and hatred or contempt. To understand how both perpetrators and victims of a historical wrong can feel shame, we need to acknowl-edge how shame can respond to different scales of social worth. While the shame

HIGH THREAT TO EXTENDED SELF

Unworthiness shame
(about ingroup
disadvantage)

Defensive
shame (about ingroup
disadvantage)

Anger (about injustice
of ingroup–outgroup
relation)

Hatred and contempt
(about bad character
of outgroup)

LOW THREAT TO EXTENDED SELF

Ingroup (left) vs. outgroup (right) focus

Figure 5.2 Shame, anger and hatred as felt by wronged groups.

of the perpetrators calls into doubt their group's moral worth, the shame of victims calls into doubt the worth of their social rank, and their own competence to defend themselves. This dynamic of shame has been noted in research on stigmatization. Victims of sexual abuse, for one, often experience a complex mixture of self-critical feelings, both about the fact of abuse and attributions of the abuse to the self rather than the abuser (Feiring, Taska, & Lewis, 1996). Another form of shame, humiliation, was shown in a study of Palestinians to lead to passivity; it was negatively related to support for any action, be it violent action against Israel or reconciliation with that country (Ginges & Atran, 2008). This, perhaps, reflects unworthiness shame that has become accepted as a marker of low standing. Other findings, though, show how being humiliated or shamed can fuel aggressive action. For example, Thomaes, Bushman, Stegge, and Olthof (2008) gave adolescents evidence that they had done poorly against a low-ranked opponent in a game. This led to higher aggression, as measured by willingness to blast the opponent with noise, but only among those with narcissism and high self-esteem. The crucial role of self-esteem suggests that aggression is born from defensive instead of unworthiness shame, fighting against a threat to the valued self rather than accepting what the feedback says about one's incompetence.

In Toni Morrison's novel *The Bluest Eye*, the author describes the feelings of a young African-American girl after she's faced with racial contempt in a shop: "Anger stirs and wakes in her: it opens its mouth, and like a hot-mouthed puppy, laps up the dredges of her shame. Anger is better" (1970, p. 38). This literary example shows one difference between the victim's and perpetrator's emotions. As the victim's emotions become more other-centred, they turn toward anger, hatred, and contempt rather than guilt and sympathy. These other-condemning emotions arise from blame of the other rather than the self (Weiner, 1995). One response to the humiliation of victimization is to transform shame's feelings of inferiority into anger toward the victimizer, in line with research and theory showing that unacknowledged shame can erupt into anger (Scheff & Retzinger, 2001; Tangney, Wagner, Fletcher, & Gramzow, 1992).

A distinction can also be drawn between anger focused on the relationship between victim and victimizer, and the more completely other-centred hostile feelings such as hatred or contempt. In this context, anger, like guilt, emphasizes the self–other relation, and the wrongness of a single action within that relationship. Hatred and contempt, however, work to break instead of restore the relationship. Those feelings focus on the evil and unworthy nature of the other individual or group. In support of this analysis, Fischer and Roseman (2007) also found that anger, versus contempt, was more often felt toward a friend than stranger, and that contempt had more of a distancing quality. In a way, hatred and contempt are reflections of shame, rejecting the judgment of self-unworthiness by reflecting it completely onto the other. Overall, the other-focused emotions felt by someone in the victim role work against reconciliation rather than for it.

Other group-relevant contexts for guilt and shame

Guilt and shame that might be felt for not being a good enough ingroup member have not been studied as much as guilt and shame felt between groups. However, the two situations are similar. As I argued in chapter 3, the emotions of the powerful-group member come from the conflict between the more parochial membership (the ethnic group, nation, and so on), and a more universal pan-human group membership. Actions that promote the smaller group risk guilt and shame because they are less moral in the light of the larger, universal group. Likewise, an individual risks guilt and shame by promoting the self in the light of the smaller group. So, merely being given undeserved high status in a small group should be enough to trigger equality guilt, if the person focuses on the need for the self–group relation to be more equal. And claims on too high a social value in a group should lead to unworthiness shame, while threats to a legitimate social value in the group should lead to defensive shame.

Most of these ideas remain to be tested empirically. While there is evidence that guilt and shame can prompt more pro-social behaviour toward individuals (de Hooge et al., 2008; Ketelaar & Au, 2003; Nelissen et al., 2007), findings on group-level morality are more mixed. Some studies find evidence that guilt-proneness in a setting of intergroup competition relates to a more universalistic morality, which comes through in less ingroup favouritism (Pinter, Insko, Wildschut, Kirchner, Montoya, & Wolf, 2007). Others find that guilt-proneness promotes acts that benefit the group (Cohen et al., 2006). Whether guilt and shame work in the service of the smaller group or the larger, universal morality might then depend on how an individual frames the situation.

Finally, shame and guilt can be felt within a group on the basis of other group members' actions. This vicarious context for emotions has been studied extensively in research led by Brian Lickel and Toni Schmader. In a number of group types, including nationality, ethnicity, and family, they find reliable differences between the kind of ingroup-member actions that elicit shame, and those that elicit guilt (Lickel et al., 2011). To feel shame, it is enough to have an essential connection to the misbehaving ingroup member; to be American if he is American, or to be related even if you have never met her. Guilt, though, requires a sense of responsibility for failing to prevent the other's behaviour. I may feel shame for the offensive behaviour of a fellow national who I see on television, but I might feel guilt if the boor is sitting next to me on a tour bus and I haven't said something. The vicarious context presents a particularly clear-cut illustration of the relationship of shame to social value, and of guilt to responsibility. Because of this, participants in these studies can clearly distinguish between the two emotions in their vicarious contexts using only the plain English labels "guilt" and "shame." This is probably because the context removes the confusion between standing in a moral hierarchy and responsibility, which usually leads to the confusion between guilt and shame language. A stranger doing immoral things far away brings moral shame on my group, lowering me; but I don't bear responsibility for his or her acts, so I feel no guilt.

Self-regulation by shame and guilt: Barriers to action

With all forms of group-based guilt and shame, a number of problems emerge in getting from the bad deed to taking effective action and correcting it. As we have seen, the appraisal function as expressed in unworthiness shame can lead to accepting rather than fighting against low social worth. But even given the impulse to fight, another set of problems arises, because the self-regulation function in guilt and shame conflicts with the associative learning function of these emotions. As self-aware beings, through associative learning, we create self-reassuring emotional attitudes. We attach positive feelings to the self and ingroup, and negative feelings to disliked others. But guilt and shame can threaten this arrangement by linking negative feelings to the individual and extended self. When guilt and shame are painfully unpleasant and threaten the self-concept by association, these emotions can be regulated by the self as much as they regulate the self, as I observed in chapter 2. So, people often try to avoid guilt and shame in a number of ways, even when they've actually done something guilty or shameful.

When guilt or shame can't be avoided, they can still fail to create constructive action. Studies of intergroup guilt find mixed results on this score. Some find that guilt, as opposed to anger and shame, leads to little support for collective action to help victims of injustice (Allpress et al., 2010, Study 1; Iyer et al., 2007; Mari, Andrighetto, Gabbiadini, Durante, & Volpato, 2010), while others find that guilt predicts support for group-level reparative action (Doosje et al., 1998) even when compared to shame (Allpress et al., 2010, Study 2; Brown et al., 2008). It should also be noted that many of these studies that have found behavioural consequences of group-based guilt and shame have measured attitudes rather than actual helping behaviour. For example, Doosje et al. (1998) measured agreement with the sentiment that the Dutch government should compensate victims of its colonial past. Arguably, support for government policy, rather than personal offers of assistance, is the appropriate way to measure the consequences of national-level emotion. But the suspicion remains that collective guilt and shame are not doing all they could do if they allow individuals to foist the problem off on their government while doing nothing themselves.

There are four main barriers blocking intergroup guilt and shame from their most productive behavioural consequences. The first barrier is the existence of defences against self-threat and ingroup threat, when self-critical feelings become overly strong. The second barrier happens if guilt or shame is actually felt, but leads to inhibition rather than action when the intergroup situation is seen as a matter of personal self-control, rather than interpersonal justice. A third barrier arises when guilt or shame is felt and leads to action, but that action is only symbolic, aimed more at relieving bad feelings than actually helping the harmed group or restoring relations. This process goes hand-in-hand with the fourth and final barrier, in which people can judge the actions needed to restore good relations as too difficult, and escape the emotions that warrant such action. Like Scylla and Charybdis, these latter two barriers jointly constrain action, causing people to shy away from difficult actions and embrace easy but ineffective solutions.

Defences

Bandura (1999) identified numerous mechanisms of moral disengagement that defend against moral guilt and shame on an individual level. For example, people can insist that their actions in fact served a different code of morality; they can deny responsibility for it or point to worse actions that have been committed by other people; they can deny that the victims are worthy of moral concern, denying them status as fully human agents or even as moral objects able to feel pain (the animalistic and mechanistic modes of dehumanization described by Haslam, 2006). Alternatively, they can deny legitimacy to their victims by demonizing them (Bar-Tal, 1989; Giner-Sorolla et al., 2012), painting them as fundamentally immoral people who deserve anything they get. These disengagement mechanisms are said to preserve equanimity, reducing anxiety, guilt, and other negative self-centred emotions in the face of threats to the view of the person or group as moral.

So far, only some of these defences have been studied specifically in a group context, and their function in reducing guilt and moral shame has been studied only indirectly. Being told that one's group is responsible for near-genocidal action against another group, for example, leads people to indirectly dehumanize the victim group by denying them the ability to feel complex emotions (Castano & Giner-Sorolla, 2006) or sometimes by denying them the ability to feel emotions at all (Leidner et al., 2010). At other times, being told of ingroup responsibility for such crimes can lead to morality shifting. Just as juvenile delinquents can justify their crimes by appealing to a notion of "honour among thieves," Americans reminded of their nation's moral misdeeds in the Middle East respond by endorsing, and having more accessible, moral values related to ingroup protection, such as loyalty (Leidner & Castano, 2011).

None of these manipulations increased or decreased self-reported guilt or shame. But experiments have a difficult time pinning down any conscious emotion as a causal element in moral disengagement, because defences are efficient. Feeling responsible may make people feel guilty, but if defensive processes react quickly, there will be no measurable change in guilt. However, describing victim group suffering as caused by the ingroup's deliberate action, rather than other groups' action or ingroup-caused accidents, was necessary to activate moral disengagement in our experiments. This means that morally disengaging from the victims was a motivated response to the ingroup's responsibility. And, because of the key role of responsibility, it is likely that the negative feelings being defended against would have the emotional nature of guilt, more so than shame.

All these defences should be more likely to occur when self-critical emotions threaten the view of the ingroup's morality. This threat, as with many failures of emotion to contribute to individual self-control, comes from an overextension of guilt and shame's associative "stickiness." Some worldviews may see any of these negative emotions as threatening the association of positive feelings with the country, and by extension the self. As an example, take an American who learns that the country's government had been responsible for infecting Guatemalan prisoners with syphilis without consent as part of medical experiments in the 1940s. If this person's guilt and shame become associated only with the specific act, then those feelings have worked effectively as ingroup-regulating emotions. They motivate action to repair the wrong, and validate the largely positive image of America in that person's mind—a country that makes mistakes, but also learns from them. However, another American might learn of the same tragic history and feel threatened by a more general association between the negative feelings aroused and the concept of America. Perhaps the threat of guilt and shame is stronger for this person. Perhaps this person's national self-image is simpler and more monolithic, based on a rigid view of the countries as either morally perfect or villainous. In any event, guilt and shame become threats, because they imply that the whole country might be morally wrong or morally inferior. The association between the country and the worthlessness implied by these emotions is unbearable, and so needs to be defended against.

Research bears out this interpretation of identification and defensive processes. Those US Whites who identify highly with their racial group respond to reminders of their group's privilege over Blacks—threatening inequality guilt—with increased endorsement of beliefs denying that racial differences are unfair. Whites who do not identify strongly as Whites, however, endorse modern racist beliefs less when reminded of their group privilege (Branscombe, Schmitt, & Schiffhauer, 2007). Likewise, high-identifying Americans in two studies used justifying cognitions to reduce the amount of guilt they felt when told of their country's aggressive acts (Maitner, Mackie, & Smith, 2007, Studies 2 and 3). However, in a different research study, identification was positively related with shame as an American, but only when confronted with very serious instances of Americans' prejudice against Arabs after September 11, 2001; for less serious instances, high identification predicted lower shame (Johns, Schmader, & Lickel, 2005). This suggests that the defences of high identifiers may be easier to deploy if the ingroup's injustice is not blatant and severe.

As I mentioned in chapter 3, some people show a basic love of country that can acknowledge faults, while others have a more rigid view that emphasizes superiority over others. Indeed, the construct of glorification versus attachment has an important bearing on defensive processes. Glorifiers, those who insist on their country's material and moral supremacy, are more likely to use mechanisms of moral disengagement than those who are simply attached to the country. They are more likely to come up with rationalizing beliefs when confronted with their own group's misdeeds; for example, Israeli glorifiers were more likely to point to the misdeeds of Arabs or insist upon the necessity of a tough line for national survival (Roccas, Klar, & Liviatan, 2006). High glorifiers also were shown, in Leidner et al. (2010), to be more likely to deny the emotional suffering of those their own group had harmed, using another technique of moral disengagement.

The role of shame in victim as well as perpetrator emotions implies that victims may also have an interest in defending themselves against shame. Converting shame into anger, as I've discussed, is one defence that brings at least a sense of moral rightness and certainty, if not calm and equanimity. But there are other ways to handle shame without accepting its judgment. If the shame's cause can be remedied, and the shame is not overly strong, it may spark action to recover face and honour; working harder, paying more attention to appearance. But if the shame is strong or based on a deep-rooted cause, its pain can be mitigated by beliefs that reduce its sting, whether or not they affect the responsibility that's crucial to guilt.

Social identity theory emphasizes the flexibility and creativity with which individuals handle identification with social groups (Ellemers, Spears, & Doosje, 2002; Turner & Oakes, 1989). Part of this creativity is the possibility of reinterpreting a despised social group more positively. Members of victimized groups often embrace an alternative hierarchy of social value that puts them in a high rather than low slot. If they are seen as untrustworthy, they may revel in being hard-working and clever; if seen as uneducated, they may take pride in a folk wisdom superior to the fancy theories of big-shot professors. Selective evaluation of social dimensions has been shown in research on artificially manipulated groups as well as real-life ones (Jackson, Sullivan, Harnish, & Hodge, 1996). For example, people in disadvantaged regions embrace the "complementary stereotypes" that they are happier and friendlier than the cold folks in richer parts of the country, as shown by research on southern and northern Italians (Jost, Kivetz, Rubini, Guermandi, & Mosso, 2005). Such "poor but happy" and "poor but honest" stereotypes serve a more general function of reducing social conflict by legitimizing the ruling system (Kay & Jost, 2003). But they also may work as personal defence mechanisms against the threat of competence-based shame felt by the poor.

A group identity that gives its holder shame or guilt can be dealt with using a final and most drastic defence mechanism: the person can cut off all identification with the group. This is a defence mechanism unique to the kind of shame and guilt generated by the actions of an ingroup. When a person feels shame and guilt for his or her own acts, denying one's own selfhood is not really an option, except via psychopathology. However, when an individual's own group is the source of shame and guilt, a number of socially creative responses become available, as social identity theorists have observed (e.g., Tajfel & Turner, 1979).

In an interview with the magazine *The Atlantic*, Christian Lander, founder of the humour blog "Stuff White People Like," explains the urge to break off identification with a morally questionable group identity. "Like, I'm aware of all the horrible crimes that my demographic has done in the world," Lander says. "And there's a bunch of white people who are desperate—*desperate*—to say, 'You know what? My skin's white, but I'm not one of the white people who's destroying the world.'" (Hsu, 2009). Faced with an undeniably pale complexion, some Whites feel a need to split themselves off from the group of "white people" responsible for those "horrible crimes." An even more extreme solution can be embraced when national identity is the cause of guilt. Thus Garry Davis, a US bomber pilot in the Second World War who felt remorse for the death and destruction the bombing caused among civilians in Germany, renounced his national citizenship in 1948 and became a "Citizen of the World," eventually registering more than half a million "world citizens" and issuing a world passport.

Acts of disidentification, be they public or private, are one way out for people who derive guilt and shame from their identity. This escape route has been much mentioned in social identity theory. Usually, the examples given are of group members trying to escape a low-status, rather than high-status but morally questionable, group identity (Ellemers et al., 2002; Tajfel & Turner, 1979). A person who refuses to accept the troublesome group identity of his or her birth— say, a remorse-stricken American—can instead start identifying as a member of a different group (e.g., "world citizens"), a more exclusive group (e.g., "non-typical Americans"), or simply as an individual (Jackson et al., 1996). These re-identification strategies are more available if the identity is seen as less stable and more flexible (Mummendey, Kessler, Klink, & Mielke, 1999). For example, gender offers less purchase for re-identification than does the less stable concept of political identification.

Yet another defence against guilt is to build a wall between past and present, isolating the perpetrators of past crimes from the moral identity of the group today. Instead of asserting personal distance from the group, a person can subjectively oust the criminals from the group instead. In a recent study of Belgian historical memory for the country's often brutal colonial legacy in the Congo, Licata and Klein (2010) found that while members of older Belgian generations avoided guilt by emphasizing the benefits brought to Africa by colonialism, younger people relied instead on the idea that those who committed atrocities in the Congo were not typical Belgians. This reasoning can be applied to contemporary misdeeds, as when US Deputy Defense Secretary Paul Wolfowitz asserted in an interview that the prisoner abuse at Abu Ghraib in Iraq came from "a few bad apples" and shouldn't reflect badly on the whole military (US Department of Defense, 2004). Creative redefinition of identity and responsibility, like self-redefinition, is only available when the possibility of guilt and shame arises in a collective context.

The flexibility of identification and the unpleasantness of remorseful feelings, taken together, can explain why findings about the relationship of group identity to guilt and shame have been inconsistent. Intergroup emotion theory asserts that emotions will be felt most strongly on a group level by those who identify strongly with the group (Mackie & Smith, 2002). For emotions as a whole, this has been shown to be true (Smith, Seger, & Mackie, 2007). However, to feel group-based guilt a person must either not identify too highly, or must identify in a flexible way that allows recognition of the group's faults. Too strong or rigid a group identification, and evidence of the group's crimes will be met with defensive thoughts. For this reason, some studies find highest levels of ingroup-based guilt at moderate levels of identification (Doosje et al., 1998), while others find that making a problematic national identity salient reduces guilt (Halloran, 2007) or that high identifiers feel less guilt (Branscombe et al., 2007; Doosje, Branscombe, Spears, & Manstead, 2006, Study 2; Maitner et al., 2007). When the source of criticism is the ingroup, excuses are less available, and high identifiers are the ones who feel most guilt (Doosje et al., 2006, Study 1).

Inhibition

Even if feelings of guilt or shame break through the initial defences, they can fail to lead to action because of their inhibiting, self-paralysing effect. This comes about principally when these feelings are experienced in an individual context, rather than a social one. In a recent article on the role of guilt feelings within the law, the legal philosopher Scott A. Anderson (2009) draws a distinction between the emphases of two theoretical approaches to guilt in Western thought. One, which he labels the *legalistic* tradition, sees guilt as arising from a personal failure to live up to abstract standards of justice. Indeed, a number of social psychological perspectives on guilt see it as coming from a discrepancy between the self and a desired standard (Higgins, 1987; Monteith et al., 2002). Gonzalez and Tyler (2007) likewise argue that guilt, unlike shame, responds to violation of standards and rules; in their view, shame is the emotion that responds to threatened relationships. This terminology, however, is at odds with numerous theoretical and empirical arguments that guilt is most characteristically awakened by a threat to one's existence in a moral relationship or community, such as those advanced by

Baumeister et al. (1995), Gilbert (2003), Lewis (1971), or van Vugt and van Lange (2006). Anderson (2009) sees just such a relational sense of guilt as an important dimension of morality in the law, beyond strictly legalistic transgression.

Undeniably, many people do feel guilt at breaking one of their personal rules, and shame at what this lapse of self-control might mean for their position on hierarchies of competence and morality, even if the rule is relevant to nobody else and no other group. Dieting is one common guilt-provoking rule violation, especially among women in the West (Chamove, Graham, & Wallis, 1991; Steenhuis, 2009). Advertisements promise "guilt-free" dessert with a low-calorie recipe that nonetheless lets you have it all, for it is "sinfully" good tasting. Guilt over personal sexual feelings and masturbation, too, exists at varying levels from generation to generation (e.g., Wells & Twenge, 2005). Finally, the balance of studying versus having fun is a personal issue that students associate with guilty feelings; among American university students studied in Giner-Sorolla (2001), sex, eating, and partying vs. studying were the three most frequently named arenas of individual self-control.

Because abstract, individualized guilt involves departure from an impersonal moral standard, it should really lie more toward self-focus on our graph, compared with the kind of guilt that focuses on injustice or inequality toward another person. On this dimension, individual "guilt" doesn't look much different from moral shame. Research on individual self-control and emotions doesn't clarify things much, using a variety of different self-conscious emotion words ("guilt," "shame," "regret") lumped under the category "compunction" or "self-conscious negative affect" (e.g., Giner-Sorolla, 2001; Monteith, 1993; Monteith & Voils, 1998; Monteith, Devine, & Zuwerink, 1993; Richard, de Vries, & van der Pligt, 1998).

Nonetheless, individual compunction is important in the study of group-based attitudes because it is sometimes proposed as a way to control one's own prejudice. The majority of research in this area shows that being reminded of personal complicity in prejudice can lead to feelings of compunction, and to behaviour aimed at inhibiting or correcting the prejudice. For example, people told they have been prejudiced rate bigoted jokes as less funny (Monteith & Voils, 1998) or take longer to respond to questions with potentially prejudiced responses (Monteith, 1993). These longer response times point to inhibition as an outcome of guilt in this context, which seems to be a short-term reaction. In one study, participants who were told they had been prejudiced showed brain activity typical of inhibition and avoidance the more they reported feeling guilty. But when later presented with an opportunity to seek out information on how to reduce their own prejudice, their guilt was related to more approach-motivated behaviour and brain activity (Amodio, Devine, & Harmon-Jones, 2007).

It should be noted that most of these demonstrations of the effects of compunction involve inhibiting or correcting one's own behaviour, rather than seeking to restore relations with other people. A closer look at this literature reveals that few studies actually show compunction feelings playing a causal or mediating role between a manipulation of standard violation and positive action to compensate for the misdeed. One apparent exception (Monteith et al., 2002, Experiment 4) showed that greater compunction after taking an implicit anti-Black prejudice test was related, later on, to increased self-reported liking for Black names. However, compunction feelings were not manipulated, but were related to how prejudiced the person's actual results had been. Compunction's effect on liking was weakened to a marginal level of significance when this was taken into account. Our own lab's experiments have used a similar prejudice feedback paradigm and have shown no direct link between feelings of compunction and either personal prejudice reduction or a task assigning funds to discriminated-against groups, although our manipulation of prejudice feedback separately increased both of these outcomes as well as compunction (Giner-Sorolla et al., 2011b).

We have seen that compunction from breaking prejudice-related personal standards works most immediately and reliably to inhibit responses. Guilt and related feelings play a delayed and possibly weaker part in motivating symbolic gestures of compensation such as rating jokes or names, and in self-centred responses such as attention to self-corrective techniques. But none of these outcomes involve dealing with another member of the group involved in the prejudice. In fact, there is indirect evidence that group-based inhibition and compunction can lead to avoidance of other people from the wronged group, and awkward, inhibited silence when interacting with them. Non-Black people who find themselves in a social interaction with a Black person in fact show more depletion of mental resources, ironically tend to appear more prejudiced, and have less successful interactions if they approach the task in a prevention-focused way with the primary goal to avoid being racist (Plant, Devine, & Peruche, 2010; Shelton, Richeson, Salvatore, & Trawalter, 2005; Trawalter & Richeson, 2006).

These limits of compunction are also shown by research done in our lab to test the social guilt hypothesis (Giner-Sorolla, Piazza, van Vugt, & Derbyshire, 2011c): the idea that feelings of guilt in particular are most likely to arise, and trigger compensatory behaviour, in social rather than individual situations. Indeed, social context has been shown to characterize guilt as opposed to regret in imaginary situations (Berndsen et al., 2004; Zeelenberg & Breugelmans, 2008). Our own research put participants into an actual situation where they believed they harmed either their own prospects or someone else's in an economic game. Feelings of guilt were stronger and predicted increased compensatory behaviour in a later task when another person, whom the participant had met in person, had been harmed. These effects were not found for regret or shame. Guilt, then, may simply work better to encourage attention to harmed individuals and groups when it is expressed through pro-social behaviour toward those individuals and groups, rather than experienced as a violation of commandments such as "Don't be prejudiced" or "Don't be too proud of your country." This may be a consequence of the self-centred, inhibitory nature of individual guilt, and the more functional nature of guilt in a relational setting.

Tokenistic responses

A third barrier blocks the way from compunction to action, not by inhibiting action, but by being satisfied with relatively little action. If bad feelings motivate us to do good things such as help other people or put right our own failings, perhaps those feelings can be fooled. The more self-centred the guilt or moral shame of the wrongdoing group, the more it might be bought off by symbolic or tokenistic acts that do not really help other people. Researchers have not yet demonstrated this feature of guilt in an intergroup context, but they have shown that irrelevant affirmations of self-worth can soothe the effects of moral transgression (e.g., O'Keefe, 2002; Sherman & Cohen, 2006). In a more direct demonstration of tokenism's ability to soothe the conscience of a dominant group, a recent study by Richard and Wright (2010) manipulated whether US university students were led to focus on the collective concerns of students from developing countries (other-focus) or of US students (self-focus). With the goal being to increase the representation of African students at the university, self-focused students were more likely to approve of a programme that only produced a tokenistic effect, with 2% of eligible students actually being accepted. Other-focused students, though, saw the tokenistic programme as just as bad as one that admitted no African students at all. Accepting tokenistic solutions reassures the conscience of the self-focused person, but without requiring any real change.

Hopelessness from difficult reparations

If guilt and shame can be bought off by a too-easy attempt at reparation, they can also be stifled by the prospect of too-difficult reparations, a fourth and final barrier. This, at least, is the conclusion of research findings that the more difficult proposed reparations in a group context are, the less guilt is felt (Berndsen & McGarty, 2010; Schmitt, Miller, Branscombe, & Brehm, 2008). Compare this with the way that anger works in collective action; in one well-supported model, anger is a separate path to action from perceptions of the action's efficacy (van Zomeren et al., 2008), meaning it promotes action independently of its perceived difficulty. Guilt may not be so robust in the face of adversity because it is unpleasant to feel. So, in the spirit of moral disengagement, people may use the difficulty or impossibility of reparations as a final excuse not to feel guilty. This analysis also suggests that defensive moral shame should be less affected by the difficulty of reparations. Unlike injustice and inequality guilt, which focus on the relations between groups, defensive shame's goal is to improve the moral standing of the group more broadly speaking. However, the flexibility of this goal also means it can be achieved without necessarily improving the lot of the injured group, for example, by giving to a different group, or through merely symbolic means.

With these four detours available—emotional defences, individual-guilt paralysis, tokenistic action, and the difficulty of reparation—the road between guilty feelings and effective reconciliation between persons and groups looks difficult and convoluted. This is especially true on the group level, where identity-based defences are additionally available, and where the nature of effective action may not be as clear as when communicating with another individual. Shame is overall less concerned with remedying a specific action than with restoring the standing of the self or ingroup, but carries a greater threat to the self in its unworthiness form. Its relative merits over guilt remain unclear. While some studies have found guilt and shame both promote action toward group reconciliation, though through different means (Brown et al., 2008), others find that shame has more to do with action than guilt does (Iyer et al., 2007). It may be that full clarity comes when researchers take on a more schematic approach to guilt and shame, looking beyond specific terms and theories to manipulate the underlying dimensions of emotional intensity and self-focus.

Communication functions of shame and guilt

If guilt and shame have a hard time motivating social actions such as reparation or image repair, this may be because part of their function is expressive and communicative. One reason these emotions feel so bad, making people want to avoid them, is because they have to be believable to other people as self-imposed sanctions for wrongdoing. Communicating guilt and shame tells other people two things. One message is that your intention to reform your own behaviour in a specific situation is genuine. But more generally, those feelings show that you are a moral person, pushed by internal sanctions to flinch from wrongdoing even when nobody is looking. Compunction feelings bind us into a signalling system that ultimately works to strengthen trust in relationships and societies (Nesse, 2001; van Vugt & van Lange, 2006). It is these communication-based functions that explain why such strong and seemingly implacable feelings as existential guilt and unworthiness shame persist in humans, even when they create associations that get in the way of the individual's rational appraisal-based and self-regulatory behaviour.

At first glance, it is easier to see how shame is communicated than guilt. Shame has a characteristic set of expressions in many cultures. Many of its expressive features convey the idea of lowered social status, much as submissive displays in social animals do. Thus, shame can be expressed by lowering or averting the gaze, lowering or covering the face, crouching, kneeling, or prostrating the body (Keltner & Buswell, 1996; Tracy et al., 2009b). At the group level, these behaviours of self-abasement are sometimes shown by political leaders on truly exceptional occasions where shame is called for. In 1970, the German Chancellor Willy Brandt fell to his knees in an expression of contrition when he visited a monument to the dead of the Warsaw Ghetto uprising against the Nazis (see this book's cover photo). Even more astoundingly, after the fall of apartheid in South Africa, the former justice minister Adriaan Vlok carried out a public washing of the feet of one of the men he had ordered imprisoned, Reverend Frank Chikane. Direct and indirect expressions of shame through language are also a part of public apology. Most strikingly, a number of Catholic Church figures, including Pope Benedict XVI and bishops in Northern Ireland and Scotland, have made public, verbal expressions of shame in response to the ongoing scandal of sexually abusive clergy.

Guilt, however, is harder to see. To begin with, it's just not as strong an emotion as shame. This is evident from a close look at comparative studies of emotions looking at numerous traits, for example, Roseman et al. (1994). While shame showed high ratings on subjective physical feelings, guilt rated very low, and showed no characteristic physical expression distinct from shame. To "look guilty," at a minimum, involves expressing discomfort in a situation where one might be responsible for a misdeed. If there is anything distinctive about a guilty look, it comes from the borrowing of some of shame's expressions—for example, the averted gaze. More distinctively, guilty feelings can be communicated verbally, either by directly expressing guilt or by using apologetic language. But the verbal communication has to be seen as sincerely expressing a state of pain to register as guilt. Offering a perfunctory "I'm sorry" is not enough.

Most theories of apology (e.g., Lazare, 2005; Scher & Darley, 1997; Tavuchis, 1991) require the sincere expression of remorse as a necessary component for the apology to be accepted. Although "remorse" is usually understood to be an expression of emotions, which emotional expressions constitute remorse is not always clear. The most important message to be conveyed by remorse is that the person is experiencing a painful emotion, one that is both punitive of the past wrong and a deterrent to future wrongs. To the extent that they convey suffering, stronger emotional expressions that are more indicative of a true change in character should work better in apologies. In fact, self-punishment has been shown to be an important behavioural outcome of guilt (Nelissen & Zeelenberg, 2009b). A further study suggests that self-punishment in guilt works to communicate remorse, because it is expressed more readily to people who have been harmed by the guilt-inducing act than to other audiences (Nelissen, 2011).

An emotional expression can also convey responsibility, which figures as an element in most theories of apology. This is important because even though apology may express suffering, it can do so in an impersonal way, as if the issuer of the apology had nothing to do with the wrong. Often, official or corporate apologies will shirk any sign of responsibility-taking, with the aim of limiting legal liability. At its worst, a "non-apology apology" can end up foisting off responsibility onto the body being apologized to, as in this satirical note by writer Bruce McCall:

> I am deeply sorry that you have decided that my term paper was not submitted in time, even if the fact that my watch had stopped would, as you know, hold up in any legitimate court of law. Nonetheless, I wish to express my heartfelt sympathy for the university's distress in believing that its rules have been violated, and trust that as a token of your equal good will my term paper will be accepted.
>
> (McCall, 2001)

McCall offers this as an example of how "you can get what you want by seeming to express regret while actually accepting no blame." Indeed, the emotion of regret is expressed frequently in official apologies because, while feelings of regret are typical of apologies, they do not actually signify taking on responsibility. I can regret something completely impersonal—for example, that Leonardo da Vinci never built a working helicopter. Even if I regret something I did, it could just be that I regret the consequences for myself, or am sorry I got caught. However, expressions of shame and guilt are more directly self-implicating, being self-conscious emotions. For this reason, perhaps, they are effective; I will discuss more of our research addressing this point in chapter 7. But it's also worth noting that shame and guilt expressions are rarely found in official statements of apology.

Guilt, shame, and their functional conflicts

The complexity and contradictions of guilt and shame can be better understood by distinguishing among the multiple appraisals that can give rise to each emotion, and by recognizing the conflict between these appraisals and the other functions of emotion. The appraisals of guilt and shame are closely linked to their self-regulatory function, because both emotions focus the attention on the self. At the same time, guilt and shame are not solitary, desert island emotions. In each type of guilt and shame, this self-focused attention is evaluated against a backdrop of standards, relationships and audiences. Guilt principally looks toward the self's relationship and responsibility toward another, while shame looks toward the self's position on a more abstract hierarchy of social value. Shame's appraisals either warn of rising too high from one's deserved position in that hierarchy (unworthiness shame) or warn of falling too low from that position (defensive shame). Further complicating matters, both of these appraisals can be applied to a number of different dimensions of social worth, so that shame can be felt simply for low status, for incompetence at a non-moral task, or for one's own moral failings. This latter application of shame may help explain why the feeling is so often confused with guilt.

Guilt is a fundamentally moral emotion. In our own research (Giner-Sorolla et al., 2011c) perceptions of the immorality of an act formed part of a cohesive scale measuring guilt feelings, but not shame or regret. As a moral emotion, guilt is most typically felt by the perpetrators or beneficiaries of unfair relations. Indeed, while one common appraisal of guilt emphasizes one's own responsibility for an unfair or harmful outcome to another person, another appraisal that defines existential guilt focuses only on the unfairness of the situation and not one's own responsibility. Because of this, guilt can have a narrow focus on a single wrong that lies between groups, or a broader focus on patterns of inequality. Some cases of irrational guilt come about when the inequality appraisal of guilt is triggered by a difference that can't easily be amended. Survivor guilt is felt about the gulf between the living and dead; existential guilt, about one's own position in the large-scale structure of society. But to repair this error, the cure would be worse than the disease if we allowed considerations of responsibility entirely to determine our guilt. Responsibility, as we've seen, can be subjectively avoided with self-serving beliefs and excuses. There is probably something adaptive for society at large in an emotion that, for at least some people, causes disquiet at the existence of too large a gap between the self's prosperity and others' misery, no matter what.

From our examination of anger and disgust, we saw that each of those emotions has its own way of perpetuating itself; anger by creating self-fuelling cognitive justifications, disgust by being contagious and beyond the grasp of reason to refute. Guilt and shame, however, exist in a much more precarious position within people's minds. The more they are unpleasant, the more they cause unpleasant associations to one's own self or important group memberships. Often, guilt and shame are undesirable emotions, to be fought against instead of perpetuated. This conflict between the associative function of these emotions and their self-regulatory function often undermines the power of guilt and shame to drive meaningful long-term self-regulation. Thus, remorseful feelings can be avoided by creating excuses and justifications for one's acts; when they are felt, they might cause inhibition of action rather than positive action, if the social context does not give an immediate opportunity to make amends; and they can be bought off with token gestures, or excused if the action required turns out to be too demanding.

In spite of all these barriers to effective action on the basis of guilt and shame, it is the final function, communication, that goes a long way to explaining why they are still part of our social life. Sometimes, only communication and not action will do the job of expressing sincere repentance. After all, material rewards can be misinterpreted as payoffs, or rejected as inadequate exchange for the death of millions. While a strong critical emotion expressed through signs of self-abasement feels bad for the individual, it is good for the communication of sincere remorse to others. The variety of unworthiness shame that clinical perspectives label as pathological may in fact be a survival of hierarchical social relations, laid down in early family and peer environments, and better adapted to a hierarchical culture than to the West's relentlessly egalitarian norms.

The communication function of guilt is more limited, but it also works to underscore the genuineness of apologies that focus more specifically on an act of wrongdoing. Guilt thus helps to restore reciprocal relations between peers by undoing or correcting an act that comes between them. However, it may be less appropriate when real, systematic inequalities of power exist. Here, a more thorough examination of existential guilt is in order. This feeling responds to the mere fact of being on the privileged end of a situation of inequality, and in a small village or tribe would plausibly lead to sharing and solidarity. But it remains to be seen whether existential guilt reliably leads to the redistribution of power in a large-scale society. Judging from the many ways in which guilt can be undermined and sabotaged, the prospects that existential guilt can lead to improved relations and communication between groups seem slim at best. Research on interracial communication suggests, instead, that a focus on positive promotion goals rather than negative prevention goals is best able to lead to better relations in a personal intergroup encounter (Murphy et al., 2011). Perhaps, then, all this focus on the negativity of guilt and shame is blinding us to the potential of positive morally relevant feelings to create change? In the next chapter I will examine the potential of the positive moral emotions.

6 Positive moral emotions

The four emotions I have examined in detail—anger, disgust, guilt, and shame—are all seen as negative feelings. These negative emotions have been of the most interest to my own research. In this fascination, I don't claim to be different from most other people. Negative things are intrinsically more attention-getting, and research usually shows that "bad is often stronger than good" in our minds (Baumeister, Bratslavsky, Finkenauer, & Vohs, 2001). However, it's also worth looking at positive moral emotions, if only because each of the four negative moral emotions has shown its limitations as an encouragement to moral behaviour. Anger, while it creates activity aimed toward justice, can become over-generalized and self-justifying. Disgust operates without regard for justification. Guilt and shame themselves are vulnerable to numerous defences and misinterpretations. Could it be that positive emotions can do better at promoting moral action?

Positive emotions present a challenge for my functional conflict theory, because they are qualitatively different from negative emotions. In her influential "broaden-and-build" theory of positive emotions, psychologist Barbara Fredrickson argues that while negative emotions are tightly focused on a single threat, positive emotions function by providing a more general signal that things are all right. When felt over a longer period of time, good feelings help people to relax and apply their creativity to problem-solving, coping, and relationships (Fredrickson, 2005). This analysis holds some truth, even accepting that the negative moral emotions are less single-mindedly focused on threats than Fredrickson suggests. As we have seen, each emotion is adapted to not one function but several, and can respond to appraisals indicating very different kinds of concern. Nonetheless, it is the very specificity of negative emotions that allows their different functions to mingle and interfere with each other inappropriately. Positive emotions, because they respond to more general circumstances, are less prone to this failing. Being blocked in traffic makes me angry, which then fuels an inappropriate moral condemnation of someone who has done nothing wrong. However, if I have a nice ride in the morning, I can still interpret an unrelated, negative immoral act correctly. It is precisely because negative things in the environment grab our attention so effectively that they can snap us out of an inappropriate positive mood. Negative feelings are more difficult to dispel.

In this way, positive emotions let us know that things are proceeding as they should, a foundation for normal and healthy life. This analysis should not, however, lead us to ignore their complexity. Viewed from the perspective of functional conflict theory, all the functions can have a positive side. We sometimes need to appraise something as good for a certain goal; to associate things with good feelings; to acknowledge the good results of ourselves and our actions in self-regulation; and to communicate happiness and closeness in a sincere way to others. Specific positive emotions arise from distinctive kinds of especially positive occurrences. A few that have been studied include joy, amusement, awe, pride, and love (in all the varieties that this simple English word conceals). Some of them, such as amusement, awe, and pride, have distinctive facial and bodily displays (Shiota, Campos, & Keltner, 2003).

As with negative emotions, only some specific positive emotions are associated with moral concerns. These can generally be divided into emotions that evaluate the self and those that evaluate other people (Haidt, 2003a). Beyond this division, though, the parallel to negative emotions ends. There aren't different terms for what we feel toward someone who upholds the virtues whose violation make us angry, versus those whose violation makes us disgusted. Instead, we categorize our other-upholding moral feelings by whether the person is doing morally good things (admiration, trust, respect, elevation, or awe), or requires our own moral concern (sympathy, compassion, or pity). Shame and guilt, as self-critical emotions, are opposed only by a single self-affirming emotion, pride—although the true nature of pride, as we will see, may be more complicated than this single term allows.

Approval emotions: Admiration, gratitude, elevation

Most of the time, when someone acts exceptionally well, we form a positive impression of that person. At times, this positive attitude becomes emotional. It can set off physical sensations as well as motivate action. But what is the exact nature of this emotion? Research to date has studied a number of positive moral emotions that focus on other people. Haidt (2003a) proposed that the expansive feeling when witnessing an act of virtue be called "elevation," in line with the centuries-old observations of Thomas Jefferson. This is distinguished from the non-moral emotion of admiration, in which the exemplary act shows competence, as well as from the moral emotion of gratitude in which the act is moral, but directed from another person towards the self. We may also consider feelings of trust, like gratitude, to bind the self relationally to another person. The difference is that trust is felt in anticipation of future selfless relations, while gratitude is felt as a reaction to a selfless act that has occurred. Ortony et al. (1990) list several more "appreciation emotions" that, while they can be moral in nature, are not necessarily so, among them respect and awe. I will use the term "approval emotions" to cover all the positive feelings that can have a moral agent or action as their target.

The English language has some peculiarities in describing approval feelings. For instance, a distinction like the one between gratitude, admiration, and elevation is not observed for negative acts. "Anger" suffices to condemn acts inflicted on the self and on others, both moral and non-moral. The English vocabulary also shows limits when lay people describe positive moral emotions. In one study distinguishing between gratitude, elevation, and admiration, "happiness" was the most frequent response to each of the situations that theoretically would elicit each of the emotions, though more differentiated terms were used in second place (Algoe & Haidt, 2009). The Jeffersonian term "elevation," not surprisingly, was also little used in everyday descriptions of the emotion. What is missing from our language is a mid-level term like "anger" or "shame" that collects together positive approval feelings, recognizing their similarities. But such a concept would only be justified if, like the different forms and contexts of anger, the different approval emotions had features of expression, experience, and biology shared in common, distinct from other positive emotions. As with the different forms of anger or disgust, the common status of the approval emotions would also be more evident if one of them could be shown to lead to another; if, say, moral elevation could increase gratitude, or lead to trusting acts.

Although research on this topic is still in its infancy, initial findings do support some common themes among the emotions of approval. Algoe and Haidt's (2009) studies found, in general, that gratitude, admiration, and elevation had more features in common than all of them shared with the non-social positive emotion of joy. Participants remembered times in their lives when the conditions theoretically required by each emotion had happened to them. The approval emotions had much weaker physical sensations than joy did. The differences that were found among their physical experiences did not generally conform to expectations (e.g., elevation did not show a special warm feeling in the chest compared with the other emotions). The motivational tendencies among these emotions likewise were distinct as a group from joy. All three led people to want to affirm their close relationships through praise and affiliation. All three also reduced the desire to express happiness outright.

In another study, participants watched videos either of a mentor for children, a talented athlete, or just some jokes. The first two videos both created a desire to be like the admired person, but differed in context-specific sensations and motivations: watching the athlete jump, not surprisingly, created greater feelings of energy and desire to be successful, while watching the mentor instead motivated participants to want to help others. These motivational effects were mainly explained by admiration for the other, and in the case of the moral example, by warm feelings for him or her as well. A common biological factor in these emotions may be the hormone oxytocin. Increased levels of oxytocin have been shown to increase trust (Kosfeld, Heinrichs, Zak, Fischbacher, & Fehr, 2005) and in turn respond to elevation feelings in nursing mothers, increasing breast milk secretion and close contact with their babies (Silvers & Haidt, 2008).

Studies of the incidental effects of approval emotions, aroused in one context and influencing another, also show the fluid boundaries among them. Bartlett and DeSteno (2006) made people grateful in the lab; this increased pro-social behaviour even towards someone who was not the target of the original gratitude.

Two studies by Schnall, Roper, and Fessler (2010), likewise, show increases in helping the experimenter as a result of watching film clips designed to provoke moral elevation, as opposed to mere happiness. Algoe and Haidt's (2009) third study compared the effects of gratitude and admiration, induced by having participants write letters on different topics to someone they knew well. Both these feelings again increased their specific motivations: admiration toward self-improvement, and gratitude toward repayment. Gratitude, however, showed a generalized effect related to moral elevation, in that it induced participants to want to chat with a morally praiseworthy fellow student who volunteered time to various causes, rather than one who just wanted to make friends. Gratitude, as a positive feeling, has been distinguished from negative feelings of obligation in part because, like elevation, it leads to a general wish to help rather than just an uncomfortable need to repay (McCullough, Kilpatrick, Emmons and Larson, 2001). These results underscore this point.

Broad similarities as well as some differences of context exist among the approval emotions. All three boost a person's desire to affiliate with and praise the good moral actor. They work in varying degrees to start or strengthen relations with him or her. By encouraging the "paying forward" of good deeds, they also work to strengthen relations with the larger social group. Elevation and admiration are described in similar lay language, and both increase desire to emulate the target. They differ in the domain of social value their context refers to, specifically whether the model's excellence is moral or non-moral; but we don't make a similar distinction in our vocabulary about anger, disgust, or shame, for example, which can apply to either kind of context. It also seems that elevation requires not just good intentions but success in carrying them out with some degree of competence. At least, I wouldn't feel elevated to hear of a man who spent his whole life mentoring inner-city kids only for each and every one of them to end up a hardened career criminal. This corresponds with Algoe and Haidt's (2009) finding that admiring as well as warm feelings are involved in the motivational consequences of elevation. Thus, to be elevated, a good person may have to carry out good deeds with an admirable amount of competence as well.

Gratitude and elevation are both activated in morally relevant contexts, and both have carry-over effects increasing pro-social behaviour. Gratitude focuses on the relationship between the individual and the other, and distinctively, it activates concerns about reciprocity within that particular pair. Just as the differences between elevation and admiration depend on the context, so the differences between gratitude and elevation hinge on whether the self is directly involved in the relationship or not. It is not too hard to see a morally elevating person as also engaging our gratitude if we think of ourselves as grateful to be a member of the same species, for example. In this sense, taking a group- or relationship-level perspective might be a critical difference between what we call "gratitude" and what we call "elevation."

I have already analysed guilt as an emotion that largely responds to concerns about the self's reciprocal relationship with another, while shame tracks concerns about one's own social and moral standing relative to others. What happens if we keep these situations where the self is relatively worse than another person, and change perspective on them, so that we now think of them as situations where the other person is relatively better than us? This would reverse the valence of guilt and shame, from negative feelings about the self to positive feelings about the other. This mental exercise generates two main motivations that underlie the emotions of approval.

The first motivation is a different way of looking at a situation that might lead to shame. We acknowledge that another person has higher standing than ourselves, but in a way that focuses on the excellence of the other rather than the low or threatened status of the self. As with defensive shame, this discrepancy can lead to a quite active motivation, but framed positively as "rising to meet" the exemplary person, rather than "pulling one's self up" to regain a lost level of worth. On the other hand, if the outcome of watching the example is to focus on the self and its faults, as sometimes happens through contrast effects in self-evaluation (Blanton & Stapel, 2008; Mussweiler & Strack, 2000), then some form of shame will occur.

Like shame, the approval emotions can be felt on moral or non-moral grounds. Indeed, when another person presents an extreme example of greatness to follow, some aspects of the non-social emotion of awe might be felt. Awe involves feelings of the smallness of the self, the greatness of the other, and the realignment of the self's patterns of thought in light of the great example (Keltner & Haidt, 2003; Shiota, Keltner, & Mossman, 2007). Perhaps the awe we feel at a starry night or magnificent waterfall is a re-application of a social emotion that originally positioned the self to support and emulate its superiors in a hierarchy. Adaptively, the social function of this emotion is clearer than the more existential function. Perhaps, too, social awe is a positive re-imagining of unworthiness shame, in the same way that elevation re-imagines defensive shame. Socially, awe is a positive emotion that puts the self in its place, rather than leading it to strive to make up lost ground. Sometimes, people react to an incredible role model by thinking "I could never do that," rather than "I want to do that." The same thoughts that underlie unworthiness shame are likely to underlie this self-limiting function of social awe as well.

The second motivation found among the emotions of approval is not hierarchical, as shame is, but reciprocal, as guilt is. This motive focuses not on bettering the self or giving way to the other's magnificence, but on improving the relationship between self and other. The primary target of this motive is the person approved of. However, as we have seen, it can also extend to other individuals or group members. In the most direct material terms, a relational concern motivates helping others who share an important connection to the self, be that a two-person relationship, a small group, a national group, or just fellow human beings. It also leads to expressions of closeness to the other person or group, which encourages the positive actions of other people that led to the feeling in the first place. Unlike guilt, however, it's not the failing of the self but the benevolence of the other that sparks further motivation to strengthen social relations.

The role of group identity in the approval emotions could also be examined more closely. One evolutionary explanation of gratitude, for example, is that it encourages helping behaviour among non-kin groups (McCullough, Kimeldorf, & Cohen, 2008; Trivers, 1971). Looking back at the results of Bartlett and DeSteno (2006), they induced gratitude by having student participants in an experimental procedure save time through the helpful act of a fellow student. Their helping was then extended not just to the student who helped them, but a different student who approached them with a request for help. Was this, then, gratitude on a group level? Would a non-student have been helped as readily? Indeed, a helpful act from a member of an unknown or disliked group might never get to the stage of gratitude. It might instead be met with suspicion or distaste. Even when gratitude does not necessarily involve exact repayment of the person to whom we are grateful, its effects tend to reinforce larger group relationships, as demonstrated by a study of gratitude among sorority sisters at a US university (Algoe, Haidt, & Gable, 2008).

Four functions of the approval emotions and their conflicts

Some of the functions of gratitude have already been noted by McCullough et al. (2001). Here, I integrate these with other potential functions of approval emotions more generally, using the functional conflict theory model. First, the appraisal function of approval emotions is straightforward. Each of these feelings responds to the perception that another person or group has done something with social value. This appraisal calls forth the adaptive social response to strengthen relations with that person or group, which has shown itself to be worthy of closer ties. Strengthening relations can take the form of acts specific to the situation, such as thanking the person, or expressions of benevolence and emulation more generally. In fact, kindness begets kindness through these emotions; appraisals and productions of generous acts can spread throughout a whole social group (Haidt, 2003c). Someone seeing the closeness and generosity prompted by these emotions could start to feel the emotions themselves and act accordingly, inspiring more people to benevolence, and setting in motion a virtuous circle that stops only when competing concerns of self-interest interrupt it.

   The approval emotions also create positive attitudes about other people or groups through associative learning. Ultimately, these attitudes are based on judgments of positive social worth, and create a basis of trust in judging future actions, which is mutually beneficial. The value of associative learning is particularly clear when trust is learned on the grounds of group membership, and good feelings extend to a whole set of people from a single person's acts. Reviewing research in organizational and social psychology, Williams (2001) argues that getting positive feelings from individual acts within a group, and generalizing these feelings from the group to its individual members, is a critical process for developing trust within an organization. Positive emotional attitudes are particularly important for trust building because they allow some of the benefits of approval emotions to happen without having to witness virtuous behaviour. This can jump-start the virtuous cycle of mutual helping.

   While the approval emotions focus on other people, they also carry implications for self-regulation. The cuing of appropriate behaviour, such as returning gratitude, is a way to regulate responses to a social situation. The self-regulation processes that control these feelings, however, are less clear. Just as shame and guilt feel bad and risk being avoided, the approval emotions feel good, contributing to long-term well-being (Emmons & McCullough, 2003). So people should seek them out. But a contrary motivation can explain why gratitude and its cousins are sometimes hard to come by. If your trust, gratitude, or admiration is inspired by a person who is not sincere, your social closeness and helping have made you more vulnerable to exploitation. Although these emotions feel good, it also makes functional sense that they can be disrupted by doubts or distrust. This fits in with Fredrickson's (2005) analysis of positive emotions as good in the long-term but subject to interruption by the more pressing short-term concerns of negative emotions.

Finally, as McCullough et al. (2001) also note, the approval emotions work as spontaneous communications that strengthen their own social impact, reinforcing and rewarding the virtuous behaviour that prompted them in the first place. While verbal expressions most precisely communicate the different forms of gratitude, admiration, and elevation, there may be some non-verbal signals that underscore the words' sincerity. For example, a facial expression of awe, or other symptoms such as speaking with a lump in the throat (being "choked up"), may help to convey elevation. More generally, in the Duchenne smile, an easy-to-fake grin is made sincere by the hard-to-fake contraction of the muscle surrounding the eyes. Duchenne smiles signal heartfelt positive affect in many contexts, including admiration and gratitude. Communicating gratitude in turn can tighten social bonds and further cooperation. For example, Raggio and Folse (2009) evaluated a gratitude-based tourism campaign for the state of Louisiana that referred to the voluntary efforts made by the rest of the US to help that state after its devastation by Hurricane Katrina in 2005. They found that the gratitude-based appeal was effective in generating positive attitudes, feelings, and economic intentions toward Louisiana, especially among those who had themselves contributed to relief efforts. Grant and Gino (2010) also found in a variety of laboratory and field settings that grateful expressions increased further cooperation by increasing people's perceptions of their own effectiveness and social value.

Caring emotions: Sympathy and pity

There is another group of other-focused emotions in which the other person is not the source of a morally good act, but the potential recipient of a helpful act from the self. Terms that describe this feeling include "sympathy," "compassion," and "pity." The term "empathy" is also often used to speak of this process. However, it has been argued that "empathy" should refer to the process of understanding and feeling what another person is feeling; whereas "sympathy" along with related terms such as "compassion" and "pity" should refer to a feeling of concern for a threat to another person's well-being (Eisenberg, 2000; Goetz, Keltner, & Simon-Thomas, 2010). Empathy is therefore more of a way of feeling emotions than an emotion by itself. Empathic anger, distress, joy, pride, disgust, or any other emotion can be envisioned, each with different consequences. When another person's threatened well-being comes from that person's own emotional distress, some amount of empathy will help an onlooker to experience sympathy.

This common situation probably leads to the confusion between empathy and sympathy. But to understand the difference more fully, let's conjure up the image of a small child who sits happily playing with a live hand grenade. While a person feeling only empathy would laugh along with the child, a person feeling sympathy would see a situation of danger, and move to take the grenade away. This shows a concern for the child's well-being that doesn't depend on mirroring the child's own feelings. Likewise, the distress of someone being apprehended for a crime they committed in cold blood might arouse no moral sympathy in our eyes—even if we can empathize for a while with the criminal's anxious feelings.

Sympathy is also different from empathic distress, with an experiential and physiological profile low in arousal. Sympathy is closer to sadness than distress is, although it's also distinct from sadness in a number of physiological indicators. Measures of sympathy form a statistically different factor from sadness in reports of experience, but sympathy also often shows high correlations with measures of sadness, and expressions of the two emotions are most frequently mistaken for one another (Eisenberg et al., 1988, 1989; Goetz et al., 2010).

Even though this affinity lends a partly negative valence to sympathetic feelings, sympathy nonetheless is counted among the positive moral emotions on the basis of its outcome. This is the same reason that anger falls among the negative emotions, even though it can feel good to express. Sympathy's behavioural outcome tends toward helping and closeness, rather than punishment or distancing. It also does not involve a negative evaluation of anyone, unlike guilt or shame. Whether another person, one's self, or impersonal fate caused the suffering of the other is not important in sympathy. However, seeing another person's suffering as intentionally self-caused or deserved can undermine compassionate feelings (e.g., Feather & Sherman, 2002; Weiner, 2005). It makes adaptive sense that our compassionate feelings respect judgments of whether their object deserves sympathy and is likely to improve on the basis of our help. Overall, other-focused sympathy is most likely to emerge when emotional concern for the other is neither so low as to be absent, nor so high that it creates strong distress and a selfish focus on relieving it (Eisenberg, Valiente, & Champion, 2004).

Like the emotions of approval, the caring emotions also combine reciprocal and hierarchical social considerations. Sympathy, like gratitude or admiration, increases the desire to strengthen the relationship between one's self and someone else by helping. As with approval emotions, sympathy involves increased levels of oxytocin (Barraza & Zak, 2009; Zak, Stanton, & Ahmadi, 2007; although these researchers use the term "empathy," their measures more closely resemble sympathy as we have defined it). This desire to help, however, seems to be quite tightly focused on the suffering other, rather than generalized to helping others. This makes functional sense. If we are grateful or admiring toward someone, we may wish to do good things for him or her, but the person may not need our help. However, sympathy implies a threat to the other person's well-being, so it would not be useful to wander away and help someone else. In summary, while the approval emotions build social relations in a more general sense, sympathy works similarly to the negative emotions in Frederickson's analysis (2005), in that it motivates a response to an immediate crisis, although a crisis affecting someone else.

The other dimension of the caring emotions is hierarchical. Here we see a clear difference between sympathy and the approval emotions. Sympathy casts the self in the active role of moral agent, and the other in the passive role of moral recipient, reversing the scenario that gives rise to gratitude. Sympathy can be increased not just through similarity, but also through nurturance—that is, the appraisal of someone as belonging to a class of beings in need of help, whether children or pets (Batson, Lishner, Cook, & Sawyer, 2005). While admiration and elevation respond to others who hold high social value, viewing another person's misfortune or suffering can lead to the assumption that they're of lower social value than the self, at least temporarily.

The term most strongly conveying the hierarchical nature of these feelings is "pity," implying that its object is deserving of help but also somewhat wretched. In the account of group-focused emotions given by the stereotype content model, pity is an ambivalent feeling corresponding to ambivalent stereotypes; numerous studies have linked it to seeing a group as warm and friendly, but low in competence (Cuddy, Fiske, & Glick, 2008). Because of this "false superiority" from pity (Florian, Mikulincer, & Hirschberger, 2000), the term has a derogatory tone, unlike its near-synonyms "sympathy" or "compassion." The writer Dorothy Sayers said as much, through a character in the mystery novel *Gaudy Night*: "Nobody likes being pitied. Most of us enjoy self-pity, but that's another thing" (1936, p. 39). Helping a member of a lower-status group who hasn't called for help was labelled "assumptive helping" in studies by Schneider, Major, Luhtanen, and Crocker (1996). A short summary of the results, taking as their background the racial situation in the United States: Black people don't respond well when Whites offer them assumptive help (see also Nadler, 2002). Sayers might have also added that other-pity can also be enjoyable. If a caring emotion includes this kind of downward comparison, it may boost the ego (e.g., Taylor & Lobel, 1989), making it even more suspect as a morally valid emotion.

However, the suspicion of pity can also contaminate expressions of sympathy offered in a comradely spirit. Offers of help promise immediate material benefit, but accepting help can have longer-term costs, reducing a person's standing in the social hierarchy (Ackerman & Kenrick, 2008). This explains why even compassionate offers can be interpreted as a social threat and refused. Here again we see a key difference between sympathy and empathy. A sympathetic person only wants to help; an empathetic person will relate to the other's desire not to be helped, and back away. The call for "empathy, but not sympathy" is therefore sometimes heard from people with various stigmas, including physical disability, incarceration, and being a woman in the male-dominated field of science (e.g., Cumberbatch, 2010; Gibilisco, 2010; Sinha, 2009). But as we have seen, sympathy and not empathy may be the more appropriate response to someone who doesn't understand, or refuses to understand, the impending threat.

Four functions of the caring emotions and their conflicts

There is more scope for conflict among the caring emotions' functions than there was among approval emotions, because of the ambivalent goals and messages that characterize sympathy and its cousins. In its appraisal of another person's need and its action tendency to help the person, sympathy has the forthright function of directing social help to where it is needed. However, the associative learning of attitudes toward that person may depend on which element prevails in sympathy. If the focus is on the good feelings that come from helping, then a supportive and warm attitude will be formed, which will encourage further caring efforts, much as when approval emotions are felt. However, with a strong focus on the hierarchical nature of the helping, or the wretched condition of the person being helped, it is also possible that negative associations might be formed. The person's misfortune becomes distressing, and he or she appears weak and incapable. Both of these will lead to the association of negative feelings with the person (Uhlmann et al., 2006). This will certainly reduce affiliative feelings with the person, if not the actual helping behaviour. But even the helping will take on a condescending tone, as a way to demonstrate both moral and material superiority. This potential conflict between warm and cold outcomes of helping deserves more examination in research.

If helping might make the other seem more negative, might it also make the self seem more positive? Considering the self-regulatory function, a boost to self-esteem might follow from helping another. However, as I will discuss in more detail when considering pride, a positive self-regarding emotion can lead to less pro-social effort and not more—"resting on one's laurels" as it were, having been given feedback that the goal is complete. Also, the more that the situation is seen in terms of status, the more likely it is that the self and other will be thought of in the kind of all-or-none terms that leads to what's been called "hubristic" pride (Tracy & Robins, 2007). The self is cast as the good, strong helper, and the other as the weak recipient. This attaches a negative emotional attitude to the other, and a positive attitude to the self, one that doesn't have to be proven through further good works. Thinking of the act of kindness as just one act, or thinking of self and other as part of a relationship that has been strengthened, may be less likely to lead to a hubristic outcome from good deeds. However, while this self-regulatory difference between sympathy and downward-looking pity potentially has important consequences for the aftermath of helping behaviour, it has not been examined in research to date.

The communication of sympathy and compassion through facial expressions, vocal tone, and even touch has also been extensively studied (for a recent review, see Goetz et al., 2010). Here, too, mixed messages can be sent from these emotions. Thus, a gentle, caressing touch sends a signal of sympathy (Hertenstein, Keltner, App, Bulleit, & Jaskolka, 2006); and leaning forward, shortening the physical distance while keeping attention fixed on the suffering person, also conveys sympathy. Interestingly, the vocal tone that conveys kindness has features in common with the kind of tone that is taken with infants, such that kinder utterances are also judged as more "babyish" (Berry, 1991). But baby-talk can come across as condescending, if the listener doesn't want to be cared for. Nevertheless, a sincere signal of sympathy can let a recipient of help know that the helping is not motivated by less admirable motivations, such as personal distress or contempt. Although research is lacking on this point, it is likely that the kind of personal compassion expression that communicates equal status unequivocally will consist more of the facial and bodily cues of attentiveness, and less of the cooing vocal tones associated with power differences, as between parent and child.

Approval emotions, caring emotions, and groups

Emotions of approval and sympathy clearly share one important motivational feature, approaching others in a spirit of closeness. Because of this, the strong role they can both play in cementing the social bonds within a group is hard to argue against. This is most evident from the body of research on emotional trust within organizations (Dirks & Ferrin, 2002; Schoorman, Mayer, & Davis, 2007). Emotional trust, as distinct from more rational expectations of reciprocity, is often classified together with the approval emotions. For example, manipulations of gratitude, but not pride, lead to increased trust in others (Dunn & Schweitzer, 2005). Also, like the approval emotions, trust increases with levels of oxytocin (Kosfeld et al., 2005).

Feelings are particularly important in the absence of a prior history with another person. The feeling of trust in this situation can mean the difference between accepting or declining a profitable relationship with someone we have no rational basis to trust. Preconceptions, then, play a large part. A few cues to shared membership in a social group are enough to create a limited amount of instant trust (Tanis & Postmes, 2005; Yuki, Maddux, Brewer, & Takemura, 2005). Furthermore, group members who follow the group's norms and exemplify its values are trusted more, while members of an outgroup are seen with distrust (for a review, see Hogg, 2007). In turn, trust among members of a group is simultaneously an appraisal that allows for more efficient cooperation; an associative attitude that allows for rapid emotional tagging of fellow group members; and a self-regulatory feeling that creates greater feelings of existential security in the face of risk. Likewise, communications of positive emotion between group members create a basis for trust. Emotional facial displays are especially effective in allaying the doubts of those whose initial trust in a group is low (Tanghe, Wisse, & van Der Flier, 2010).

Could these positive emotions also play a role in relations between different groups? In the previous chapter, I outlined some of the benefits and pitfalls of sympathy as an alternative to shame and guilt, when considering emotional responses to unjust dominance or exploitation of a less powerful group. We have seen in this chapter that sympathy expressions, while other-focused, are not automatically free of self-serving motives. Pity that is based on false assumptions about the other's needs, or that reinforces the dominant group's hierarchical position, is likely to backfire. The approval emotions convey the closeness that sympathy does, but with the effect of elevating rather than lowering the target.

But approval can backfire, too. Overly fulsome praise about the moral nobility of an oppressed people, coming from the oppressor group, might be seen as an attempt to justify an unfair system by attributing special, magical powers to the impoverished. Indeed, stereotypes that work to defend a hierarchical system often advance the idea that women, the poor, or minorities are especially moral and honest (Kay et al., 2007). Ultimately, the best kind of encounter between groups might involve other-focused, level dialogue: listening to what the other has to say, but answering to their accusations of responsibility made against one's own group without denial or equivocation. Certainly, recent research on interracial interaction in the US supports the idea that other-focused motivation with the intent to learn works better than self-focused motivation with the intent to prove or disprove one's own worthiness (Murphy et al., 2011).

Moral pride

Pride, like shame, is an emotion that can evaluate the self on moral or non-moral grounds. But unlike shame, pride tells the self good news, not bad. Because of this, pride may be seen more positively in self-valuing individualistic cultures than in collectivistic ones. For example, one study showed that persuasive appeals involving personal pride were more convincing to Americans than to Chinese, who prefer more sympathetic persuasive themes (Aaker & Williams, 1998). Chinese do take pride, but their pride is more often extended to the vicarious accomplishments of a friend or family member, while Americans (and probably other Westerners) take more pride in their personal accomplishments (Stipek, 1998). While they almost always feel good, proud feelings can either undercut group relationships or strengthen them, depending on whether they are felt on behalf of the individual or the collective.

Even at the individual level, there is a two-edged aspect to pride. Tangney and colleagues originally included items measuring two different kind of pride in the well-known TOSCA scale, more usually used to measure guilt and shame (Tangney & Dearing, 2002). These two subtypes extended the attributional logic behind guilt and shame to positive self-evaluations. Like guilt, one type of pride responds to one's own actions, but positively rather than negatively. Like shame, the other type of pride responds to evaluations of the whole self, but instead of feeling like a rat, the person feels great. Tracy and Robins (2007) expand on this distinction, measuring feelings of "hubristic" pride with adjectives like "conceited" and "arrogant" and feelings of "authentic" pride with adjectives like "confident." They showed hubristic pride to respond to more stable attributions of personal success such as ability, while authentic pride is associated with more desirable personality traits and more controllable attributions of success to things like effort. One problem with this research, though, is that the hubristic pride scale required people to label their feelings with terms that are socially negative, to the point of yielding average responses that were close to the scale minimum of 1. This may mean that hubristic pride is associated with low rather than high self-esteem, or at the very least a negative retrospective evaluation of the way one acted (Piazza, Holbrook, & Fessler, 2011).

Stepping beyond the term "pride" for a moment, there is also a wealth of research on hubristic and authentic forms of general positive self-evaluation. For instance, narcissism has been distinguished from genuine self-esteem, and linked back to different forms of pride (Paulhus & John, 1998; Tracy, Cheng, Robins, & Trzesniewski, 2009a). To sum up some general themes across these approaches, socially "good" pride follows from a person's achievements, makes no comparison with others, and allows for the acknowledgement of flaws. However, socially "bad" pride presumes superiority, elevates the self above others, and rigidly denies the possibility of anything bad about the self. In fact, it is this diagnosis that group researchers apply on a collective level as they separate constructive from destructive forms of group identification (e.g., Roccas et al., 2006), sometimes treating national pride as a form of evaluative identification (e.g., Mummendey et al., 2001). Some, such as the investigators of the collective narcissism construct (Golec de Zavala et al., 2009), even extend the terminology of individual self-aggrandizing pathology to the group level.

Four functions of pride and their conflicts

The emotion of pride presents several contradictions. These, I believe, can best be understood in terms of its multiple functions. As a self-conscious emotion, the appraisal function of pride is linked to, but different from, the self-regulation function. A key difference within these functions rests on whether feelings of pride signal that a moral goal is worthy of continued commitment, or that it has already been achieved (Fishbach, Eyal, & Finkelstein, 2010). That is, does pride perpetuate the same appraisal function that generated it—judging one's activity to be good, and continuing the activity? Or does pride follow a goal-oriented, self-regulation logic—judging one's activity to be good *enough*, and so ending the activity?

The first outcome is predicted by a number of attribution-appraisal theories of pride (Weiner, 1985), as well as by Frederickson's concept of the "upward spiral" in which good feelings breed more good feelings. Early research in motivation confirmed many of McClelland and Atkinson's hypotheses that the good feelings that come from success drive on further engagement with the task (e.g., McClelland, Atkinson, Clark, & Lowell, 1953). For example, Berkowitz and Levy (1956) showed that praising the collective performance of a group of US Air Force trainees increased pride in the group, which in turn increased performance even more. Much more recently, research by Williams and DeSteno (2008) has shown a more specific motivational role of emotional pride, not just positive feelings or cognitive beliefs about one's own effectiveness, in getting people to approach a difficult task. These studies manipulated pride by having an experimenter congratulate the subject heartily on his or her good performance on a previous task, versus delivering the same information in a monotone. One feature of these experiments that seemed to help was the fact that the pride comes from the same domain of ability as the task (in both cases, cognitive ability), suggesting that moral pride might both spring from and encourage further moral acts.

However, good feelings can also be seen as a feedback signal to the self that a goal has been achieved. Instead of working harder at being morally good, a self-satisfied feeling from looking back on moral deeds lets me rest on my laurels, maybe indulge in a few moral peccadilloes. Indeed, an increasing number of studies on the phenomena of moral licensing and moral credentialing have shown that carrying out a morally good act can reduce the likelihood of good behaviour in the immediate future (Merritt et al., 2010). For example, people told to write a story about themselves containing words extolling their own morality ("generous," "kind") were much less likely to donate to a charity, or favour cooperation in an environmental cause, than when they were told to include more self-critical terms (Sachdeva, Iliev, & Medin, 2009); and Whites who were given a chance to select a Black candidate for a job were more likely to make a selection in a second, unrelated task that favoured Whites (Monin & Miller, 2001, Experiment 3). Although the role of positive emotions in this moral coasting remains unclear, the implication is that feeling good about yourself gives a signal to go ahead and be morally bad.

To figure out when people will strive or coast after positive feedback from pride, a number of findings in the motivation literature might be helpful. A meta-analysis of 23 separate experiments (Rawsthorne & Elliot, 1999) showed that giving people positive external feedback undermines their motivation to strive mainly when they take the approach of proving the self (performance goal) rather than learning and understanding the task (mastery goal). Fishbach et al. (2010) draw a conceptually similar distinction between the motivating effects of positive feelings that act as a commitment to the goal, and the demotivating effects of positive feelings that act as a judgment of goal progress (see also Wilcox, Kramer, & Sen, 2011). Even within a performance goal, positive feedback also undermines striving more when the person has the negative goal to avoid failure, rather than the positive goal to achieve.

Some authors also make a further distinction between a more external, "introjected" motivation, in which people work to gain internal rewards such as pride and self-esteem, and more intrinsically driven motives, in which the pride instead comes from attaining the goal (Ryan & Deci, 2000). Using this distinction, some people might see feeling proud as a stopping point because they focus on themselves. Pride for them works as a self-regulation message that the goal is achieved. Others, perhaps, see feeling proud as a cue to continue because they want more positive feelings from pursing the goal. Here, the good feelings from pride work as appraisal information that the goal is worthy and attainable. A cynical conclusion from moral licensing experiments, perhaps, is that most of the participants in those studies saw pro-social and anti-racist goals as a way to prove their worth or feel good about themselves, rather than as a way to help other people or right historic wrongs.

The associative function of pride labels the self, or the group, with positive feelings. Repeated over time, these experiences help to create a positive attitude toward the self, known as self-esteem. Self-esteem, too, can exist on a group level (Crocker & Luhtanen, 1990). However, the logic of associative learning means that self-esteem or group-esteem can also be learned by means other than pride. Seeing other people praise us gives us a good feeling; seeing the group and its symbols praised, respected, and celebrated gives us a good feeling about the group. Many adolescents go through a crisis when this kind of simple pride in a cherished group collides with appraisal-based evidence that the actions of the group are not all that pride-worthy (for me, it was the Boy Scouts). In the aftermath of such a collision, the distinction between glorification and attachment becomes very useful. A glorifier wants to hold on to the positive view of the group, and denies or explains away the evidence against it. A person who is attached to the group without glorifying it, however, sees the group's failings as a cause for real concern. Instead of seeing the group as a source of a never-ending stream of positive feelings, the group elicits concern for its weaknesses and failings—including moral failings.

Finally, pride also can be communicated socially, most vividly through a characteristic posture of chest thrust out and chin high (Tracy & Robins, 2004). Tracy, Shariff, and Cheng (2010) argue that such signals of pride serve the adaptive function of representing high social value to others. They furthermore make a connection between hubristic pride and a dominance strategy of social influence, based on assuming a superior position. However, authentic pride is related to a prestige strategy of social influence, in which one's skills and deeds rather than dominant behaviours convey social value and result in better reproductive success.

While Tracy et al. (2010) describe a number of studies supporting this correspondence, it is worth noting that in our society dominance strategies and hubristic pride are both disapproved of. Links found between hubristic pride and dominance could reflect this simple fact. Moreover, it's hard to see why an expression of pride would be taken as a reliable signal for the high competence required by a prestige strategy. Competence, after all, is more reliably signalled by actual performance. There is disdain and not respect for someone who uses signalling in place of results to gain prestige. To resort to some folksy American expressions, such a person is "all hat and no cattle" or "talks the talk but can't walk the walk." Authentic pride and its prestige strategy are best seen, I think, as an adaptation of the pride emotion to a different function. By its homology to dominant displays in other species, pride probably started out as a communication of dominance. However, the usefulness of self-belief in motivating further action by the self led to pride's adaptation to serve appraisal and self-regulation functions.

A simple theory of functional signalling also would find it hard to explain why people tend to control expressions of pride in social company. Here, taking into account both self-regulation and communication functions can lead to a better understanding. Socially, pride elevates but also distances the individual from the group. Dominance pride may evoke resentment in others; even displays of prestige may breed envy. For dominance-based pride, a haughty expression works to convey superiority. Resentment comes as an inevitable cost of taking this route. But for prestige-based pride, the expression is irrelevant to the display of actual results, and harmful to being accepted. Self-regulation thus collides with the communication function in two ways: first, when the self-regulatory adaptation of authentic pride triggers a prideful expression better adapted to the needs of social dominance; and second, when awareness of social pressures leads the proud person to apply self-regulation against that expression, appearing humble while keeping the warm glow of self-belief inside.

Pride and groups

Most social groups realize the benefits of feeling and conveying group-based pride. Thus we see Pride parades for sexual minorities, country songs such as Lee Greenwood's "God Bless the USA" extolling American pride, or the attempts of White supremacist groups to encourage explicit pride in a majority racial identity. As I have already discussed, research to date on chronic pride in one's group has been carried out as part of larger investigations into identity. Moral pride is a dimension of this emotion particularly relevant to groups, because of the predominant importance of morality in judging one's own group and others (Leach et al., 2007). We can expect more defensive thinking and less striving for morality from people whose pride presumes that their group already reaches high moral standards (measured by the "glorification" scale of Roccas et al., 2006) than from people whose pride leads them to set a high standard for their group (measured by their attachment scale).

Because these two kinds of pride are often communicated through similar terms and expressions, it is possible for misunderstandings to arise. Pride is an external problem when its expressions rub another group the wrong way, and even an internal problem when a group becomes aware of its own historical deeds, and vows collectively to regulate its expressions of pride. A former colleague told me of the distress of her mother, who had been raised in the German post-war generation, when she (the daughter) praised something as trivial as the superiority of German pastries in the presence of people from different European countries. Just as hubristic pride threatens the community of different individuals within a group, so it threatens the coexistence of different groups in a world community. The danger, however, is that regulating this threat can leave little room for the expression of authentic pride that is vital for group identification. But in contrast to the wealth of research in social psychology on group-based guilt and shame, expressing and suppressing group pride has not been investigated in much depth.

If people can feel ashamed at group pride, perhaps they might likewise be able to take paradoxical pride in shame, guilt, humiliation, and other self-lowering emotions. In a phenomenon that Nietzsche perhaps would have appreciated, the expression of remorseful feelings at one's personal or group-based shortcomings can be shown as proof that one is morally exalted. After all, abundant research on emotional dehumanization shows a similar phenomenon in the opposite direction. Members of outgroups are usually attributed less complex emotions than members of ingroups. They are seen as less able to experience typically human and self-conscious emotions such as shame and embarrassment (Leyens et al., 2000). One example comes from liberal blogger Brian Dockstader's outburst against US conservatives on the website OurFuture.org: "That is the problem with these people, they have no sense of shame. With them there is *zero* introspection . . . They don't feel embarrassed, they don't feel shame, they don't wonder how they could have been so gullible and ignorant as to be sucked into all of that" (Dockstader, 2009). If shame's absence can be condemned in enemies, it follows that its presence in friends can be seized upon as evidence of superior morality or humanity. But as with the self-control of group-based pride expressions, little research in psychology has tried to establish or explain this phenomenon.

Conclusion

In this section I have demonstrated, perhaps, my own personal bias toward negative emotions as a topic of psychological study by finding at every turn the worm within the apple of positive emotions. However, I don't consider my approach unrealistic. In fact, in the two previous chapters I have tried to shine a positive light on negative emotions that are often seen as bothersome or counterproductive. I have argued that negative emotions fail to work as we would like because they're overburdened with too many functions that individually are useful and necessary. Likewise, positive emotions serve many good functions, but we ignore at our peril the times when their functions collide and they don't work well.

Certainly pride is a very tricky emotion for the individual, with the potential to shut down as well as energize effort. Pride becomes even more tricky when the individual is living in society. In fact, there are many societies in the world where pride is seen as a problem to be controlled, not a thing to be encouraged. The caring emotions, like pride, also have the potential to send unwanted messages of superiority. While sympathy has been identified as a healthily other-focused emotion for perpetrator group members to feel in the wake of intergroup injustice, its downside has not been as closely examined. In particular, the factors that keep sympathy from turning into pity have not been given a thorough treatment in the psychological research literature yet. I do have to admit that the least problematic emotions are the other-praising ones of gratitude, admiration, and elevation. Certainly, they have the least to offer the ego compared with the downward glance of pity and the self-congratulation of pride. All the same, even the most saintly emotions also perform their function well when they flee the scene in the face of approaching threat or sudden disillusionment. Happiness all the time is not a realistic state for humans. Both positive and negative emotions play their part in our functioning, even if it's usually better to have more pleasant feelings than unpleasant. Certainly, we could all use more positive emotions in our lives. But without negative emotions, we would be defenceless against human predators, and incapable of taking action when something is really going wrong.

7   Applications and conclusion

Behind every application of psychological theory lies a value judgment. The usefulness of our studies depends on their transition from the question of how the mind works to the question of how the mind can be changed. In placing social value on this latter question, though, we assume that we have already settled the question of why the mind should be changed. Short-sighted and irrational behaviour is thought to be bad; the habits of mind that support it should be discouraged. Some applications of psychology take improvements in the effectiveness of a process as signs of success: work groups' output, dieters' weight loss. Others count it a success if goals are not just facilitated, but actually changed: deterring violence, reducing prejudice, fostering reconciliation after a conflict.

My functional conflict theory poses some challenges for this view—not insurmountable problems, but points that need to be recognized. If we see that an emotion is misplaced, we also have to recognize that it is misplaced because it is fulfilling some other function. Often, this function predominates because it is more useful to the individual than the function that we, the psychologists, are concerned about. So for instance, a prisoner may react angrily to provocations in ways that look irrational to us. Surely something is wrong with the appraisal function here? But when we look at the prisoner's environment in the penitentiary, the benefits of communicating anger and aggression outweigh the irrationality of attacking someone for bumping him in the hall. Removing anger will then appear to be a bad voluntary move for the inmate. If anger is somehow reduced involuntarily, as by the Ludovico Technique in Anthony Burgess' *A Clockwork Orange* (1962), this will just cause other functional problems for the inmate, much as when a cat's claws are removed to stop it scratching furniture, its defences and territorial marking glands are also removed, causing other problems for the cat.

Another usual goal of applied psychology is to get people to think at a higher level of organization; to give up the interests of the individual for those of the family, those of the family for those of the nation, those of the nation for those of the world. This purpose is on more solid ground, functionally speaking, and it is here that the moral emotions play a special part. Anger, shame, sympathy, and the other emotions we have surveyed, all work in one way or another to motivate the individual to put long-term, high-level social concerns above short-term, personal advantage. Emotions make these moral concerns compelling, and because they are so compelling, they are often treated as moral mandates in personal and policy decision-making (Mullen & Skitka, 2006), overriding the material concerns that classical economics place at people's hearts.

But here, too, the existence of a many-layered social structure means that moral emotions do not automatically fall on one side or the other of many social issues. The citizens of a country that emits greenhouses gases above the norm may be confronted with anger at the country's actions, urged to feel guilt about them, or cajoled with the possibility of pride and admiration if the country abandons its short-term interests for the long-term good of the planet. However, opposing these moral emotions will be equally strong moral emotions defending national prosperity, and chafing at unfair limitations on competition. Likewise, a war that is opposed morally in the name of peace and cooperation may be supported morally in the name of vengeance, punishment, and loyalty to the group for whose interests the war is fought.

With these conflicts and paradoxes in mind, the rest of this chapter will consider two social issues that benefit from the insights of functional conflict theory: people's judgments of sexual morality, and apologies between groups.

Applications to sexual morality

Worldwide, the moral judgment of sexual and reproductive behaviour is central to many hotly contested issues. Tolerance of same-sex relationships ranges from full recognition of marriage rights to the death penalty. Other boundaries of sexual expression are also regulated as both moral and legal issues. Certainly a sense of morality underlies laws that fix the age of sexual consent, define and enforce the crime of rape, and regulate or outlaw the various forms of sex work. Yet sexual issues often confuse people looking for the clear dichotomy of a left–right political divide. In sexual politics, a non-moral perspective often confronts two different forms of moral condemnation. These two moralities sometimes oppose and sometimes support each other, depending on which side of the issue they are on.

To simplify matters, I'll outline these three distinctive stances broadly, although many points of compromise and ambivalence can be found between them.

1   The sexual libertarian viewpoint seeks to minimize the moral concerns attaching to sex. For example, prostitution and pornography are seen as matters of the free market, so that exchanging some form of sexuality for pay is not inherently morally wrong.
2   In contrast, the social conservative viewpoint is moral. It sees sexuality as sacred, modesty and chastity as virtues, and acts that violate these virtues as intrinsically wrong.
3   The rights-based viewpoint sees sex as sometimes morally problematic, not because anything about it is intrinsically bad, but because it can foster a particularly vicious form of the unjust domination of the powerless by the powerful. This last moral stance is characteristic of, if not entirely limited to, feminist thought.

While all three points of view have access to the repertoire of moral anger and disgust, their sensitivities differ. The libertarian viewpoint has a high tolerance for outrage. Direct, forcible threats to person and property are worthy of serious moral concern, but very little else in the realm of sexuality is. Social conservatives, however, see violations of sexual norms and taboos principally in terms of disgust, following the logic that disgust responds to the mere fact of the violation of a norm that regulates the body (see chapter 4). Finally, people who subscribe to the rights-based viewpoint have a different range of problems with sexuality. Like social conservatives, they see prostitution, pornography, and underage sex as morally wrong; however, they have few or no problems with consensual same-sex relations between equals in status. Unlike social conservatives, they do see as a problem any kind of sexuality that involves the use of power, even when this is culturally normal. This can be especially unseemly when a man exercises sexual power over a woman, due to the overall position of advantage that men enjoy. In the rights-based view, sexual relations between bosses and subordinates in a company are wrong, a man can be guilty of rape against his wife, and the accuser in ambiguous cases of rape is more likely to be believed. Libertarians and conservatives, on the other hand, tend to see less of a problem in the context of sexual encounters that may involve inequality.

In the field of political psychology, the three-cornered conflict is rarely acknowledged, although sometimes writers will look at one side of the triangle. For example, Haidt and Hersh (2001) found that political conservatives were less tolerant of victimless sexual acts than liberals were. However, the "conservative–liberal" dichotomy in sexual politics glosses over what kind of "liberal" we are speaking about—is it a libertarian, espousing maximum freedom from external interference into sexual matters (cf. Flanagan & Lee, 2003, contrasting authoritarian and libertarian social values), or an egalitarian, who accepts some degree of interference in order to balance an unequal playing field between men and women? Duggan (2002) does identify all three tendencies in a review of the struggle for gay and lesbian rights, showing how a libertarian gay-rights movement seeking privacy and normality has coexisted and conflicted with more militant "queer" movements that actively promote difference. Moreover, in the wake of the 1960s sexual revolution, the debates within the feminist movement over the acceptability of sexual expressions such as pornography and sadomasochism led to a comparatively early and very clear distinction between what Cohen (1986) termed "libertarian" and "radical" feminists.

A rough parallel can be drawn between the two disapproving viewpoints (rights-based and conservative) and the moral emotions of anger and disgust (Giner-Sorolla & Russell, 2009). Recall that moral disgust is most characteristically evoked by violations of a bodily norm, while moral anger responds to concepts such as harm and rights. In the moral scheme I reviewed in chapters 1 and 4 (Graham et al., 2009; Rozin et al., 1999b), moral disgust responds to "divinity" (purity) concerns, while moral anger responds to "autonomy" (harm and fairness) concerns. In politics, conservatives endorse divinity concerns more than liberals do (Graham et al., 2009) and a link has been shown between the personality trait of disgust proneness and various manifestations of conservative ideology, especially as it relates to sexuality (e.g., Inbar, Pizarro, & Bloom, 2009; Olatunji, 2008). Legislation on such issues as outlawing extreme pornography, too, has been justified both in terms of preventing harm and in protecting the public morality from disgusting images (Johnson, 2010). With this background, we might speak of a sexual morality of disgust and a sexual morality of anger.

Disgust morality responds to the kind of sexual act that is done, rather than its context or circumstances. Be it incest, homosexual acts, or heterosexual "sodomy" as defined for many years in US state law, there is no mitigating circumstance that can make such an act morally acceptable. This is the logic of bodily-moral disgust, which as our studies have shown resists reconsideration and mitigating circumstances (Russell & Giner-Sorolla, 2011c). However, among conservatives another one of our findings may be open to qualification. The lack of elaborated reasons among our student participants' justifications for their moral disgust may not hold for social conservatives. In particular, conservatives often advance religious reasons for being against homosexuality, in the form of the word of living or scriptural authorities. Indeed, Olatunji (2008) found that moral and religious concerns, rather than biological concerns, largely accounted for conservative attitudes against homosexuality in a US population. Notably, however, these religious reasons are also phrased in terms of absolute pronouncements. While the rules maintaining sexual taboos can be explicitly stated, they are just as inflexible as the emotion of disgust that helps to maintain them.

Admittedly, there is another class of sexual activities that social conservatives oppose, one that is more defined by context than content. Prostitution, pornography, and displays of sexuality are not so much defined by what is being done as by the fact that money is changing hands for it, or that it is being done in public. Disgust attaches to these activities in part because of the view that what is sacred and private is being treated as something commercial and public. Prostitution and pornography are also opposed by rights-based groups for a different reason, in that they can involve exploitation. The concern is not that money is contaminating sex in and of itself, but that money enters into it unfairly.

While this view of emotional disapproval of sexual morality is complex, there is initial evidence that disgust in sexual attitudes responds to perceptions of abnormality, while anger responds to rights violation and injustice. As mentioned in chapter 4, two studies in our lab have looked at the contribution of anger and disgust to sexual attitudes (Giner-Sorolla et al., 2011a). The first study presented participants with a variety of sexual acts that might be seen as immoral from either standpoint (sexual coercion in the workplace, consensual relations between a man and a transsexual woman), and measured their anger, disgust, and various appraisals. We found that both anger and disgust made separate contributions to moral judgment; anger was related to perceptions of whether rights were violated, while disgust was related to perceptions of whether the act was unnatural and abnormal. In the second study we experimentally varied the sexual nature of a brief scenario (non-sexual business relationship, heterosexual relationship, homosexual relationship) along with whether or not betrayal occurred within the relationship. When controlling for the other emotion, anger was only increased by the betrayal element, while disgust was only increased by the sexual nature of the story, being moderate in the heterosexual story but highest in the homosexual one. Furthermore, we showed that the perceptions that mediated these effects were perceptions of rights violations for anger, and perceptions of abnormality—not bad character or contamination—for disgust.

Of course, people who aren't violating anyone's rights can also be the targets of angry and punitive acts. Anger, for example, is instrumental in the link between anti-gay attitudes and anti-gay aggression among heterosexual men (Parrott & Peterson, 2008). Zeichner and Reidy (2009) found that men with strong homophobic attitudes felt more anger, and actually felt less disgust, than other heterosexual men did when presented with male–male erotica. How can our view of emotions in sexual morality account for this anger, which prepares a person for verbal and physical aggression against gay and transgender people? It is here, beyond the limits of moral anger's injustice appraisal, that the other appraisals of anger we considered in chapter 4 can provide answers. As we have seen, anger can arise from personal threats and frustration as well as injustice. The common currency of angry emotions explains why these non-moral causes can end up promoting moralized hostility. Research has implicated the perception of threat from gay men as one instigator of heterosexual men's anti-gay aggression. This covers both the threat of unwanted sexual advances and a more general threat gay men pose to gender identity (for a review see Parrott, 2008).

Anger against people who break sexual norms can also serve a self-regulation function, increasing certainty and shoring up a shaky personal identity. This function is different from simply responding to threat. The aggression can be expressive or symbolic, more about proving something about the self than dealing with a threat from without. Recall from chapter 4 that evidence for scapegoating of racial minorities in response to economic uncertainty is limited; the area of anti-gay attitudes, however, shows more solid grounds for the role of defensive processes (e.g., Glick et al., 2007). Research and theory in this area has generally moved away from the literal assumption that gay-haters are dealing with their own repressed homosexual urges. Instead, a more well-supported idea is that anti-gay aggression is not just an appraisal response to a cultural or interpersonal threat, but also a self-regulatory response to a threatened personal gender identity (Parrott, 2008).

Because masculinity, at least in North American culture, constantly needs to be proven, it makes up a precarious but valued element of a man's identity (Vandello, Bosson, Cohen, Burnaford, & Weaver, 2008). Therefore, aggression against gay men can be intensified for personal self-regulatory reasons. Beating up a sexual nonconformist re-establishes masculinity both in general, because aggression is macho, and specifically, by enforcing the boundaries of gender and sexuality. These conjectures are supported by survey, interview, and experimental data in which measures or manipulations of threatened masculinity, together with pre-existing anti-gay attitudes, predict anti-gay aggression in interaction. For example, in one line of research (Parrott, 2009; Parrott & Zeichner, 2005), straight men were exposed to images of same-sex male affection or erotic activity. This threat increased aggression and anger against a gay man in a subsequent experimental setting, but this primarily happened among participants with strong anti-gay and anti-feminine attitudes.

It's possible, too, that the associative learning function helps to establish angry attitudes against sexual nonconformists. Most moral judgment against sexual practices that aren't culturally normal, as we have seen, rests on disgust rather than anger. This points to a possible division of labour in a homophobic society. Thus, most people who subscribe to anti-gay prejudice merely express disgust and the wish to avoid gays, but a smaller group of men with highly hostile attitudes express anger. But it's possible to learn anger associatively, at least in theory, and this might happen if people are exposed to peers or parents who express anger at sexual minorities. The association of anger with the breaking of a taboo could spread throughout a culture, in much the same way that Tapias et al. (2007) showed anger to be associated with Blacks in the US and disgust to be associated with gay men.

The associative process may explain why participants in Gutierrez and Giner-Sorolla (2007) reacted with higher levels of anger, along with much higher levels of disgust, when a scientist was described as eating cloned human meat from her own cells, versus a non-disgusting powder. The scenario, I have to admit, was probably a completely novel one for participants. Up until that point, every single instance of eating human meat that they had thought or heard of had been made possible by the taking of a human life, or at least by the violation of a corpse's rights. Such a monstrous injustice stirs up anger. Possibly, then, the thought of eating human meat, even if cruelty-free, was associated not just with disgust, but also anger. This can explain why judgments that the meat-eating violated other people's rights also increased in the human steak vs. control condition. These judgments were apparently an elaborated response to anger rather than a cause of it, because they disappeared when participants were cognitively distracted, while the anger remained.

Mere associations with anger can be "caught" socially from people who have a stronger, more appraisal-based anger, and this may explain some angry attitudes toward violators of sexual norms. For example, a group of boys may pick up anti-gay anger from a popular boy whose male sex role is threatened at home; or a woman might pick up anger at promiscuous men from her grandmother, who believes they harm women's reputations, even though times have changed. If enough people in the peer group feel that expressing anger at gays is appropriate, then the social communication function also can explain how the attitude might take on a life of its own as a mark of group membership, encouraging conformity through prejudiced expression. Likewise, disgust reactions can be learned and transmitted socially, as we have seen in chapter 4.

To sum up, attitudes toward sexual behaviour exist at the intersection of moral, group, and emotional demands. We have seen how attitudes respond to socially conservative moral concerns about the normal use of the body, which cultures and individuals can use as a large-scale solution to existential concerns. Sex also involves openness and vulnerability. Oxytocin, a hormone that we have seen to accompany increased trust and other pro-social moral emotions, is also intimately connected to sexual response and orgasm (Carter, 1992; Neumann, 2008). This connection between trust and sex raises special concerns about rights, consent, and exploitation in the rights-based approach to sexual morality. Although the overall trend of evidence from studies shows that disgust accompanies body-related bases of disapproval for sexual acts, and anger accompanies trust-related bases of disapproval, I have also pointed out some ways in which anger can arise from threats to bodily norms. Finally, some groups are constituted by their sexual preference or behaviour, making sexuality obviously relevant to group processes and intergroup prejudice. Even groups that are not sexually constituted still can be bound together through expressing common cultural attitudes about sexuality. Males, at least in patriarchal societies, seem to be one group that builds an identity by rejecting and attacking deviants, in an ideology that mingles gender and sexual norms indiscriminately.

As we have seen, all four functions of my theory help explain sexual attitudes. Appraisal deals directly with the source of perceived threats and injustices. Associative learning picks up socially transmitted information connecting an emotion with a group or act. Self-regulation responds to threatened identities by symbolically expressing feelings of hostility, bolstering the self rather than realistically meeting a threat. Social communication transmits attitudes to make an impression on others and to create group solidarity.

The complexity of sexual attitudes cannot be dealt with using a simplistic model of moral emotions. For example, reducing anti-gay feelings to any one element—realistic threat concerns, ideological cultural defence, motivated psychological self-defence, or socially learned norms—will leave unexplained the attitudes of people who are driven to condemn gays via one of the other functions of emotion. Some of the irrational aspects of moralized sexual attitudes can be explained by functional conflicts inherent to the moral emotions. For example, self-regulatory defences and cultural associations can hijack the anger system's appraisal of realistic threats. This anger, activating thoughts of injustice, can lead people to make a presumption of harm about acts that harm nobody except those who are offended by them. A satirical website, *The Onion*, recently lampooned the misplaced fear and anger that was seen to drive support for legislation outlawing same-sex marriage in this headline: "Marauding gay hordes drag thousands of helpless citizens from marriages after Obama drops Defense of Marriage Act" (*The Onion*, 2011). The vision of such a moral threat, though exaggerated, is a memorable summary of the kind of arguments that anger produces in its own defence. Although sexual tolerance has made great advances in the past 50 years, further progress will have to be content with opposition strongly rooted in the moral emotions.

Applications to intergroup apology

In chapter 5, I outlined how feelings of shame and guilt can drive people to offer apologies. Guilt takes on the goal of fixing a relationship. Defensive shame serves the related goal of getting back to the high moral standing a person or group deserves in a moral hierarchy. Unworthiness shame, however, is a more profound expression of appeasement to another group, and acts more as an admission than a correction of inferiority. I also noted that expressions of shame and guilt, if they are seen as spontaneous and sincere, can improve the acceptance of apologies and reparations, and may even be able to take the place of apologies and reparations. Guilt, shame, and related emotions are communications with the potential to convey two important messages: I am suffering internally as a result of my own bad behaviour; and I take responsibility for it. Research in my lab has looked in more detail at the effect of different kinds of wrongdoers' emotional expressions on satisfaction among people collectively wronged. Taking apologies to a group level, the number of questions already answered in psychology is far outnumbered by the number that remain (for a review see Blatz & Philpot, 2010). Here I will focus on the role of specific emotional expressions in apologies.

Official apologies for national and international issues have become a part of politics since the Second World War (Barkan, 2000), and increasingly in recent years: Brooks (2003) characterized the 1990s as an "age of apology." Just as I was writing this, I decided to search for stories about apologies on the British Broadcasting Corporation news website (http://news.bbc.co.uk) and found at least one apology a day for the past week. Most of these newsworthy apologies involved groups, either as the source of an official apology, or an offended group receiving an individual's apology. The daily apologies for 28 March 2011 included one from the UK Census for failing to count a mobile home park, and another from the British Government for the killing of a 12-year-old girl in Northern Ireland in 1976. A feature story about the US internment of Japanese-Americans during the Second World War also mentions the official apology for that injustice. Other issues sparking apologies in the news that week included disrespectful treatment of dead combatants by US and Australian troops in Afghanistan, the Tokyo Electric Power Company's mishandling of the Fukushima reactor crisis, and the lack of ethnic diversity in the television drama "Midsomer Murders."

Apologetic statements risk sounding hollow without an adequate expression of remorse. But moving from individual to group communication, it becomes difficult to meet the requirement of remorse emphasized in most apology theories (e.g., Lazare, 2005; Scher & Darley, 1997; Tavuchis, 1991). How can a whole group express an emotion? It usually falls to the leader of a nation or group to make the apology personally, but some groups have no leader (who leads the group of White Europeans, for example?). More generally, an official apology is difficult to communicate in a way that leads to reconciliation and forgiveness. One study of official intergroup apologies in a number of contexts found no effect of apology on forgiveness at all, only satisfaction; apologies from representative members of a group, however, did increase individual forgiveness (Philpot & Hornsey, 2008).

Nonetheless, our lab has found that different emotional expressions do make a difference to the acceptance of apologies in a group context, beginning with guilt and shame (Giner-Sorolla, Castano, Espinosa, & Brown, 2008). Even though shame is rarely expressed in official apologies, we found in two studies in the US and Spain in which an expression of unworthiness shame attributed to the CEO of a company responsible for an ecological disaster was overall more satisfactory than an expression of guilt focused merely on the event. Moreover, shame had a very specific effect in one experimental condition in which the CEO was from a different nation than the respondents and had offered reparations. A guilt expression in this context led to levels of insult among the participants that were as high as if no emotion had been expressed. However, a shame expression worked to reduce insult in this condition. These results were replicated in another study looking at the reaction of Black British people to hypothetical apology and reparation offers from the London police for racial discrimination (Giner-Sorolla, Kamau, & Castano, 2010). There, too, only when reparations were offered did shame reduce insult taken. However, these results were only found among Black people who attributed high levels of blame to the police for racial discrimination.

People take insult from reparation attempts when they perceive them as controlling or reassertions of an unfair, unchangeable, and unequal power dynamic (Nadler & Liviatan, 2006). Because unworthiness shame implies a reduction in social standing, it conveys self-abasement and appeasement. Guilt, as we manipulated it, focuses only on a single act, without larger implications for the standing of the person expressing it. So while it may be more functional in the short term for an individual to feel guilt rather than shame, the expression of shame is a stronger sign of appeasement, which can work to balance unequal social relations in the larger picture. Although the studies I've described were conducted before I'd developed the distinction between defensive and unworthiness shame, it would be interesting to present expressions of defensive shame to people who'd been collectively wronged (e.g., "I feel ashamed that we have let down this country's great ideals"). My suspicion is that defensive shame looks too self-aggrandizing, too focused on the ingroup, to satisfy outgroup victims. At the same time it may be more appealing to fellow ingroup members precisely for that reason.

Further evidence for the importance of emotional expressions in apology comes from a series of studies in which we varied only single emotion words in the statement of a typical, anonymous smoker when confronted with evidence of the health hazards of second-hand smoke to non-smokers (Giner-Sorolla, Zebel, Zaiser, Vasiljevic, & Yamamoto, 2011d). Non-smoking participants read the statement, and rated it on a number of criteria, including how much suffering it expressed, how much responsibility the smoker was taking for harm to non-smokers, and how satisfied they were, a measure that included forgiveness and expectations of reparative action from the smoker. In three countries—the United Kingdom, Netherlands, and Japan—satisfaction was independently predicted across the different conditions by inferences of suffering and responsibility-taking. These two factors also explained differences in satisfaction among different emotions, and between emotional and non-emotional expressions in general. For example, in the Netherlands, "shame" and "guilt" both led to greater satisfaction than "regret," because they created higher inferences of suffering and responsibility-taking; however, in the United Kingdom, "guilt" led to lower inferences of these two factors, and so to lower satisfaction. These results show that even a single emotion word in an apology can not only express remorse and suffering, but also imply the taking of responsibility, in a way that leads to greater satisfaction among those who receive it.

Despite these initial findings, there remains a great deal to be explored about the role of shame, guilt, and other emotional expressions in relations between groups. As we saw earlier in this chapter, much research has focused on what drives people to feel guilt and shame, but there is relatively little research into how these expressed feelings of guilt and shame are received. One important factor is likely to be the goal of the group member receiving the apology. Attitudes toward historical wrongs can vary between wronged groups and also within them. For example, in responding to the wrong of slavery, some African-American political figures such as W. E. B. DuBois argued for integration and reconciliation with White America, while others such as Marcus Garvey argued for separation and independence as the only way to counteract White supremacy.

In the analysis of political scientist Melissa Nobles (2008), an important consideration in offering apologies and reparation for historic wrongs is whether these moves are seen as "opening the door" to further equalization of status and integration of the two groups, or "closing the door" and drawing a line under history, leaving each group to go its own way. An expression of guilt, assuming it is seen as sincere, conveys the goal that a closer relationship is desired. An expression of shame, on the other hand, is inherently distancing, but favourable to its recipient the more appeasement is inferred from it. Offering guilt, an emotion characteristic of close reciprocal relationships, may come off as patronizing to people who want to keep their distance. This may especially be true when considering reparations, if these are seen as a further affirmation of status difference. On the other hand, shame may not be the most appropriate emotion to offer to people who want a closer relationship—what is the good of joining together with people who are expressing their unworthiness?

People can also misunderstand each other because they apply different standards for the adequacy of an emotional communication. As we have seen, people can see a tokenistic action as fulfilling their collective moral obligation. The same action may not, however, be enough to satisfy the demands of the wronged group. What they want may be unacceptable to the perpetrator group, leading to a permanent impasse. Add to this the difference in cultural and language approaches to the expression of self-conscious emotion that often exist in intergroup settings, and a truly vast gap of understanding looms. For example, the statement made in 1990 by Emperor Akihito in apology for Japan's treatment of Korea during its occupation contained the carefully considered phrase "tsuseki no nen" or "deepest regret." For the semi-divine, symbolic figure of an Emperor to express such feelings was considered a controversial move in Japan. But some Korean advisors balked at the statement, considering it "devised by bureaucrats" and unnatural-sounding when translated into Korean (Makino, 2010; Ruoff, 2003). To this day, 97% of Koreans (as opposed to 30% of Japanese) don't think Japan has apologized enough (Asahi Shimbun/Dong-A Ilbo Joint Public Opinion Poll,

June 2010), in spite of numerous statements from the Prime Minister and Emperor beginning in 1990. Indeed, in 2008 the Korean Prime Minister spoke approvingly of the idea of the Japanese Emperor coming to Korea and kneeling in atonement, explicitly mentioning Willy Brandt's famous kneeling gesture in Warsaw (Parry, 2008).

One problem with shame expressions of the kind offered by Brandt, though, is that they risk offending internal political sentiment. The dilemma of the apologizing leader is neatly summed up by the author of a rhetorical analysis of Japanese post-war apologies: "National apologies for past wrongdoing must gain acceptance from the domestic audience and with its demeaning dimensions, the threat to identity, pride and heroic historical myths that apology represents, this is not easy" (Yamazaki, 2006, p. 88). Yamazaki identifies two rhetorical devices that can justify apology internally. First, in the spirit of responsibility-based guilt, the shameful behaviour can be sealed off in the past, while the apology augurs a new future for the nation. Second, in the spirit of defensive rather than unworthiness shame, the past behaviour can be presented as a black mark against the nation's true greatness that must be expunged. However, both of these strategies risk diluting the strength of the apology to the wronged audience, who may wish a more complete abasement. The tension is inescapable. Gestures of shame work on a group level to smooth external relations, but just as expressions of shame threaten individuals' self-concept, so they may threaten the group self.

We have not yet tested the reactions of ingroup members to apologies containing guilt or other emotions from their leaders. However, a number of studies in our lab have shown that two separate concerns predict ingroup members' satisfaction with apologies and reparations to a wronged group: the perception that an apology improves the ingroup's image, and that it "puts the ball in the other court" by shifting the obligation of forgiveness to the other group (Zaiser & Giner-Sorolla, 2011). These concerns were found to be important among British nationals for a variety of topics in which hypothetical or real British apologies or reparations were presented, ranging from Second World War landmines left in North Africa to Prime Minister David Cameron's apology for the Bloody Sunday incident in Northern Ireland. Obligation shifting, but not image improvement, also predicted lower desire to help the wronged country in ways beyond the immediate apology or reparations. Also, how much the apology or reparations affected the power balance between these two countries did not seem to be a factor in preference. If we were to continue this research with studies that varied the emotional expressions of ingroup leaders, we might predict that expressions of unworthiness shame would lead to less satisfaction among the apologizing group. Because they involve admission of the group's immoral and incompetent status, they may be seen as downgrading the image of the group, which is important to the apologizing official's clientele, even at the same time that unworthiness shame might attract the most approval from the apology's recipients.

Although sympathy doesn't present the same defensive conflict that guilt and shame do, it can also be dangerous to express in a situation of reconciliation, as hinted at by some of the considerations from chapter 6. It conveys concern for another group, but also can send a message of unwanted closeness, familiarity, and even dominance, shading into contempt and pity. Because sympathy is other-focused, it can also fail to express responsibility-taking in the same way that guilt or shame do; imagine the message being sent by a Mafia assassin sending a condolence card to the family of one of his victims. Like the mixed messages sent by remorseful apologies, the message of a sympathetic expression has to be carefully calibrated.

Functional conflict theory, then, offers a structure for unpacking the "remorse" concept within apologies, understanding it in terms of the specific emotions involved and their multiple functions. As I explained in chapter 5, people's reluctance to feel remorse in general has its roots in defensive processes that patrol the boundary between the associative and self-regulation functions of guilt and shame. When it comes to valuable national identities, the emotional commitment to apology and reparation demanded by self-regulation comes into conflict with the desire to keep the national identity clean of unfavourable associations. Likewise, within the communication function, there is a tension between the demands of different audiences when a national or organizational leader makes an apologetic statement. While the outgroup audience demands a strong and self-blaming demonstration of appeasement, which may best be served by unworthiness shame, an ingroup audience wants to know that its valued national identity is being rescued from moral jeopardy. It may well be that more painful and more responsible expressions of emotion are needed to satisfy an outgroup versus an ingroup audience.

Conclusion: Matters of perspective

My first published paper in social psychology (Giner-Sorolla & Chaiken, 1994) tested and confirmed an insight I'd had about the nature of the hostile media phenomenon (Hastorf & Cantril, 1954; Vallone, Ross, & Lepper, 1985). Previous studies had found that partisans on opposing sides tended to see a neutral body in the middle as biased toward the other side—whether a football referee in the Hastorf and Cantril study, or US network news coverage of the Israeli invasion of Lebanon in the study by Vallone and colleagues. These authors concluded that partisans selectively perceived events—that they literally saw and remembered different things about the film of the game, or the videotape of the news coverage. I wasn't so sure. With the help of my doctoral advisor, Shelly Chaiken, we devised a study to test directly what people on two sides of an issue were seeing and remembering about non-partisan news coverage of the Israeli response to the killing of a Jewish settler in the Palestinian Occupied Territories.

The results of our study were not auspicious for reconciliation in poisonous political conflicts. Pro-Israelis and pro-Palestinians, recruited from the student population at New York University, showed the same amount of memory for the news coverage in a test afterward, and no memory bias either for events that favoured Israel or the Palestinians. However, we found the hostile media effect among them; pro-Israelis saw the media report as pro-Palestinian, and pro-Palestinians saw it as pro-Israeli. Part of this biased judgment of bias could be explained by preconceived notions about the mainstream media that participants had picked up from their own partisan sources, which we measured beforehand. But it seemed that the rest of the hostile media perceptions could only be explained by a more fundamental difference in perspective. The partisans disapproved of even-handed coverage because it was even-handed. They believed the truth was all on the side of the Israelis, or of the Palestinians. Any departure from that would be doing a disservice to the truth and helping the other side. This chasm in perspective could not be bridged just by making sure that people paid attention to the right set of facts.

The Nazi moralization of the invasion of Poland, with which I opened this book, presents a similar challenge of perspective. Far from being unfeeling and amoral, the propaganda presented to the German people and foreign powers at the start of September 1939 sought to engage their moral sense. On the previous day, Germans were told that the Poles had attacked them; in the previous years, they were told that ethnic Germans in Poland had been oppressed; and on the historical scale of decades, Germany was shown to be the victim of betrayal and injustice after the First World War. The same emotions and concerns that mobilized the world against the Axis also mobilized the Axis against the world. If the Germans used disgust and contempt against their racial enemies, these sentiments were returned in Allied propaganda; US cartoons portrayed the Japanese as buck-toothed sub-humans, flying monkeys and octopi. Does our current designation of Hitler as the epitome of evil really only depend on our particular perspective? Would there be a very different moral understanding in the world if the wrong side had won the war?

The way out of this hall of mirrors, with its moral equivalencies and reflective perspectives, is to look up. The definition of morality that we have arrived at in chapter 1 involves the imposition of concerns from a wider scope of social and personal organization to a narrower one. Thus, self-control is moral in nature, because it values the concerns of an entire lifetime over those of a single moment. Morality can also be attached to the demands of the group on the individual, because this privileges the concerns of the many over the few. However, the highest and most universal morality pre-empts even the demands of the group in favour of the concerns of all humanity. It is this test of universalism over parochialism that the Nazis could not pass, but that the United Nations during and after the war did, by adopting principles of rights and sovereignty for all nations, and giving aid and reconstruction to the conquered nations. If Stalin doesn't stand today as such an epitome of evil as Hitler was, it is not necessarily because the victors write history; after all, his system of Soviet Communism also now lies in ruins. Rather, Stalin's millions of murders were committed in the name of the universalistic ideology of international Communism, although one that was ruthlessly parochial in practice. The Party, in the name of the proletariat, was privileged to deprive everyone else of life and freedom. Everyone in theory could be a Communist, but not everyone could join the German *Volk*. This, I think, is why the conventional wisdom is kinder to Stalin than to Hitler, even though there's also a case to be made that Stalin's crimes were more monstrous because he violated a more universalistic ideal. Probably the best we can ask of future Stalins and Hitlers is to stop abusing morality and moralization, and present themselves honestly as being driven by the parochial interest of a nation or a clique, in the style of a Genghis Khan. Of course, they're not likely to comply; it's too easy and profitable to hide behind a screen of halfway-adopted morality.

Like morality, emotion works to bridge perspectives. Scherer (1994) points out that emotion, unlike reflex, can "decouple stimulus and response"—that is, it prepares a quick action while allowing time to intervene for processing and modification of the stimulus. The moral emotions work in a similar but more specific way. Each of the functions in my model of emotions allows perspectives from different times and scales to intersect. Appraisal weighs and considers the goals of the present. Associative learning efficiently brings up emotional knowledge from the past, and gives the self a stable anchor of certainty. Self-regulation allows the concerns of the future self and of the social sphere to weigh in upon the individual's actions. And social communication allows the self to reply to others in an outward direction, giving off signals of good faith that allow social interaction to proceed beyond a constant struggle of testing and doubt. Of course these functions conflict; but each of them is there for a reason.

To summarize the functional conflicts that I have sketched out in my treatment of each of the individual emotions, I've put together Table 7.1. None of these conflicts is easy to resolve. Let's consider them row by row.

1   When appraisal clashes with the learned associations of experience, the present fights the past. Sometimes things have actually changed, sometimes they stay the same; the radical and the conservative view are both important in any individual or society.

2   and (3) The way in which self-regulatory feelings conflict with associations and appraisals is another struggle where neither perspective is always right. A person who is constantly controlled by concerns about other people and the future lacks the basis to assert a stable and active self-image. Sometimes defences against self-regulation are desirable.

4   The assertion of self against others, and others against self, is also present when social communication subverts realistic appraisal. An audience can bring out a person's anger over a tempest in a teapot, just to attract sympathy and social capital.

5   and (6) By the same token, an audience's communication of disapproval can create social reality, causing feelings of shame or guilt in a person who admits no actual wrong.

7   Finally, a person's need to associate good things with the self and keep bad things away can conflict with the needs of communication where apology is required. This can lead them to embrace a more self-serving emotion than the audience requires. The self-abasement that the audience really wants would be rejected as too threatening to self-esteem.

Table 7.1 Summary of seven functional conflicts that are manifested in different emotions

	Function 1	Function 2	Manifestation	Relevant emotions
1	Appraisal	Associative	Inflexible learned emotional reactions are independent of, and even bias, more flexible appraisals	Disgust, anger, pride
2	Appraisal	Self-regulation	Appraisal of self motivates behaviour consistent with self-image; this conflicts with self-regulation, which motivates behaviour to change self-image	Guilt, shame, pride
3	Associative	Self-regulation	Motivated manipulation of self-regulatory feelings: defence against negative associations with self and ingroup, and promotion of positive associations	Guilt, shame, pride
4	Appraisal	Communication	Communicative uses of emotion to get social benefits conflicts with appraised situation	Anger, guilt, shame, admiration
5	Associative	Communication	Moral rightness for self looks self-serving to others	Sympathy, guilt, defensive shame
6	Associative	Communication	Loss of image for self is moral rightness to others	Unworthiness, shame
7	Self-regulation	Communication	Approval of own action sends unwanted dominance signals to others	Pride

The engraving of a crowned conglomerate giant that prefaced the original edition of Thomas Hobbes' treatise on the state, *Leviathan* (1651), illustrates literally the metaphorical truth that a group is built from a myriad of individual bodies. All these functional conflicts thus can be copied on the mass level among thousands or millions of people who hold a particular group identification. Like individual persons, persons who think of themselves as group members are likely to see the appraisal of the group's world as their world. They are likely to have learned positive associations to group-favouring concepts, and negative associations to enemies or underlings of the group. They may come to see self-regulating feedback about the competence and morality of the group as relevant, and act to restore a desired balance point for the group. And ultimately, they may endorse or reject emotion-laden communications from the group to others, made by official representatives as well as average members. Although it is individuals who feel each of these conflicts, the phenomena they create are extended to the group level. The main difference is that when unpleasant group-level feelings become hard to bear, the nature of identification with the group can change, in addition to the large array of psychological defences otherwise available to the person.

I've always believed that conflict is built into human nature. In fact, back in high school I entered a local synagogue's essay contest; the topic was "My Vision of Peace," but I submitted an essay titled "A Dark Vision of Peace," which made the point that to achieve complete peace in the world, we would have to give up other aspects of our self-expression and freedom that make us human. The essay took second place, despite being somewhat off-mission for the point that Temple Sholom might have wanted to make. Some 30 years later, this is a point I still want to make.

To the extent that our behaviour exists to transmit our genes, there is conflict between the genes of our own organism and the larger genetic good of the family or species (Slavin & Kriegman, 1992). Individual interests also conflict with collective interests in dilemmas of material resource distribution, and when cultural freedom fights against cultural stability and conformity. The intelligence that allows us self-awareness adds another layer of conflict to our existence. Our awareness of our actual self—frail, fallible, mortal—conflicts with the fantasies and ideals our imagination constructs, and with the demands placed upon us by society. Although it may be tempting to escape subjectively from all these conflicts of the self by identifying utterly with a nation, religion, or ideology, we find that the group level merely magnifies these conflicts, rather than resolving them. At first glance, the moral emotions of admiration for others, elevation, and gratitude may seem free of conflict. But to feel nothing but those emotions would be just as detrimental as to feel nothing but anger. The first scoundrel to happen upon such a society would find it ripe for exploitation. If tranquillity can only be achieved by giving up our essential humanity, then I opt for conflict—but a conflict that we understand, so that we can make informed and rational choices within it. I hope this book has led you some small way toward such an understanding.

References

Aaker, J. L., & Williams, P. (1998). Empathy versus pride: The influence of emotional appeals across cultures. *Journal of Consumer Research*, *25*, 241–261.

Abrahms, M. (2006). Why terrorism does not work. *International Security*, *31*, 42–76.

Ackerman, J. M., & Kenrick, D. T. (2008). The costs of benefits: Help-refusals highlight key trade-offs of social life. *Personality and Social Psychology Review*, *12*, 118–140.

Adams, E. S. (2001). Threat displays in animal communication: Handicaps, reputations, and commitments. In R. M. Nesse (Ed.), *Evolution and the capacity for commitment* (pp. 99–119). New York: Russell Sage Foundation.

Adorno, T., Frenkel-Brunswik, E., Levinson, D., & Sanford, R. (1950). *The authoritarian personality*. New York: Harper & Row.

Algoe, S. B., & Haidt, J. (2009). Witnessing excellence in action: The other-praising emotions of elevation, admiration, and gratitude. *Journal of Positive Psychology*, *4*, 105–127.

Algoe, S. B., Haidt, J., & Gable, S. L. (2008). Beyond reciprocity: Gratitude and relationships in everyday life. *Emotion*, *8*, 425–429.

Alicke, M. D. (2000). Culpable control and the psychology of blame. *Psychological Bulletin*, *126*, 556–574.

Allport, G. (1954). *The nature of prejudice*. Reading, MA: Addison-Wesley.

Allpress, J. A., Barlow, F. K., Brown, R., & Louis, W. R. (2010). Atoning for colonial injustices: Group-based shame and guilt motivate support for reparation. *International Journal of Conflict and Violence*, *4*, 75–88.

Alonso-Arbiol, I., Shaver, P. R., Fraley, R. C., Oronoz, B., Unzurrunzaga, E., & Urizar, R. (2006). Structure of the Basque emotion lexicon. *Cognition and Emotion*, *20*, 836–865.

Amodio, D. M., Devine, P. G., & Harmon-Jones, E. (2007). A dynamic model of guilt: Implications for motivation and self-regulation in the context of prejudice. *Psychological Science*, *18*, 524–530.

Andersen, S. M., & Glassman, N. S. (1996). Responding to significant others when they are not there: Effects on interpersonal inference, motivation, and affect. In R. M. Sorrentino & E. T. Higgins (Eds.), *Handbook of motivation and cognition*, Vol. 3: *The interpersonal context* (pp. 262–321). New York: Guilford Press.

Anderson, C., Keltner, D., & John, O. P. (2003). Emotional convergence between people over time. *Journal of Personality and Social Psychology*, *84*, 1054–1068.

Anderson, C. A., Anderson, K. B., & Deuser, W. E. (1996). Examining an affective aggression framework: Weapon and temperature effects on aggressive thoughts, affect, and attitudes. *Personality and Social Psychology Bulletin*, *22*, 366–376.

Anderson, S. A. (2009). Rationalizing indirect guilt. *Vermont Law Review*, *33*, 519–783.

Antonaccio, O., & Tittle, C. R. (2008). Morality, self-control and crime. *Criminology*, *46*(2), 479–510.

Appleton, K. M., & McGowan, L. (2006). The relationship between restrained eating and poor psychological health is moderated by pleasure normally associated with eating. *Eating Behaviors*, *7*, 342–347.

Aquino, A., & Reed, K. F. (2003). Moral identity and the expanding circle of moral regard toward out-groups. *Journal of Personality and Social Psychology*, *84*, 1270–1286.

Arendt, H. (1963). Eichmann in Jerusalem. *The New Yorker*, March 16, p. 58.

Arnold, M. B. (1960). *Emotion and personality*. New York: Columbia University Press.

Asahi Shimbun/Dong-A Ilbo Joint Public Opinion Poll (June 2010). Retrieved from http://www.mansfieldfdn.org/polls/2010/poll-10-21.htm

Asch, S. E. (1951). Effects of group pressure upon the modification and distortion of judgment. In H. Guetzkow (Ed.), *Groups, leadership and men* (pp. 177–190). Pittsburgh, PA: Carnegie Press.

Ashburn-Nardo, L., Voils, C. I., & Monteith, M. J. (2001). Implicit associations as the seeds of intergroup bias: How easily do they take root? *Journal of Personality and Social Psychology*, *81*, 789–799.

Ask, K., & Granhag, P. A. (2007). Hot cognition in investigative judgments: The differential influence of anger and sadness. *Law and Human Behavior*, *31*, 537–551.

Ask, K., & Pina, A. (2011). On being angry and punitive. *Social Psychological and Personality Science, 2*(5), 494–499.

Ausubel, D. P. (1955). Relationships between shame and guilt in the socializing process. *Psychological Review*, *62*, 378–390.

Baeyens, F., Vansteenwegen, D., De Houwer, J., & Crombez, G. (1996). Observational conditioning of food valence in humans. *Appetite*, *27*, 235–250.

Bandura, A. (1999). Moral disengagement in the perpetration of inhumanities. *Personality and Social Psychology Review*, *3*, 193–209.

Barkan, E. (2000). *The guilt of nations: Restitution and negotiating historical injustices*. Baltimore, MD: Johns Hopkins University Press.

Baron, J. (2003). Value analysis of political behavior. Self-interested: moralistic: altruistic: moral. *University of Pennsylvania Law Review*, *151*, 1135–1167.

Barraza, J. A., & Zak, P. J. (2009). Empathy toward strangers triggers oxytocin release and subsequent generosity. *Annals of the New York Academy of Sciences*, *1167*, 182–189.

Barrett, L. F. (2006). Solving the emotion paradox: Categorization and the experience of emotion. *Personality and Social Psychology Review*, *10*, 20–46.

Barsade, S. G. (2002). The ripple effect: Emotional contagion and its influence on group behavior. *Administrative Science Quarterly, 47*(4), 644–677.

Bar-Tal, D. (1989). Delegitimization: The extreme case of stereotyping and prejudice. In D. Bar-Tal, C. Graumann, A. W. Kruglanski, & W. Stroebe (Eds.), *Stereotyping and prejudice: Changing conceptions* (pp. 169–188). Bristol, IN: Wyndham Hall Press.

Bartlett, M. Y., & DeSteno, D. (2006). Gratitude and prosocial behavior: Helping when it costs you. *Psychological Science*, *17*, 319–325.

Basil, D., Ridgway, N., & Basil, M. (2008). Guilt and giving: A process model of empathy and efficacy. *Psychology & Marketing*, *25*, 1–23.

Batson, C., Kennedy, C., Nord, L., Stocks, E., Fleming, D., Marzette, C., Lishner, D., Hayes, R., Kolchinsky, L., & Zerger, T. (2007). Anger at unfairness: Is it moral outrage? *European Journal of Social Psychology*, *37*, 1272–1285.

Batson, C. D., Lishner, D. A., Cook, J., & Sawyer, S. (2005). Similarity and nurturance: Two possible sources of empathy for strangers. *Basic and Applied Social Psychology, 27,* 15–25.

Batson, C. D., Turk, C. L., Shaw, L. L., & Klein, T. R. (1995). Information function of empathic emotion: Learning that we value the other's welfare. *Journal of Personality and Social Psychology, 68,* 300–313.

Baumeister, R. F., & Exline, J. J. (1999). Virtue, personality, and social relations: Self-control as the moral muscle. *Journal of Personality, 67,* 1165–1194.

Baumeister, R. F., & Heatherton, T. F. (1996). Self-regulation failure: An overview. *Psychological Inquiry, 7,* 1–15.

Baumeister, R. F., Bratslavsky, E., Finkenauer, C., & Vohs, K. D. (2001). Bad is stronger than good. *Review of General Psychology, 5,* 323–370.

Baumeister, R. F., Campbell, J. D., Krueger, J. I., & Vohs, K. D. (2003). Does high self-esteem cause better performance, interpersonal success, happiness, or healthier lifestyles? *Psychological Science in the Public Interest, 4,* 1–44.

Baumeister, R. F., Reis, H. T., & Delespaul, P. A. E. G. (1995). Subjective and experiential correlates of guilt in daily life. *Personal and Social Psychology Bulletin, 21,* 1256–1268.

Baumeister, R. F., Stillwell, A. M., & Heatherton, T. F. (1994). Guilt: An interpersonal approach. *Psychological Bulletin, 115,* 243–267.

Baumeister, R. F., Stillwell, A., & Wotman, S. R. (1990). Victim and perpetrator accounts of interpersonal conflict: Autobiographical narratives about anger. *Journal of Personality and Social Psychology, 59,* 994–1005.

Baumeister, R. F., Vohs, K. D., DeWall, C. N., & Zhang, L. (2007). How emotion shapes behavior: Feedback, anticipation, and reflection, rather than direct causation. *Personality and Social Psychology Review, 11,* 167–203.

Beck, A. T. (1967). *Depression: Clinical, experimental, and theoretical aspects.* New York: Hoeber.

Becker, E. (1973). *The denial of death.* New York: Simon & Schuster.

Becker, J. C., Tausch, N., & Wagner, U. (2011). Emotional consequences of collective action participation: Differentiating self-directed and outgroup-directed emotions. *Personality and Social Psychology Bulletin.* E-publication ahead of print, 7 July 2011.

Benedict, R. (1946). *The chrysanthemum and the sword.* Boston: Houghton Mifflin.

Bergsieker, H. B., Shelton, J. N., & Richeson, J. A. (2010). To be liked versus respected: Divergent goals in interracial interactions. *Journal of Personality and Social Psychology, 99,* 248–264.

Berkowitz, L. (1990). On the formation and regulation of anger and aggression: A cognitive-neoassociationistic analysis. *American Psychologist, 45,* 494–503.

Berkowitz, L., & Harmon-Jones, E. (2004). Toward an understanding of the determinants of anger. *Emotion, 4,* 107–130.

Berkowitz, L., & Heimer, K. (1989). On the construction of the anger experience: Aversive events and negative priming in the formation of feelings. In L. Berkowitz (Ed.), *Advances in experimental social psychology* (pp. 1–37). New York: Academic Press.

Berkowitz, L., & Levy, B. I. (1956). Pride in group performance and group-task motivation. *Journal of Abnormal and Social Psychology, 53,* 300–306.

Berndsen, M., & McGarty, C. (2010). The impact of magnitude of harm and perceived difficulty of making reparations on group based guilt and reparation towards victims of historical harm. *European Journal of Social Psychology, 40,* 500–513.

Berndsen, M., van der Pligt, J., Doosje, B., & Manstead, A. (2004). Guilt and regret: The determining role of interpersonal and intrapersonal harm. *Cognition & Emotion, 18,* 55–70.

Bernhard, H., Fehr, E., & Fischbacher, U. (2006). Third-party punishment within and across groups: An experimental study in Papua New Guinea. *American Economic Review, Papers and Proceedings, 92*, 217–221.

Berry, D. S. (1991). Accuracy in social perception: Contributions of facial and vocal information. *Journal of Personality and Social Psychology, 61*, 298–307.

Berthoz, S., Armony, J. L., Blair, R. J. R., & Dolan, R. J. (2002). An fMRI study of intentional and unintentional (embarrassing) violations of social norms. *Brain, 125*, 1696–1708.

Berthoz, S., Grezes, J., Armony, J. L., Passingham, R. E., & Dolan, R. J. (2006). Affective response to one's own moral violations. *Neuroimage, 31*, 941–950.

Björklund, F., Haidt, J., & Murphy, S. (2000). Moral dumbfounding: When intuition finds no reason. *Lund Psychological Reports, 1*, 1–15.

Blair, R. J. R. (1999). Psychophysiological responsiveness to the distress of others in children with autism. *Personality and Individual Differences, 26*, 477–485.

Blanchard, D. C., & Blanchard, R. J. (2003). What can animal aggression research tell us about human aggression? *Hormones and Behavior, 44*, 171–177.

Blanton, H., & Stapel, D. A. (2008). Unconscious and spontaneous and complex: The three selves model of social comparison assimilation and contrast. *Journal of Personality and Social Psychology, 94*, 1018–1032.

Blatz, C. W., & Philpot, C. (2010). On the outcomes of intergroup apologies: A review. *Social and Personality Psychology Compass, 4*(11), 995–1007.

Blechner, M. (2005). Disgust, desire, and fascination: Psychoanalytic, cultural, historical, and neuroscientific perspectives. *Studies in Gender and Sexuality, 6*, 33–45.

Bloom, A. H. (1986). Psychological ingredients of high-level moral thinking: A critique of the Kohlberg-Gilligan paradigm. *Journal for the Theory of Social Behavior, 16*, 89–103.

Boardley, I., & Kavusannu, M. (2007). Development and validation of the Moral Disengagement in Sport Scale. *Journal of Sport and Exercise Psychology, 29*, 608.

Bodenhausen, G. V., Sheppard, L. A., & Kramer, G. P. (1994). Negative affect and social judgment: The differential impact of anger and sadness. *European Journal of Social Psychology, 24*, 45–62.

Bond, R., & Smith, P. B. (1996). Culture and conformity: A meta-analysis of studies using Asch's (1952b, 1956) line judgment task. *Psychological Bulletin, 119*, 111–137.

Bourgeois, P., & Hess, U. (2008). The impact of social context on mimicry. *Biological Psychology, 77*, 343–352.

Braithwaite, J. (2000). Shame and criminal justice. *Canadian Journal of Criminology – Review of Canadian Criminology, 42*, 281–298.

Brandt, A. M., & Rozin, P. (Eds.). (1997). *Morality and health.* New York: Routledge.

Branscombe, N. R., Schmitt, M. T., & Schiffhauer, K. (2007). Racial attitudes in response to thoughts of White privilege. *European Journal of Social Psychology, 37*, 203–215.

Brewer, M. B. (1999). The psychology of prejudice: Ingroup love or outgroup hate? *Journal of Social Issues, 55*(3), 429–444.

Brooks, R. L. (2003). The age of apology. In R. L. Brooks (Ed.), *When sorry isn't enough: The controversy over apologies and reparations for human injustice* (pp. 3–12). New York: New York University Press.

Brown, L. M., Bradley, M. M., & Lang, P. J. (2006). Affective reactions to pictures of ingroup and outgroup members. *Biological Psychology, 71*, 303–311.

Brown, R. J. (2000). Social identity theory: Past achievements, current problems and future challenges. *European Journal of Social Psychology, 30*(6), 745–778.

Brown, R., González, R., Zagefka, H., Manzi, J., & Ćehajić, S. (2008). Nuestra culpa: Collective guilt and shame as predictors of reparation for historical wrongdoing. *Journal of Personality and Social Psychology, 94*, 75–90.

Burgess, A. (1962). *A clockwork orange*. London: Heinemann.

Burris, C. T., & Rempel, J. K. (2004). 'It's the end of the world as we know it': Threat and the spatial-symbolic self. *Journal of Personality and Social Psychology, 86*, 19–42.

Bushman, B. J., Bonacci, A. M., Pedersen, W. C., Vasquez, E. A., & Miller, N. (2005). Chewing on it can chew you up: Effects of rumination on triggered displaced aggression. *Journal of Personality and Social Psychology, 88*, 969–983.

Cacioppo, J. T., & Berntson, G. (2001). The affect system and racial prejudice. In *Unraveling the complexities of social life: A festschrift in honor of Robert B. Zajonc* (pp. 95–110). Washington, DC: American Psychological Association.

Cain, D. M., Loewenstein, G., & Moore, D. A. (2005). The dirt on coming clean: Perverse effects of disclosing conflicts of interest. *The Journal of Legal Studies, 34*, 1–25.

Campbell, D. T. (1958). Common fate, similarity, and other indices of the status of aggregates of person as social entities. *Behavioural Science, 14*–25.

Cappella, J. N. (1997). Behavioral and judged coordination in adult informal social interactions: Vocal and kinesic indicators. *Journal of Personality and Social Psychology, 72*, 119–131.

Carter, C. S. (1992). Oxytocin and sexual behavior. *Neuroscience & Biobehavioral Reviews, 16*, 131–144.

Carver, C. S., & Harmon-Jones, E. (2009). Anger is an approach-related affect: Evidence and implications. *Psychological Bulletin, 135*, 183–204.

Carver, C. S., & Scheier, M. F. (1990). Origins and functions of positive and negative affect: A control-process view. *Psychological Review, 97*, 19–35.

Carver, C. S., & Scheier, M. F. (1998). *On the self-regulation of behavior*. New York: Cambridge University Press.

Carver, C. S., Lawrence, J. W., & Scheier, M. F. (1996). A control-process perspective on the origins of affect. In L. L. Martin & A. Tesser (Eds.), *Striving and feeling: Interactions among goals, affect, and self-regulation* (pp. 11–52). Mahwah, NJ: Lawrence Erlbaum Associates.

Carver, C. S., Sutton, S. K., & Scheier, M. F. (2000). Action, emotion, and personality: Emerging conceptual integration. *Personality and Social Psychology Bulletin, 26*, 741–751.

Castano, E., & Giner-Sorolla, R. (2006). Not quite human: Infra-humanization as a response to collective responsibility for intergroup killing. *Journal of Personality and Social Psychology, 90*, 804–818.

Castelfranchi, C., & Poggi, I. (1990). Blushing as a discourse: Was Darwin wrong? In R. Crozier (Ed.), *Shyness and embarrassment: Perspectives from social psychology* (pp. 230–252). New York: Cambridge University Press.

Chamove, A. S., Graham, P. A. M., & Wallis, C. M. (1991). Guilt and obsessive compulsive traits in female dieters. *Journal of Human Nutrition and Dietetics, 4*, 113–119.

Chekroun, P. (2008). Social control behavior: The effects of social situations and personal implication on informal social sanctions. *Social and Personality Psychology Compass, 2*, 2141–2158.

Cheung, A. S. Y. (2009). China Internet going wild: Cyber-hunting versus privacy protection. *Computer Law & Security Review, 25*, 275–279.

Church, A. T., Katigbak, M. S., Reyes, J. A. S., & Jensen, S. M. (1998). Language and organisation of Filipino emotion concepts: Comparing emotion concepts and dimensions across cultures. *Cognition and Emotion, 12*, 63–92.

Cialdini, R. B., & Kenrick, D. T. (1976). Altruism as hedonism: A social development perspective on the relationship of negative mood state and helping. *Journal of Personality and Social Psychology, 34*, 907–914.

Cisler, J. M., Olatunji, B. O., & Lohr, J. M. (2009). Disgust, fear, and the anxiety disorders: A critical review. *Clinical Psychology Review, 29*, 34–46.

Cohen, C. H. (1986). The feminist sexuality debate: Ethics and politics. *Hypatia, 1*, 71–86.

Cohen, T. R., Montoya, R. M., & Insko, C. A. (2006). Group morality and intergroup relations: Cross-cultural and experimental evidence. *Personality and Social Psychology Bulletin, 32*, 1559–1572.

Cook, K. S., & Hegtvedt, K. (1983). Distributive justice, equity, and equality. *Annual Review of Sociology, 9*, 217–241.

Cooley, C. H. (1964/1902). *Human nature and the social order*. New York: Schocken Books.

Cosmides, L., & Tooby, J. (1990). The past explains the present: Emotional adaptations and the structure of ancestral environments. *Ethology and Sociobiology, 11*, 375–424.

Costafreda, S. G., Brammer, M. J., David, A. S., & Fu, C. H. (2008). Predictors of amygdala activation during the processing of emotional stimuli: A meta-analysis of 385 PET and fMRI studies. *Brain Research Reviews, 58*, 57–70.

Costello, K., & Hodson, G. (2010). Exploring the roots of dehumanization: The role of animal–human similarity in promoting immigrant humanization. *Group Processes and Intergroup Relations, 13*, 3–22.

Cottrell, C. A., & Neuberg, S. L. (2005). Different emotional reactions to different groups: A sociofunctional threat-based approach to 'prejudice'. *Journal of Personality and Social Psychology, 88*, 770–789.

Cox, C. R., Goldenberg, J. L., Arndt, J., & Pyszczynski, T. (2007). Mother's milk: An existential perspective on negative reactions to breast-feeding. *Personality and Social Psychology Bulletin, 33*, 110–122.

Craigie, J. (2011). Thinking and feeling: Moral deliberation in a dual-process framework. *Philosophical Psychology, 24*, 52–71.

Cramer, D., & Jowett, S. (2010). Perceived empathy, accurate empathy and relationship satisfaction in heterosexual couples, *Journal of Social and Personal Relationships, 27*, 327–349.

Crandall, C. S. (2000). Ideology and lay theories of stigma: The justification of stigmatization. In C. S. Crandall, T. F. Heatherton, & R. E. Kleck (Eds.), *The social psychology of stigma* (pp. 126–150). New York: Guilford Press.

Crandall, C. S., & Martinez, R. (1996). Culture, ideology, and antifat attitudes. *Personality and Social Psychology Bulletin, 22*, 1165–1176.

Crano, W. D., & Prislin, R. (2005). Attitudes and persuasion. *Annual Review of Psychology, 57*, 345–374.

Creighton, M. R. (1990). Revisiting shame and guilt cultures: A forty year pilgrimage. *Ethos, 18*, 279–307.

Crites, S., Fabrigar, L., & Petty, R. (1994). Measuring the affective and cognitive properties of attitudes: Conceptual and methodological issues. *Personality and Social Psychology Bulletin, 20*, 619–634.

Crocker, J., & Luhtanen, R. (1990). Collective self-esteem and ingroup bias. *Journal of Personality and Social Psychology, 58*, 60–67.

Crocker, J., Thompson, L. L., McGraw, K. M., & Ingerman, C. (1987). Downward comparison, prejudice, and evaluations of others: Effects of self-esteem and threat. *Journal of Personality and Social Psychology, 52*, 907–916.

Cross, J., & Guyer, M. (1980). *Social traps*. Ann Arbor, MI: University of Michigan Press.

Crozier, W. R. (1998). Self-consciousness in shame: The role of the 'other'. *Journal for the Theory of Social Behaviour, 28,* 273–286.

Cuddy, A. J. C., Fiske, S. T., & Glick, P. (2008). Warmth and competence as universal dimensions of social perception: The stereotype content model and the BIAS map. *Advances in Experimental Social Psychology, 40,* 61–149.

Cumberbatch, A. (2010). The inside perspective: Empathy, not sympathy. Fortune Society Blog. Retrieved from http://fortunesociety.org/fortune-clients/the-inside-perspective-empathy-not-sympathy/

Curtis, V., & Biran, A. (2001). Dirt, disgust, and disease. Is hygiene in our genes? *Perspectives in Biology and Medicine, 44,* 17–31.

Dalal, F. (2001). Insides and outsides: A review of psychoanalytic renderings of difference, racism and prejudice. *Psychoanalytic Studies, 3,* 43–66.

Damasio, A. (1999). *The feeling of what happens: Body and emotion in the making of consciousness*. San Diego, CA: Harcourt.

Dasgupta, N., DeSteno, D. A., Williams, L. A., & Hunsinger, M. (2009). Fanning the flames of prejudice: The influence of specific incidental emotions on implicit prejudice. *Emotion, 9,* 585–591.

Davis, J. I., Senghas, A., Brandt, F., & Ochsner, K. N. (2010). The effects of botox injections on emotional experience. *Emotion, 10,* 433–440.

de Cremer, D., & Tyler, T. R. (2005). Am I respected or not? Inclusion and reputation as issues in group membership. *Social Justice Research, 18,* 121–153.

de Hooge, I. E., Breugelmans, S. M., & Zeelenberg, M. (2008). Not so ugly after all: Endogenous shame acts as a commitment device. *Journal of Personality and Social Psychology, 95,* 933–943.

de Hooge, I. E., Nelissen, R., Breugelmans, S. M., & Zeelenberg, M. (2011). What is moral about guilt? Acting 'prosocially' at the disadvantage of others. *Journal of Personality and Social Psychology, 100,* 462.

de Hooge, I. E., Zeelenberg, M., & Breugelmans, S. M. (2007). Moral sentiments and cooperation: Differential influences of shame and guilt. *Cognition and Emotion, 21,* 1025–1042.

de Silva, P. (2000). *An introduction to Buddhist psychology*. Lanham, MD: Rowman & Littlefield.

De Vos, G. A., & Wagatsuma, H. (1966). *Japan's invisible race: Caste in culture and personality*. Berkeley, CA: University of California Press.

Dennett, D. C. (1996). *Darwin's dangerous idea: Evolution and the meanings of life*. New York: Simon and Schuster.

DeSteno, D. A., Bartlett, M. Y., Baumann, J., Williams, L. A., & Dickens, L. (2010). Gratitude as moral sentiment: Emotion-guided cooperation in economic exchange. *Emotion, 10,* 289–293.

DeSteno, D. A., Dasgupta, N., Bartlett, M. Y., & Cajdric, A. (2004). Prejudice from thin air: The effect of emotion on automatic intergroup attitudes. *Psychological Science, 15,* 319–324.

Deutsch, R., Gawronski, B., & Strack, F. (2006). At the boundaries of automaticity: Negation as reflective operation. *Journal of Personality and Social Psychology, 91,* 385–405.

Dirks, K. T., & Ferrin, D. L. (2002). Trust in leadership: Meta-analytic findings and implications for research and practice. *Journal of Applied Psychology, 87,* 611–628.

Ditto, P. H., & Lopez, D. F. (1992). Motivated skepticism: Use of differential decision criteria for preferred and nonpreferred conclusions. *Journal of Personality and Social Psychology, 63,* 568–584.

Dockstader, B. (2009). Post-speech: Conservatives, how stupid do you feel now? Campaign for America's Future. Retrieved from http://www.ourfuture.org/blog-entry/2009093708/post-speech-conservatives-how-stupid-do-you-feel-now

Dollard, J., Miller, N. E., Doob, L. W., Mowrer, O. H., & Sears, R. R. (1939). *Frustration and aggression.* New Haven, CT: Yale University Press.

Doosje, B., Branscombe, N. R., Spears, R., & Manstead, A. S. R. (1998). Guilty by association: When one's group has a negative history. *Journal of Personality and Social Psychology, 75,* 872–886.

Doosje, B., Branscombe, N. R., Spears, R., & Manstead, A. S. R. (2006). Antecedents and consequences of group-based guilt: The effects of ingroup identification. *Group Processes & Intergroup Relations, 9,* 325.

Dostoyevsky, F. (1866/1945). *Crime and punishment* (trans. C. Garnett). London: Heinemann.

Duggan, L. (2002). The new homonormativity: The sexual politics of neoliberalism. In R. Castronovo & D. D. Nelson (Eds.), *Materializing democracy: Toward a revitalized cultural politics* (pp. 175–194). London: Duke University Press.

Dumont, M., Yzerbyt, V. Y., Wigboldus, D., & Gordjin, E. H. (2003). Social categorization and fear reactions to the September 11th terrorist attacks. *Personality and Social Psychology Bulletin, 29,* 1509–1520.

Dunn, J. R., & Schweitzer, M. E. (2005). Feeling and believing: The influence of emotion on trust. *Journal of Personality and Social Psychology, 88,* 736–748.

Dunsmore, J., Bradburn, I., Costanzo, P., & Fredrickson, B. L. (2009). Mothers' expressive style and emotional responses to children's behavior predict children's prosocial and achievement-related self-ratings. *International Journal of Behavioral Development, 33,* 253–264.

Eagly, A. H., & Chaiken, S. (1993). *The psychology of attitudes.* Fort Worth, TX: Harcourt Brace Jovanovich College Publishers.

Echterhoff, G., Higgins, E. T., & Levine, J. M. (2009). Shared reality. *Perspectives on Psychological Science, 4,* 496.

Eisenberg, N. (2000). Emotion, regulation, and moral development. *Annual Review of Psychology, 51,* 665–697.

Eisenberg, N., & Miller, P. A. (1987). The relation of empathy to prosocial and related behaviors. *Psychological Bulletin, 101,* 91–119.

Eisenberg, N., Fabes, R. A., Miller, P. A., Fultz, J., Shell, R., Mathy, R. M., & Reno, R. R. (1989). Relation of sympathy and personal distress to prosocial behavior: A multimethod study. *Journal of Personality and Social Psychology, 57,* 55–66.

Eisenberg, N., Schaller, M., Fabes, R. A., Bustamante, D., Mathy, R. M., Shell, R., & Rhodes, K. (1988). Differentiation of personal distress and sympathy in children and adults. *Developmental Psychology, 24,* 766–775.

Eisenberg, N., Valiente, C., & Champion, C. (2004). Empathy-related responding: Moral, social, and socialization correlates. In A. G. Miller (Ed.), *The social psychology of good and evil* (pp. 386–414). New York: The Guilford Press.

Ekman, P. (1992). An argument for basic emotions. *Cognition and Emotion, 6,* 169–200.

Ekman, P. (1994). Strong evidence for universals in facial expressions: A reply to Russell's mistaken critique. *Psychological Bulletin, 115,* 268–287.

Elfenbein, H. A., & Ambady, N. (2002). On the universality and cultural specificity of emotion recognition: A meta-analysis. *Psychological Bulletin, 128,* 203–235.

Elison, J. (2005). Shame and guilt: A hundred years of apples and oranges. *New Ideas in Psychology, 23*, 5–32.

Ellemers, N., Spears, R., & Doosje, B. (2002). Self and social identity. *Annual Review of Psychology, 53*, 161–186.

Ellsworth, P. C., & Smith, C. A. (1988). From appraisal to emotion: Differences among unpleasant feelings. *Motivation and Emotion, 12*, 271–302.

Ellsworth, P. C., & Tong, E. M. (2006). What does it mean to be angry at yourself? Categories, appraisals, and the problem of language. *Emotion, 6*, 572–586.

Emde, R. N., Johnson, W. F., & Easterbrooks, M. A. (1987). The do's and don'ts of early moral development: Psychoanalytic tradition and current research. In J. Kagan & S. Lamb (Eds.), *The emergence of morality in young children* (pp. 245–276). Chicago: University of Chicago Press.

Emmons, R. A., & McCullough, M. E. (2003). Counting blessings versus burdens: An experimental investigation of gratitude and subjective well-being in daily life. *Journal of Personality and Social Psychology, 84*, 377–389.

Esses, V. M., Haddock, G., & Zanna, M. P. (1993). Values, stereotypes, and emotions as determinants of intergroup attitudes. In D. M. Mackie & D. L. Hamilton (Eds.), *Affect, cognition, and stereotyping: Intergroup processes in group perception* (pp. 137–166). San Diego, CA: Academic Press.

Fabrigar, L., & Petty, R. (1999). The role of the affective and cognitive bases of attitudes in susceptibility to affectively and cognitively based persuasion. *Personality and Social Psychology Bulletin, 25*, 363–381.

Faulkner, J., Schaller, M., Park, J. H., & Duncan, L. A. (2004). Evolved disease-avoidance mechanisms and contemporary xenophobic attitudes. *Group Processes and Intergroup Relations, 7*, 333–353.

Fazio, R. H. (1986). How do attitudes guide behavior? In R. M. Sorrentino & E. T. Higgins (Eds.), *Handbook of motivation and cognition: Foundations of social behavior* (pp. 204–243). New York: The Guilford Press.

Fazio, R. H. (2007). Attitudes as object-evaluation associations of varying strength. *Social Cognition, 25*, 603.

Fazio, R. H., & Powell, M. C. (1997). On the value of knowing one's likes and dislikes. *Psychological Science, 8*, 430–437.

Feather, N. T., & Sherman, R. (2002). Envy, resentment, schadenfreude, and sympathy: Reactions to deserved and undeserved achievement and subsequent failure. *Personality and Social Psychology Bulletin, 28*, 953–961.

Fehr, E., & Gächter, S. (2002). Altruistic punishment in humans. *Nature, 415*, 137–140.

Fein, S., & Spencer, S. J. (1997). Prejudice as self-image maintenance: Affirming the self through derogating others. *Journal of Personality and Social Psychology, 73*, 31–44.

Feiring, C., Taska, L., & Lewis, M. (1996). A process model for understanding adaptation to sexual abuse: The role of shame in defining stigmatization. *Child Abuse & Neglect, 20*, 767–782.

Ferguson, M. J., & Bargh, J. A. (2004). Liking is for doing: The effects of goal pursuit on automatic evaluation. *Journal of Personality and Social Psychology, 87*, 557–572.

Ferguson, T. J., Brugman, D., White, J., & Eyre, H. L. (2007). Shame and guilt as morally warranted experiences. In J. L. Tracy & R. W. Robins (Eds.), *The self-conscious emotions: Theory and research* (pp. 330–348). New York: Guilford Press.

Feshbach, S. (1987). Individual aggression, national attachment, and the search for peace: Psychological perspectives. *Aggressive Behaviour, 13*, 315–325.

Fessler, D. M. T. (2007). From appeasement to conformity: Evolutionary and cultural perspectives on shame, competition, and cooperation. In J. L. Tracy, R. W. Robins, & J. P. Tangney (Eds.), *The self-conscious emotions: Theory and research* (pp. 174–193). New York: Guilford.

Fessler, D. M. T. (2010). Madmen: An evolutionary perspective on anger and men's violent responses to transgression. In M. Potegal, G. Stemmler, & C. D. Spielberger (Eds.), *International handbook of anger: Constituent and concomitant biological, psychological, and social processes* (pp. 361–381). Secaucus, NJ: Springer.

Fine, C. (2006). Is the emotional dog wagging its rational tail, or chasing it? *Philosophical Explorations, 9*, 83–98.

Fischer, A. H., & Roseman, I. J. (2007). Beat them or ban them: The characteristics and social functions of anger and contempt. *Journal of Personality and Social Psychology, 93*, 103–115.

Fishbach, A., & Shah, J. Y. (2006). Self control in action: Implicit dispositions toward goals and away from temptations. *Journal of Personality and Social Psychology, 90*, 820–832.

Fishbach, A., Eyal, T., & Finkelstein, S. R. (2010). How positive and negative feedback motivate goal pursuit. *Social and Personality Psychology Compass, 4*, 517–530.

Fiske, A. P. (1992). Book review of *Personality and the cultural construction of society* (David K. Jordon and Marc J. Swartz, eds.). *American Ethnologist, 20*, 395–396.

Fiske, S. T., Cuddy, A. J. C., & Glick, P. (2007). Universal dimensions of social cognition: Warmth and competence. *Trends in Cognitive Sciences, 11*, 77–83.

Flanagan, S. C., & Lee, A. R. (2003). The new politics, culture wars, and the authoritarian-libertarian value change in advanced industrial democracies. *Comparative Political Studies, 36*, 235–270.

Florian, V., Mikulincer, M., & Hirschberger, G. (2000). The anatomy of a problematic emotion: The conceptualization and measurement of the experience of pity. *Imagination, Cognition and Personality, 19*, 3–26.

Fontaine, J. R. J., Luyten, P., De Boeck, P., & Corveleyn, J. (2001). The test of self-conscious affect: Internal structure, differential scales and relationships with long-term affects. *European Journal of Personality, 15*(6), 449–463.

Fontaine, J. R. J., Scherer, K. R., Roesch, E. B., & Ellsworth, P. C. (2007). The world of emotions is not two-dimensional. *Psychological Science, 18*, 1050–1057.

Frank, R. (1988). *Passions within reason*. New York: W. W. Norton & Company.

Fredrickson, B. L. (2005). The broaden-and-build theory of positive emotions. In F. A. Huppert, N. Baylis, & B. Keverne (Eds.), *The science of well-being* (pp. 217–240). Oxford, UK: Oxford University Press.

Freud, S. (1905/1962). *Three essays on the theory of sexuality* (trans. J. Strachey). London: Hogarth Press.

Frijda, N. H. (1986). *The emotions*. Cambridge, UK: Cambridge University Press.

Furnham, A. (1990). *The Protestant work ethic: The psychology of work-related beliefs and behaviours*. London: Routledge.

Galinsky, A. D., & Moskowitz, G. B. (2000). Perspective-taking: Decreasing stereotype expression, stereotype accessibility, and in-group favoritism. *Journal of Personality and Social Psychology, 78*, 708–724.

Gawronski, B., & Bodenhausen, G. V. (2006). Associative and propositional processes in evaluation: An integrative review of implicit and explicit attitude change. *Psychological Bulletin, 132*, 692–731.

Gawronski, B., & Bodenhausen, G. V. (2007). Unraveling the processes underlying evaluation: Attitudes from the perspective of the APE model. *Social Cognition, 25,* 687–717.

Gert, B. (2011). The definition of morality. *Stanford Encyclopedia of Philosophy.* Retrieved from http://plato.stanford.edu/entries/morality-definition/

Gibbs, J. C., Basinger, K. S., Grime, R. L., & Snarey, J. R. (2007). Moral judgment development across cultures: Revisiting Kohlberg's universality claims. *Developmental Review, 27,* 443–500.

Gibilisco, P. (2010, 29 December). Empathy not sympathy helps inclusiveness. On Line Opinion: Australia's e-journal of social and political debate. Retrieved from http://www.onlineopinion.com.au/view.asp?article=11422&page=1

Gilbert, P. (1998). What is shame? Some core issues and controversies. In P. Gilbert & B. Andrews (Eds.), *Shame: Interpersonal behavior, psychopathology and culture* (pp. 3–36). New York: Oxford University Press.

Gilbert, P. (2003). Evolution, social roles, and differences in shame and guilt. *Social Research, 70,* 1205–1230.

Gilligan, C. (1982). *In a different voice: Psychological theory and women's development.* Cambridge, MA: Harvard University Press.

Giner-Sorolla, R. (1999). Affect in attitude: Immediate and deliberative perspectives. In S. Chaiken & Y. Trope (Eds.), *Dual process theories in social psychology* (pp. 441–461). New York: The Guilford Press.

Giner-Sorolla, R. (2001). Guilty pleasures and grim necessities: Affective attitudes in dilemmas of self-control. *Journal of Personality and Social Psychology, 80,* 206–221.

Giner-Sorolla, R. (2004). Is affective material in attitudes more accessible than cognitive material? The moderating role of attitude basis. *European Journal of Social Psychology, 34,* 761–780.

Giner-Sorolla, R., & Chaiken, S. (1994). The causes of hostile media effects. *Journal of Experimental Social Psychology, 30,* 165–180.

Giner-Sorolla, R., & Espinosa, P. (2011). Social cuing of guilt by anger and shame by disgust. *Psychological Science, 22,* 49–53.

Giner-Sorolla, R., & Hewitson, N. (2011). *Disgust, fear, and anger: three emotions related to infrahumanizing prejudice.* Unpublished manuscript, University of Kent.

Giner-Sorolla, R., & Maitner, A. T. (2011). *Anger and fear as reactions to intergroup injustice and power.* Unpublished manuscript, University of Kent.

Giner-Sorolla, R., & Russell, P. S. (2009). Anger, disgust and sexual crimes. In M. A. H. Horvath & J. M. Brown (Eds.), *Rape: Challenging contemporary thinking* (pp. 46–73). Cullompton: Willan Publishing.

Giner-Sorolla, R., Castano, E., Espinosa, P., & Brown, R. J. (2008). Shame expressions reduce the recipient's insult from outgroup reparations. *Journal of Experimental Social Psychology, 44,* 519–526.

Giner-Sorolla, R., Caswell, T. A., Bosson, J. K., & Hettinger, V. M. (2011a). *Emotions in sexual morality: Testing the separate elicitors of anger and disgust.* Unpublished manuscript, University of Kent.

Giner-Sorolla, R., Kamau, C. W., & Castano, E. (2010). Guilt and shame through recipients' eyes: The moderating effect of blame. *Social Psychology, 41,* 88–92.

Giner-Sorolla, R., Leidner, B., & Castano, E. (2012). Dehumanization, demonization, and morality shifting: Paths to moral certainty in extremist violence. In M. Hogg & D. Blaylock (Eds.), *Extremism and the psychology of uncertainty* (pp. 165–182). London: Wiley.

Giner-Sorolla, R., Piazza, J., & Espinosa, P. (2011b). *What do the TOSCA guilt and shame scales really measure: Affect or action?* Unpublished manuscript, University of Kent.

Giner-Sorolla, R., Piazza, J., van Vugt, M., & Derbyshire, S. (2011c). *The social guilt hypothesis: Experimental demonstrations of the interpersonal nature of guilt.* Unpublished manuscript, University of Kent.

Giner-Sorolla, R., Zebel, S., Zaiser, E., Vasiljevic, M., & Yamamoto, C. (2011d). *Suffering and responsibility-taking inferences explain why wrongdoers' use of negative emotion words can satisfy victim group members.* Unpublished manuscript, University of Kent.

Ginges, J., & Atran, S. (2008). Humiliation and the inertia effect: Implications for understanding violence and compromise in intractable intergroup conflicts. *Journal of Cognition and Culture, 8,* 281–294.

Glick, P., Gangl, C., Gibb, S., Klumpner, S., & Weinberg, E. (2007). Defensive reactions to masculinity threat: More negative affect toward effeminate (but not masculine) gay men. *Sex Roles, 57,* 55–59.

Goetz, J. L., Keltner, D., & Simon-Thomas, E. (2010). Compassion: An evolutionary analysis and empirical review. *Psychological Bulletin, 136,* 351–374.

Goffman, E. (1971). *Relations in public: Microstudies of the public order.* Harmondsworth: Penguin Books.

Goldberg, J. H., Lerner, J. S., & Tetlock, P. E. (1999). Rage and reason: The psychology of the intuitive prosecutor. *European Journal of Social Psychology, 29,* 781–795.

Goldenberg, J. L., Goplen, J., Cox, C. R., & Arndt, J. (2007). 'Viewing' pregnancy as an existential threat: The effects of creatureliness on reactions to media depictions of the pregnant body. *Media Psychology, 10,* 211–230.

Goldenberg, J. L., Heflick, N. A., Vaes, J., Motyl, M., & Greenberg, J. (2009). Of mice and men, and objectified women: A terror management account of infrahumanization. *Group Processes and Intergroup Relations, 12,* 763–776.

Goldenberg, J. L., Pyszczynski, T., Greenberg, J., & Solomon, S. (2000). Fleeing the body: A terror management perspective on the problem of human corporeality. *Personality and Social Psychology Review, 4,* 200–218.

Goldenberg, J. L., Pyszczynski, T., Greenberg, J., Solomon, S., Kluck, B., & Cornwell, R. (2001). I am not an animal: Mortality salience, disgust, and the denial of human creatureliness. *Journal of Experimental Psychology: General, 130,* 427–435.

Goldhagen, D. (1996). *Hitler's willing executioners: Ordinary Germans and the holocaust.* New York: Alfred A. Knopf.

Golec de Zavala, A., Cichocka, A., Eidelson, R., & Jayawickreme, N. (2009). Collective narcissism and its social consequences. *Journal of Personality and Social Psychology, 97,* 1074–1096.

Gonzalez, C. M., & Tyler, T. R. (2007). Emotional reactions to unfairness. In D. de Cremer (Ed.), *Advances in the psychology of justice and affect* (pp. 109–132). Greenwich: Information Age Publishing.

Gordijn, E. H., Wigboldus, D., & Yzerbyt, V. Y. (2001). Emotional consequences of categorizing victims of negative outgroup behavior as ingroup or outgroup. *Group Processes and Intergroup Relations, 4,* 317–326.

Gould, S. J. (1987). The panda's thumb of technology. *Natural History, 96,* 14–23.

Gould, S. J. (1991). Exaptation: A crucial tool for an evolutionary psychology. *Journal of Social Issues, 47,* 43–65.

Gould, S. J. (1992). *The panda's thumb: More reflections in natural history.* New York: W. W. Norton & Company.

Graham, J., Haidt, J., & Nosek, B. A. (2009). Liberals and conservatives rely on different sets of moral foundations. *Journal of Personality and Social Psychology, 96,* 1029–1046.

Graham, S., Weiner, B., Giuliano, T., & Williams, E. (1993). An attributional analysis of reactions to Magic Johnson. *Journal of Applied Social Psychology, 23,* 996–1010.

Grant, A. M., & Gino, F. (2010). A little thanks goes a long way: Explaining why gratitude expressions motivate prosocial behavior. *Journal of Personality and Social Psychology, 98*(6), 946–955.

Gray, J. A. (1999). Cognition, emotion, conscious experience and the brain. In T. Dalgleish & M. J. Power (Eds.), *Handbook of cognition and emotion* (pp. 83–102). Chichester, UK: Wiley.

Green, D. P., Glaser, J., & Rich, A. (1998). From lynching to gay-bashing: The elusive connection between economic conditions and hate crime. *Journal of Personality and Social Psychology, 75,* 82–92.

Greenberg, J., & Kosloff, S. (2008). Terror management theory: Implications for understanding prejudice, stereotyping, intergroup conflict, and political attitudes. *Social and Personality Psychology Compass, 2,* 1881–1894.

Greenberg, J., Simon, L., Pyszczynski, T., Solomon, S., & Chatel, D. (1992). Terror management and tolerance: Does mortality salience always intensify negative reactions to others who threaten one's worldview. *Journal of Personality and Social Psychology, 63,* 212–220.

Greenberg, J., Solomon, S., & Pyszczynski, T. (1997). Terror management theory of self-esteem and cultural worldviews: Empirical assessments and conceptual refinements. *Advances in Experimental Social Psychology, 29,* 61–139.

Greene, J. D. (2009a). Dual-process morality and the personal/impersonal distinction: A reply to McGuire, Langdon, Coltheart, and Mackenzie. *Journal of Experimental Social Psychology, 45*(3), 581–584.

Greene, J. D. (2009b). The cognitive neuroscience of moral judgment. In M. S. Gazzaniga (Ed.), *The cognitive neurosciences IV* (pp. 987–1002). Cambridge, MA: MIT Press.

Greene, J. D., Morelli, S. A., Lowenberg, K., Nystrom, L. E., & Cohen, J. D. (2008). Cognitive load selectively interferes with utilitarian moral judgment. *Cognition, 107,* 1144–1154.

Greene, J. D., Nystrom, L. E., Engell, A. D., Darley, J. M., & Cohen, J. D. (2004). The neural bases of cognitive conflict and control in moral judgment. *Neuron, 44,* 389–400.

Greene, J. D., Sommerville, R. B., Nystrom, L. E., Darley, J. M., & Cohen, J. D. (2001). An fMRI investigation of emotional engagement in moral judgment. *Science, 293,* 2105–2108.

Greenwald, A. G. (1992). Unconscious cognition reclaimed. *American Psychologist, 47,* 766–779.

Greenwald, A. G., McGhee, D. E., & Schwartz, J. L. (1998). Measuring individual differences in implicit cognition: The implicit association test. *Journal of Personality and Social Psychology, 74,* 1464–1480.

Griffin, J., & Berry, E. M. (2003). A modern day holy anorexia? Religious language in advertising and anorexia nervosa in the West. *European Journal of Clinical Nutrition, 57,* 43–51.

Gruenewald, T. L., Kemeny, M. E., Aziz, N., & Fahey, J. L. (2004). Acute threat to the social self: Shame, social self-esteem, and cortisol activity. *Psychosomatic Medicine, 66,* 915–924.

Gudykunst, W. B. (2005). An anxiety/uncertainty management (AUM) theory of effective communication. In W. B. Gudykunst (Ed.), *Theorizing about intercultural communication* (pp. 281–322). Thousand Oaks, CA: Sage Publications.

Guerra, V. M., & Giner-Sorolla, R. (2010). Community, Autonomy, and Divinity Scale (CADS): Development of a theory-based moral codes scale. *Journal of Cross-Cultural Psychology, 41*, 35–50.

Gurr, T. R. (1968). A causal model of civil strife: A comparative analysis using new indices. *American Political Science Review, 62*(4), 1104–1124.

Gutierrez, R., & Giner-Sorolla, R. S. (2007). Anger, disgust, and presumption of harm as reactions to taboo-breaking behaviors. *Emotion, 7*, 853–868.

Gutierrez, R., Giner-Sorolla, R., & Vasiljevic, M. (in press). Just an anger synonym? Moral context influences predictors of disgust word use. *Cognition and Emotion*.

Hafer, C. L., & Bègue, L. (2005). Experimental research on just-world theory: Problems, developments, and future challenges. *Psychological Bulletin, 131*, 128–167.

Haidt, J. (2001). The emotional dog and its rational tail. *Psychological Review, 108*, 814–834.

Haidt, J. (2003a). The moral emotions. In R. J. Davidson, K. R. Scherer, & H. H. Goldsmith (Eds.), *Handbook of affective sciences* (pp. 852–870). Oxford: Oxford University Press.

Haidt, J. (2003b). The emotional dog does learn new tricks: A reply to Pizarro and Bloom. *Psychological Review, 110*(1), 197–198.

Haidt, J. (2003c). Elevation and the positive psychology of morality. In C. L. M. Keyes & J. Haidt (Eds.), *Flourishing: Positive psychology and the life well-lived* (pp. 275–289). Washington, DC: American Psychological Association.

Haidt, J. (2004). The emotional dog gets mistaken for a possum. *Review of General Psychology, 8*, 283–290.

Haidt, J. (2007). The new synthesis in moral psychology. *Science, 316*, 998–1002.

Haidt, J. (2010). Moral psychology must not be based on faith and hope: Commentary on Narvaez (2010). *Perspectives on Psychological Science, 5*, 182.

Haidt, J., & Hersh, M. A. (2001). Sexual morality: The cultures and emotions of conservatives and liberals. *Journal of Applied Social Psychology, 31*, 191–221.

Haidt, J., Björklund, F., & Murphy, S. (2000). Moral dumbfounding: When intuition finds no reason. *Lund Psychological Reports*, 1–15.

Haidt, J., Koller, S. H., & Dias, M. G. (1993). Affect, culture, and morality, or is it wrong to eat your dog? *Journal of Personal Social Psychology, 65*, 613–628.

Halloran, M. J. (2007). Indigenous reconciliation in Australia: Do values, identity and collective guilt matter? *Journal of Community & Applied Social Psychology, 17*, 1–18.

Halperin, E., & Gross, J. J. (2011). Intergroup anger in intractable conflict. *Group Processes & Intergroup Relations, 14*, 477–488.

Hansen, C. H., & Shantz, C. A. (1995). Emotion-specific priming: Congruence effects on affect and recognition across negative emotions. *Personality and Social Psychology Bulletin, 21*, 548–557.

Hansen, N., & Sassenberg, K. (2006). Does social identification harm or serve as a buffer? The impact of social identification on anger after experiencing social discrimination. *Personality and Social Psychology Bulletin, 32*, 983–996.

Hareli, S., & Hess, U. (2010). What emotional reactions can tell us about the nature of others: An appraisal perspective on person perception. *Cognition and Emotion, 24*, 128–140.

Hareli, S., Shomrat, N., & Hess, U. (2009). Emotional versus neutral expressions and perceptions of social dominance and submissiveness. *Emotion, 9*, 378.

Harmon-Jones, E., & Sigelman, J. (2001). State anger and prefrontal brain activity: Evidence that insult-related relative left-prefrontal activation is associated with experienced anger and aggression. *Journal of Personality and Social Psychology, 80*, 797–803.

Harris, L. T., & Fiske, S. T. (2006). Dehumanizing the lowest of the low: Neuroimaging responses to extreme out-groups. *Psychological Science, 17*, 847–853.

Harth, N. S., Kessler, T., & Leach, C. W. (2008). Advantaged group's emotional reactions to intergroup inequality: The dynamics of pride, guilt, and sympathy. *Personality and Social Psychology Bulletin, 34*, 115–129.

Haslam, N. (2006). Dehumanization: An integrative review. *Personality and Social Psychology Review, 10*, 252–264.

Haslam, S. A., & Reicher, S. (2007). Beyond the banality of evil: Three dynamics of an interactionist social psychology of tyranny. *Personality and Social Psychology Bulletin, 33*, 615–622.

Hastorf, A. H., & Cantril, H. (1954). They saw a game: A case study. *Journal of Abnormal and Social Psychology, 49*, 129–134.

Hatfield, E., Cacioppo, J. T., & Rapson, R. L. (1993). Emotional contagion. *Current Directions in Psychological Sciences, 2*, 96–99.

Hatfield, E., Cacioppo, J. T., & Rapson, R. L. (1994). *Emotional contagion*. New York: Cambridge University Press.

Hauser, M. (2006). *Moral minds: How nature designed our universal sense of right and wrong*. New York: Harper Collins.

Haviland, J. M., & Lelwica, M. (1987). The induced affect response: 10-week-old infants' responses to three emotion expressions. *Developmental Psychology, 23*, 97–104.

Heath, C., Bell, C., & Sternberg, E. (2001). Emotional selection in memes: The case of urban legends. *Journal of Personality and Social Psychology, 81*, 1028–1041.

Heine, S. J., Proulx, T., & Vohs, K. D. (2006). The meaning maintenance model: On the coherence of social motivations. *Personality and Social Psychology Review, 10*, 88–110.

Hennig-Thurau, T., Groth, M., Paul, M., & Gremler, D. D. (2006). Are all smiles created equal? How emotional contagion and emotional labor affect service relationships. *Journal of Marketing, 70*, 58–73.

Herek, G. M. (1984). Attitudes toward lesbians and gay men: A factor-analytic study. *Journal of Homosexuality, 10*, 39–51.

Hertenstein, M. J., Keltner, D., App, B., Bulleit, B. A., & Jaskolka, A. R. (2006). Touch communicates distinct emotions. *Emotion, 6*, 528–533.

Hess, R., & Torney, J. (1967). *The development of political attitudes in children*. Chicago: Aldine.

Hess, U., & Blairy, S. (2001). Facial mimicry and emotional contagion to dynamic emotional facial expressions and their influence on decoding accuracy. *International Journal of Psychophysiology, 40*, 129–141.

Higgins, E. T. (1987). Self-discrepancy: A theory relating self and affect. *Psychological Review, 94*, 319.

Higgins, E. T., Klein, R., & Strauman, T. (1985). Self-concept discrepancy theory: A psychological model for distinguishing among different aspects of depression and anxiety. *Social Cognition, 3*, 51–76.

Hoffman, M. L. (1975). Developmental synthesis of affect and cognition and its implications for altruistic motivation. *Developmental Psychology, 11*(5), 607–622.

Hoffman, M. L. (1977). Moral internalization: Current theory and research. *Advances in Experimental Social Psychology, 10*, 85–133.

Hoffman, M. L. (1989). Empathic emotions and justice in society. *Social Justice Research, 3*, 283–311.

Hogg, M. A. (2007). Social identity and the group context of trust: Managing risk and building trust through belonging. In M. Siegrist, T. C. Earle, & H. Gutscher (Eds.), *Trust in cooperative risk management: Uncertainty and scepticism in the public mind* (pp. 51–72). London: Blackwell.

Hopfensitz, A., & Reuben, E. (2009). The importance of emotions for the effectiveness of social punishment. *The Economic Journal, 119*, 1534–1559.

Horberg, E. J., Oveis, C., Keltner, D., & Cohen, A. B. (2009). Disgust and the moralization of purity. *Journal of Personality and Social Psychology, 97*, 963–976.

Horvath, M. A. H., & Giner-Sorolla, R. S. (2007). Below the age of consent: Double standards, context effects, and mediating judgments in preconceptions of adolescent–adult sexual relationships. *Journal of Applied Social Psychology, 37*, 2980–3009.

Hovland, C. I., & Sears, R. R. (1940). Minor studies of aggression: VI. Correlation of lynchings with economic indices. *The Journal of Psychology, 9*, 301–310.

Hsu, H. (2009, January/February). The end of white America? *The Atlantic Online*. Retrieved from http://www.theatlantic.com/magazine/archive/2009/01/the-end-of-white-america/7208/

Huebner, B., Dwyer, S., & Hauser, M. (2009). The role of emotion in moral psychology. *Trends in Cognitive Sciences, 13*, 1–6.

Hunt, A. (1998). The great masturbation panic and the discourses of moral regulation in nineteenth- and early twentieth-century Britain. *Journal of the History of Sexuality, 8*, 575–615.

Hyde, L. W., Shaw, D. S., & Moilanen, K. L. (2010). Developmental precursors of moral disengagement and the role of moral disengagement in the development of antisocial behavior. *Journal of Abnormal Child Psychology, 38*, 197–209.

Hymel, S., Rocke-Henderson, N., & Bonanno, R. A. (2005). Moral disengagement: A framework for understanding bullying among adolescents. *Journal of Social Sciences, 8*, 1–11.

Inbar, Y., Pizarro, D. A., & Bloom, P. (2009). Conservatives are more easily disgusted than liberals. *Cognition & Emotion, 23*, 714–725.

Inbar, Y., Pizarro, D. A., Knobe, J., & Bloom, P. (2009). Disgust sensitivity predicts intuitive disapproval of gays. *Emotion, 9*, 435–439.

Innes-Ker, A., & Niedenthal, P. M. (2002). Emotion concepts and emotional states in social judgment and categorization. *Journal of Personality and Social Psychology, 83*, 804–816.

Iyer, A., & Leach, C. W. (2008). Emotion in inter-group relations. *European Review of Social Psychology, 19*, 86–125.

Iyer, A., Leach, C. W., & Crosby, F. J. (2003). White guilt and racial compensation: The benefits and limits of self-focus. *Personality and Social Psychology Bulletin, 29*, 117–129.

Iyer, A., Leach, C. W., & Pedersen, A. (2004). Racial wrongs and restitutions: The role of guilt and other group-based emotions. In M. Fine (Ed.), *Off White: Readings on power, privilege, and resistance* (pp. 345–361). London: Routledge.

Iyer, A., Schmader, T., & Lickel, B. (2007). Why individuals protest the perceived transgressions of their country: The role of anger, shame, and guilt. *Personality and Social Psychology Bulletin, 33*, 572–587.

Izard, C. E. (2007). Basic emotions, natural kinds, emotion schemas, and a new paradigm. *Perspectives on Psychological Science, 2*, 260–280.

Jabbi, M., Bastiaansen, J., & Keysers, C. (2008). A common anterior insula representation of disgust observation, experience and imagination shows divergent functional connectivity pathways. *PLoS One, 3*, e2939.

Jackson, L. A., Sullivan, L. A., Harnish, R., & Hodge, C. N. (1996). Achieving positive social identity: Social mobility, social creativity, and permeability of group boundaries. *Journal of Personality and Social Psychology, 70*, 241–254.

Janoff-Bulman, R., & Sheikh, S. (2006). From national trauma to moralizing nation. *Basic and Applied Social Psychology, 28*, 325–332.

Janoff-Bulman, R., Sheikh, S., & Hepp, S. (2009). Proscriptive versus prescriptive morality: Two faces of moral regulation. *Journal of Personality and Social Psychology, 96*, 521–537.

Jensen, L. A. (1998). Moral divisions within countries between orthodoxy and progressivism: India and the United States. *Journal for the Scientific Study of Religion, 37*, 90–107.

Johns, M., Schmader, T., & Lickel, B. (2005). Ashamed to be an American? The role of identification in predicting vicarious shame for anti-Arab prejudice after 9–11. *Self and Identity, 4*, 331–348.

Johnson, P. (2010). Law, morality and disgust: The regulation of 'extreme pornography' in England and Wales. *Social and Legal Studies, 19*, 147–163.

Johnson-Laird, P. N., & Oatley, K. (1989). The language of emotions: An analysis of a semantic field. *Cognition & Emotion, 3*, 81–123.

Johnstone, T., & Scherer, K. R. (2000). Vocal communication of emotion. In M. Lewis & J. Haviland (Eds.), *The handbook of emotions* (pp. 226–235). New York: Guilford.

Jost, J. T., Banaji, M. R., & Nosek, B. A. (2004). A decade of system justification theory: Accumulated evidence of conscious and unconscious bolstering of the status quo. *Political Psychology, 25*, 881–919.

Jost, J. T., Kivetz, Y., Rubini, M., Guermandi, G., & Mosso, C. (2005). System-justifying functions of complementary regional and ethnic stereotypes: Cross-national evidence. *Social Justice Research, 18*, 305–333.

Jost, J. T., Pelham, B. W., Sheldon, O., & Ni Sullivan, B. (2003). Social inequality and the reduction of ideological dissonance on behalf of the system: Evidence of enhanced system justification among the disadvantaged. *European Journal of Social Psychology, 33*, 13–36.

Kahan, D. M. (2000). The progressive appropriation of disgust. In S. Bandes (Ed.), *The passions of law* (pp. 63–79). New York: New York University Press.

Katz, I., & Hass, R. G. (1988). Racial ambivalence and American value conflict: Correlational and priming studies of dual cognitive structures. *Journal of Personality and Social Psychology, 55*, 893.

Kay, A. C., & Jost, J. T. (2003). Complementary justice: Effects of 'poor but happy' and 'poor but honest' stereotype exemplars on system justification and implicit activation of the justice motive. *Journal of Personality and Social Psychology, 85*, 823–837.

Kay, A. C., Jost, J. T., Mandisodza, A. N., Sherman, S. J., Petrocelli, J. V., & Johnson, A. L. (2007). Panglossian ideology in the service of system justification: How complementary stereotypes help us to rationalize inequality. *Advances in Experimental Social Psychology, 39*, 305–358.

Kelly, J. R., & Barsade, S. G. (2001). Mood and emotions in small groups and work teams. *Organizational Behavior and Human Decision Processes, 86*, 99–130.

Keltner, D. (1995). Signs of appeasement: Evidence for the distinct displays of embarrassment, amusement, and shame. *Journal of Personality and Social Psychology, 68*, 441–454.

Keltner, D., & Buswell, B. N. (1996). Evidence for the distinctness of embarrassment, shame, and guilt: A study of recalled antecedents and facial expressions of emotion. *Cognition and Emotion, 10*, 155–171.

Keltner, D., & Haidt, J. (1999). Social functions of emotions at four levels of analysis. *Cognition and Emotion, 13*, 505–521.

Keltner, D., & Haidt, J. (2001). Social functions of emotions. In T. J. Mayne & G. A. Bonanno (Eds.), *Emotions: Currrent issues and future directions* (pp. 192–213). New York: Guilford Press.

Keltner, D., & Haidt, J. (2003). Approaching awe, a moral, spiritual, and aesthetic emotion. *Cognition & Emotion, 17*, 297–314.

Keltner, D., & Kring, A. M. (1998). Emotion, social function, and psychopathology. *Review of General Psychology, 2*, 320–342.

Keltner, D., & Lerner, J. S. (2010). Emotion. In S. T. Fiske, D. T. Gilbert, & G. Lindzey (Eds.), *Handbook of Social Psychology*, 5th Edition (pp. 312–347). Hoboken, NJ: Wiley.

Keltner, D., Ellsworth, P. C., & Edwards, K. (1993). Beyond simple pessimism: Effects of sadness and anger on social perception. *Journal of Personality and Social Psychology, 64*, 740–752.

Kemper, T. D. (1987). How many emotions are there? Wedding the social and the autonomic component. *American Journal of Sociology, 93*, 263–289.

Kenworthy, J. B., Canales, C. A., Weaver, K. D., & Miller, N. (2003). Negative incidental affect and mood congruency in crossed categorization. *Journal of Experimental Social Psychology, 39*(3), 195–219.

Kessler, T., & Hollbach, S. (2005). Group-based emotions as determinants of ingroup identification. *Journal of Experimental Social Psychology, 41*, 677–685.

Ketelaar, T., & Au, W. T. (2003). The effects of feelings of guilt on the behaviour of uncooperative individuals in repeated social bargaining games: An affect-as-information interpretation of the role of emotion in social interaction. *Cognition and Emotion, 17*, 429–453.

Koenigs, M., Young, L., Adolphs, R., Tranel, D., Cushman, F., Hauser, M., & Damasio, A. (2007). Damage to the prefrontal cortex increases utilitarian moral judgements. *Nature, 446*, 908–911.

Kohlberg, L. (1981). *The philosophy of moral development: Moral stages and the idea of justice*. New York: Harper & Collins.

Kosfeld, M., Heinrichs, M., Zak, P. J., Fischbacher, U., & Fehr, E. (2005). Oxytocin increases trust in humans. *Nature, 435*, 673–676.

Kosterman, R., & Feshbach, S. (1989). Towards a measure of patriotic and nationalistic attitudes. *Political Psychology, 10*, 257–274.

Kövecses, Z. (2003). *Metaphor and emotion: Language, culture, and body in human feeling*. Cambridge: Cambridge University Press.

Kraus, S. J. (1995). Attitudes and the prediction of behavior: A meta-analysis of the empirical literature. *Personality and Social Psychology Bulletin, 21*, 58.

Krebs, D. L. (1970). Altruism: An examination of the concept and a review of the literature. *Psychological Bulletin, 73*, 258–302.

Kross, E., Ayduk, O., & Mischel, W. (2005). When asking 'why' doesn't hurt: Distinguishing rumination from reflective processing of negative emotions. *Psychological Science, 16*, 709–715.

Kuppens, P. (2010). From appraisal to emotion. *Emotion Review, 2*, 157–158.

Kuppens, P., & van Mechelen, I. (2007). Interactional appraisal models for the anger appraisals of threatened self-esteem, other-blame, and frustration. *Cognition and Emotion, 21*, 56–77.

Kuppens, P., van Mechelen, I., & Meulders, M. (2004). Every cloud has a silver lining: Interpersonal and individual differences determinants of anger-related behaviors. *Personality and Social Psychology Bulletin, 30*, 1550–1564.

Kuppens, P., van Mechelen, I., & Rijmen, F. (2008). Towards disentangling sources of individual differences in appraisal and anger. *Journal of Personality, 76*, 969–1000.

Kuppens, P., van Mechelen, I., Smits, D. J. M., & de Boeck, P. (2003). The appraisal basis of anger: Specificity, necessity and sufficiency of components. *Emotion, 3*, 254–269.

Kurzban, R., & Leary, M. R. (2001). Evolutionary origins of stigmatization: The functions of social exclusion. *Psychological Bulletin, 127*, 187–208.

Laible, D. J., & Thompson, R. A. (2000). Mother–child discourse, attachment security, shared positive affect and early conscience development. *Child Development, 71*, 1424–1440.

Lavine, H., Thomsen, C. J., Zanna, M. P., & Borgida, E. (1998). On the primacy of affect in the determination of attitudes and behavior: The moderating role of affective-cognitive ambivalence. *Journal of Experimental Social Psychology, 34*, 398–421.

Lazare, A. (2005). *On apology*. Oxford, UK: Oxford University Press.

Lazarus, R. S. (1982). Thoughts on the relations between emotion and cognition. *American Psychologist, 37*, 1019–1024.

Lazarus, R. S. (1984). On the primacy of cognition. *American Psychologist, 39*, 124–129.

Lazarus, R. S. (1991). *Emotion and adaptation*. Oxford, UK: Oxford University Press.

Lazarus, R. S., & Folkman, S. (1984). *Stress, appraisal, and coping*. New York: Springer.

Lazarus, R., & Folkman, D. (1988). The relationship between coping and emotion: Implications for theory and research. *Social Science & Medicine, 26*, 309–317.

Leach, C. W., Ellemers, N., & Barreto, M. (2007). Group virtue: The importance of morality (vs. competence and sociability) in the positive evaluation of in-groups. *Journal of Personality and Social Psychology, 93*, 234–249.

LeDoux, J. (1996). *The emotional brain: The mysterious underpinnings of emotional life*. New York: Simon and Schuster.

Lee, E. J. (2007). Infant feeding in risk society. *Health, Risk and Society, 9*, 295–309.

Leidner, B., & Castano, E. (2011). *Morality shifting in the context of intergroup wrongdoings*. Unpublished manuscript, New School for Social Research.

Leidner, B., Castano, E., Zaiser, E., & Giner-Sorolla, R. (2010). Ingroup glorification, moral disengagement, and justice in the context of collective violence. *Personality and Social Psychology Bulletin, 36*, 1115–1129.

Leith, K. P., & Baumeister, R. F. (1998). Empathy, shame, guilt, and narratives of interpersonal conflicts: Guilt-prone people are better at perspective taking. *Journal of Personality, 66*, 1–37.

Lerner, J. S., & Keltner, D. (2001). Fear, anger, and risk. *Journal of Personality and Social Psychology, 81*, 146–159.

Lerner, J. S., & Tiedens, L. Z. (2006). Portrait of the angry decision maker: How appraisal tendencies shape anger's influence on cognition. *Journal of Behavioral Decision Making, 19*, 115–137.

Lerner, J. S., Goldberg, J. H., & Tetlock, P. E. (1998). Sober second thought: The effects of accountability, anger, and authoritarianism on attributions of responsibility. *Personality and Social Psychology Bulletin, 24*, 563–574.

Lerner, J. S., Gonzalez, R. M., Small, D. A., & Fischhoff, B. (2003). Effects of fear and anger on perceived risks of terrorism: A national field experiment. *Psychological Science, 14*, 144–150.

Levenson, R. W. (1992). Autonomic nervous system differences among emotions. *Psychological Science, 3*, 23–27.

Levenson, R. W., & Ekman, P. (2002). Difficulty does not account for emotion-specific heart rate changes in the directed facial action task. *Psychophysiology, 39*, 397–405.

Leventhal, H., & Scherer, K. R. (1987). The relationship of emotion to cognition: A functional approach to a semantic controversy. *Cognition & Emotion, 1*, 3–28.

Leventhal, H., & Tomarken, A. J. (1986). Emotion: Today's problems. *Annual Review of Psychology, 37*, 565–610.

Levy, D. N. (2006). *Robots unlimited: Life in a virtual age*. Wellesley, MA: AK Peters, Ltd.

Lewis, H. B. (1971). *Shame and guilt in neurosis*. New York: International Universities Press.

Leyens, J.-P., Paladino, P. M., Rodriguez-Torres, R., Vaes, J., Demoulin, S., Rodriguez-Perez, A., & Gaunt, R. (2000). The emotional side of prejudice: The attribution of secondary emotions to ingroups and outgroups. *Personality and Social Psychology Review, 4*, 186–197.

Licata, L., & Klein, O. (2010). Holocaust or benevolent paternalism? Intergenerational comparisons on collective memories and emotions about Belgium's colonial past. *International Journal of Conflict and Violence, 4*, 45–57.

Lickel, B., Miller, N., Stenstrom, D. M., Denson, T. F., & Schmader, T. (2006). Vicarious retribution: The role of collective blame in intergroup aggression. *Personality and Social Psychology Review, 10*, 372–390.

Lickel, B., Schmader, T., Curtis, M., Scarnier, M., & Ames, D. R. (2005). Vicarious shame and guilt. *Group Processes and Intergroup Relations, 8*, 145–157.

Lickel, B., Steele, R. R., & Schmader, T. (2011). Group-based shame and guilt: Emerging directions in research. *Social and Personality Psychology Compass, 5*, 153–163.

Lind, E. A., & Tyler, T. R. (1988). *The social psychology of procedural justice*. New York: Plenum Press.

Littell, J. (2009). *The kindly ones* (trans. C. Mandell). London: Vintage Books.

Lucock, M. P., & Salkovskis, P. M. (1988). Cognitive factors in social anxiety and its treatment. *Behaviour Research and Therapy, 26*, 297–302.

Lundqvist, L. O., & Dimberg, U. (1995). Facial expressions are contagious. *Journal of Psychophysiology, 9*, 203–211.

Lutz, C. A. (1988). *Unnatural emotions: Everyday sentiments on a Micronesian atoll and their challenge to western theory*. Chicago: University of Chicago Press.

Luyten, P., Fontaine, J. R. J., & Corveleyn, J. (2002). Does the test of self-conscious affect (TOSCA) measure maladaptive aspects of guilt and adaptive aspects of shame? An empirical investigation. *Personality and Individual Differences, 33*, 1373–1387.

Mackie, D. M., & Smith, E. R. (2002). Intergroup emotions: Prejudice reconceptualized as differentiated reactions to out-groups. In J. P. Forgas & K. D. Williams (Eds.), *The social self: Cognitive, interpersonal, and intergroup perspectives* (pp. 309–326). Philadelphia: Psychology Press.

Mackie, D. M., & Smith, E. R. (2004). *From prejudice to intergroup emotions: Differentiated reactions to social groups*. New York: Psychology Press.

Mackie, D. M., Devos, T., & Smith, E. R. (2000). Intergroup emotions: Explaining offensive action tendencies in an intergroup context. *Journal of Personality and Social Psychology, 79*, 602–616.

Maio, G. R., & Olson, J. M. (1998). Values as truisms: Evidence and implications. *Journal of Personality and Social Psychology, 74*, 294–311.

Maitner, A. T., Mackie, D. M., & Smith, E. R. (2006). Evidence for the regulatory function of intergroup emotion: Emotional consequences of implemented or impeded intergroup action tendencies. *Journal of Experimental Social Psychology, 42*, 720–728.

Maitner, A. T., Mackie, D. M., & Smith, E. R. (2007). Antecedents and consequences of satisfaction and guilt following ingroup aggression. *Group Processes & Intergroup Relations, 10*, 223.

Makino, Y. (2010, August 26). Emperor mentioned blood ties with Korea in 1990. *Asahi Shimbun*, English Online Edition. Retrieved from http://www.asahi.com/english/TKY201008250380.html

Mallett, R. K., & Swim, J. K. (2007). The influence of inequality, responsibility, and justifiability on reports of group-based guilt for ingroup privilege. *Group Processes and Intergroup Relations, 10*, 57–69.

Marcus-Newhall, A., Pedersen, W. C., Carlson, M., & Miller, N. (2000). Displaced aggression is alive and well: A meta-analytic review. *Journal of Personality and Social Psychology, 78*, 670–689.

Mari, S., Andrighetto, L., Gabbiadini, A., Durante, F., & Volpato, C. (2010). The shadow of the Italian colonial experience: The impact of collective emotions on intentions to help the victims' descendants. *International Journal of Conflict and Violence, 4*, 58–74.

Marsh, A. A., Adams, R. B., & Kleck, R. E. (2005). Why do fear and anger look the way they do? Form and social function in facial expressions. *Personality and Social Psychology Bulletin, 31*, 73–86.

Matsumoto, D., Keltner, D., Shiota, M. N., O'Sullivan, M., & Frank, M. (2008). Facial expressions of emotion. In M. Lewis, J. M. Haviland-Jones, & L. Feldman Barrett (Eds.), *Handbook of emotions* (pp. 211–234). New York: Guilford Press.

Maurage, P., Joassin, F., Philippot, P., & Campanella, S. (2007). A validated battery of vocal emotional expressions. *Neuropsychological Trends, 2*, 63–74.

McCall, B. (2001, April 22). The perfect non-apology apology. *The New York Times* (online edition). Retrieved from http://query.nytimes.com/gst/fullpage.html?res=9F02E7DA1030F931A15757C0A9679C8B63

McClelland, D. C., Atkinson, J. W., Clark, R. A., & Lowell, E. L. (1953). *The achievement motive*. New York: Appleton-Century-Crofts.

McCullough, M. E., Kilpatrick, S. D., Emmons, R. A., & Larson, D. B. (2001). Is gratitude a moral affect? *Psychological Bulletin, 127*, 249–266.

McCullough, M. E., Kimeldorf, M. B., & Cohen, A. D. (2008). An adaptation for altruism? The social causes, social effects, and social evolution of gratitude. *Current Directions in Psychological Science, 17*, 281–285.

McElreath, R. (2003). Reputation and the evolution of conflict. *Journal of Theoretical Biology, 220*, 345–357.

McGarty, C., Pedersen, A., Leach, C. W., Mansell, T., Waller, J., & Bliuc, A.-M. (2005). Group-based guilt as a predictor of commitment to apology. *British Journal of Social Psychology, 44*, 659–680.

McGregor, I. (2006). Zeal appeal: The allure of moral extremes. *Basic and Applied Social Psychology, 28*, 343–348.

McGregor, I., Zanna, M. P., Holmes, J. G., & Spencer, S. J. (2001). Compensatory conviction in the face of personal uncertainty: Going to extremes and being oneself. *Journal of Personality and Social Psychology, 80*, 472–488.

McGuire, W. J. (1983). A contextualist theory of knowledge: Its implications for innovation and reform in psychological research. *Advances in Experimental Social Psychology, 16*, 1–47.

McIntosh, D. N. (1996). Facial feedback hypotheses: Evidence, implications, and directions. *Motivation and Emotion, 20*, 121–147.

McRobbie, A., & Thornton, S. L. (1995). Rethinking 'moral panic' for multi-mediated social worlds. *British Journal of Sociology, 46,* 559–574.

Mealey, L. (1995). The sociobiology of sociopathy: An integrated evolutionary model. *Behavioral and Brain Sciences, 18,* 523–541.

Menec, V. H., & Perry, R. P. (1998). Reactions to stigmas among Canadian students: Testing an attribution-affect-help judgment model. *Journal of Social Psychology, 138,* 443–454.

Merritt, A. M., Effron, D. A., & Monin, B. (2010). Moral self-licensing: When being good frees us to be bad. *Social and Personality Psychology Compass, 4,* 344–357.

Mikulincer, M. (1988). Reactance and helplessness following exposure to unsolvable problems: The effects of attributional style. *Journal of Personality and Social Psychology, 54,* 679–686.

Milgram, S. (1974). *Obedience to authority: An experimental view.* New York: Harper Collins.

Miller, J. G., & Bersoff, D. M. (1992). Culture and moral judgment: How are conflicts between justice and interpersonal responsibilities resolved? *Journal of Personality and Social Psychology, 62,* 541–554.

Miller, N., Pederson, W. C., Earlywine, M., & Pollock, V. E. (2003). A theoretical model of triggered displaced aggression. *Personality and Social Psychology Review, 7,* 75–97.

Miron, A. M., Branscombe, N. R., & Schmitt, M. T. (2006). Collective guilt as distress over illegitimate intergroup inequality. *Group Processes & Intergroup Relations, 9,* 163.

Monin, B., & Miller, D. T. (2001). Moral credentials and the expression of prejudice. *Journal of Personality and Social Psychology, 81,* 33–43.

Monin, B., Pizarro, D. A., & Beer, J. S. (2007). Deciding versus reacting: Conceptions of moral judgment and the reason-affect debate. *Review of General Psychology, 11,* 99–111.

Monteith, M. J. (1993). Self-regulation of prejudiced responses: Implications for progress in prejudice-reduction efforts. *Journal of Personality and Social Psychology, 65,* 469–485.

Monteith, M. J. (1996). Affective reactions to prejudice-related discrepant responses: The impact of standard salience. *Personality and Social Psychology Bulletin, 22,* 48–59.

Monteith, M. J., & Mark, A. Y. (2005). Changing one's prejudiced ways: Awareness, affect, and self-regulation. *European Review of Social Psychology, 16*(4), 113–154.

Monteith, M. J., & Voils, C. I. (1998). Proneness to prejudiced responses: Toward understanding the authenticity of self-reported discrepancies. *Journal of Personality and Social Psychology, 75,* 901–916.

Monteith, M. J., Ashburn-Nardo, L., Voils, C. I., & Czopp, A. M. (2002). Putting the brakes on prejudice: On the development and operation of cues for control. *Journal of Personality and Social Psychology, 83,* 1029–1050.

Monteith, M. J., Devine, P. G., & Zuwerink, J. R. (1993). Self-directed versus other-directed affect as a consequence of prejudice-related discrepancies. *Journal of Personality and Social Psychology, 64,* 198–210.

Moors, A. (2010). Automatic constructive appraisal as a candidate cause of emotion. *Emotion Review, 2,* 139–156.

Moors, A., & De Houwer, J. (2001). Automatic appraisal of motivational valence: Motivational affective priming and Simon effects. *Cognition and Emotion, 15,* 749–766.

Morrison, T. (1970). *The bluest eye.* New York: Holt, Rinehart and Winston.

Mullen, E., & Skitka, L. J. (2006). Exploring the psychological underpinnings of the moral mandate effect: Motivated reasoning, group differentiation, or anger? *Journal of Personality and Social Psychology, 90*, 629–643.

Mummendey, A., Kessler, T., Klink, A., & Mielke, R. (1999). Strategies to cope with negative social identity: Predictions by social identity theory and relative deprivation theory. *Journal of Personality and Social Psychology, 76*, 229–245.

Mummendey, A., Klink, A., & Brown, R. (2001). Nationalism and patriotism: National identification and out-group rejection. *British Journal of Social Psychology, 40*, 159–172.

Muraven, M., Collins, R. L., Morsheimer, E. T., Shiffman, S., & Paty, J. A. (2005). The morning after: Limit violations and the self-regulation of alcohol consumption. *Psychology of Addictive Behaviors, 19*, 253–262.

Murphy, M. C., Richeson, J. A., & Molden, D. C. (2011). Leveraging motivational mind-sets to foster positive interracial interactions. *Social and Personality Psychology Compass, 5*, 118–131.

Mussweiler, T., & Strack, F. (2000). The 'relative self': Informational and judgmental consequences of comparative self-evaluation. *Journal of Personality and Social Psychology, 79*, 23–38.

Nabi, R. L. (2002). Discrete emotions and persuasion. In J. P. Dillard & M. Pfau (Eds.), *The persuasion handbook: Developments in theory and practice* (pp. 289–308). Thousand Oaks, CA: Sage Publications.

Nadler, A. (2002). Inter-group helping relations as power relations: Maintaining or challenging social dominance between groups through helping. *Journal of Social Issues, 58*, 487–502.

Nadler, A., & Liviatan, I. (2006). Intergroup reconciliation: Effects of adversary's expressions of empathy, responsibility, and recipients' trust. *Personality and Social Psychology Bulletin, 32*, 459–470.

Narvaez, D. (2010). Moral complexity. *Perspectives on Psychological Science, 5*, 163–181.

Narvaez, D., & Vaydich, J. L. (2008). Moral development and behavior under the spotlight of the neurobiological sciences. *Journal of Moral Education, 37*, 289–312.

Navarrete, C. D., Kurzban, R., Fessler, D. M. T., & Kirkpatrick, L. A. (2004). Anxiety and intergroup bias: Terror management or coalitional psychology? *Group Processes & Intergroup Relations, 7*, 370.

Nelissen, R. M. A. (2011). Guilt induced self-punishment as a sign of remorse. *Social Psychological and Personality Science* doi: 10.1177/1948550611411520

Nelissen, R. M. A., & Zeelenberg, M. (2009a). Moral emotions as determinants of third-party punishment: Anger, guilt, and the functions of altruistic sanctions. *Judgment and Decision Making, 4*, 543–553.

Nelissen, R. M. A., & Zeelenberg, M. (2009b). When guilt evokes self-punishment: Evidence for the existence of a 'Dobby Effect'. *Emotion, 9*, 118–122.

Nelissen, R. M. A., Dijker, A. J. M., & de Vries, N. K. (2007). How to turn a hawk into a dove and vice versa: Interactions between emotions and goals in a give-some dilemma game. *Journal of Experimental Social Psychology, 43*, 280–286.

Nesse, R. M. (2001). *Evolution and the capacity for commitment.* New York: Russell Sage Foundation Publications.

Neumann, I. D. (2008). Brain oxytocin: A key regulator of emotional and social behaviours in both females and males. *Journal of Neuroendocrinology, 20*, 858–865.

Neumann, R., & Strack, F. (2000). 'Mood contagion': The automatic transfer of mood between persons. *Journal of Personality and Social Psychology, 79*, 211–223.

Niedenthal, P. M., Barsalou, L. W., Winkielman, P., Krauth-Gruber, S., & Ric, F. (2005). Embodiment in attitudes, social perception, and emotion. *Personality and Social Psychology Review, 9*, 184–211.

Niedenthal, P. M., Tangney, J. P., & Gavanski, I. (1994). 'If only I weren't' versus 'if only I hadn't': Distinguishing shame and guilt in counterfactual thinking. *Journal of Personality and Social Psychology, 67*, 585–595.

Niedenthal, P. M., Winkielman, P., Mondillon, L., & Vermeulen, N. (2009). Embodiment of emotion concepts. *Journal of Personality and Social Psychology, 96*, 1120–1136.

Nietzsche, F. W. (1887/1967). *On the genealogy of morals* (trans. W. A. Kaufmann). New York: Vintage Books.

Nisbett, R., & Wilson, T. (1977). Telling more than we can know: Verbal reports on mental processes. *Psychological Review, 84*, 231–259.

Nobles, M. (2008). *The politics of official apologies*. New York: Cambridge University Press.

Novaco, R. W. (2007). Anger dysregulation. In T. A. Cavell & K. T. Malcolm (Eds.), *Anger, aggression, and interventions for interpersonal violence* (pp. 3–54). Mahwah, NJ: Lawrence Erlbaum.

Nowak, M. A. (2006). Five rules for the evolution of cooperation. *Science, 314*, 1560–1563.

Nugier, A., Niedenthal, P. M., Brauer, M., & Chekroun, P. (2007). Moral and angry emotions provoked by informal social control. *Cognition and Emotion, 21*, 1699–1720.

Nussbaum, M. C. (2000). *Women and human development: The capabilities approach*. Cambridge, UK: Cambridge University Press.

Nussbaum, M. C. (2004). *Hiding from humanity: Shame, disgust, and the law*. Princeton, NJ: Princeton University Press.

Oaten, M. J., Stevenson, R. J., & Case, T. I. (2009). Disgust as a disease-avoidance mechanism. *Psychological Bulletin, 135*, 303–321.

Oatley, K., & Johnson-Laird, P. N. (1996). The communicative theory of emotions. In L. L. Martin & A. Tesser (Eds.), *Striving and feeling: interactions among goals, affect, and self-regulation* (pp. 363–394). Mahwah, NJ: Lawrence Erlbaum Associates, Inc.

O'Connor, L. E., Berry, J. B., Lewis, T., Mulherin, K., & Yi, E. (2007). Empathy and depression. In T. F. D. Farrow & P. W. R. Woodruff (Eds.), *Empathy and mental illness* (pp. 49–75). Cambridge, UK: Cambridge University Press.

O'Connor, L. E., Berry, J. W., Weiss, J., & Gilbert, P. (2002). Guilt, fear, submission, and empathy in depression. *Journal of Affective Disorders, 71*, 19–27.

Ohbuchi, K.-I., Tamura, T., Quigley, B. M., Tedeschi, J. T., Madi, N., Bond, M. H., & Mummendey, A. (2004). Anger, blame, and dimensions of perceived norm violations: Culture, gender, and relationships. *Journal of Applied Social Psychology, 34*, 1587–1603.

Öhman, A., & Mineka, S. (2001). Fears, phobias, and preparedness: Toward an evolved module of fear and fear learning. *Psychological Review, 108*, 483–522.

O'Keefe, D. J. (2002). Guilt as a mechanism of persuasion. In J. P. Dillard & M. Pfau (Eds.), *The persuasion handbook: Developments in theory and practice* (pp. 329–344). Thousand Oaks, CA: Sage Publications.

Olatunji, B. O. (2008). Disgust, scrupulosity and conservative attitudes about sex: Evidence for a mediational model of homophobia. *Journal of Research in Personality, 42*, 1364–1369.

Olatunji, B. O., Forsyth, J. P., & Cherian, A. (2007). Evaluative differential conditioning of disgust: A sticky form of relational learning that is resistant to extinction. *Journal of Anxiety Disorders, 21*, 820–834.

Olatunji, B. O., Haidt, J., McKay, D., & David, B. (2008). Core, animal reminder, and contamination disgust: Three kinds of disgust with distinct personality, behavioral, physiological, and clinical correlates. *Journal of Research in Personality, 42*, 1243–1259.

Olson, M. A., & Fazio, R. H. (2001). Implicit attitude formation through classical conditioning. *Psychological Science, 12*, 413.

Olson, M. A., & Fazio, R. H. (2006). Reducing automatically activated racial prejudice through implicit evaluative conditioning. *Personality and Social Psychology Bulletin, 32*, 421–433.

Ortony, A., Clore, G. L., & Collins, A. (1990). *The cognitive structure of emotions.* Cambridge: Cambridge University Press.

Orwell, G. (1945). Notes on nationalism. Retrieved from http://orwell.ru/library/essays/nationalism/english/e_nat

Osgood, C. E., Suci, G. J., & Tannenbaum, P. H. (1957). *The measurement of meaning.* Chicago: University of Illinois Press.

Panksepp, J. (2007). Criteria for basic emotions: Is disgust a primary 'emotion'? *Cognition and Emotion, 21*, 1819–1828.

Park, J. H., Faulkner, J., & Schaller, M. (2003). Evolved disease-avoidance processes and contemporary anti-social behavior: Prejudicial attitudes and avoidance of people with physical disabilities. *Journal of Nonverbal Behavior, 27*, 65–87.

Parkinson, B. (1996). Emotions are social. *British Journal of Psychology, 86*, 663–683.

Parkinson, B. (1997). Untangling the appraisal–emotion connection. *Personality and Social Psychology Review, 1*, 62–79.

Parkinson, B. (1999). Relations and dissociations between appraisal and emotion ratings of reasonable and unreasonable anger and guilt. *Cognition and Emotion, 13*, 347–385.

Parkinson, B., Fischer, A. H., & Manstead, A. S. (2005). *Emotion in social relations: Cultural, group, and interpersonal processes.* London: Psychology Press.

Parkinson, B., Roper, A., & Simons, G. (2009). Appraisal ratings in diary reports of reasonable and unreasonable anger. *European Journal of Social Psychology, 39*, 82–87.

Parrott, D. J. (2008). A theoretical framework for antigay aggression: Review of established and hypothesized effects within the context of the general aggression model. *Clinical Psychology Review, 28*, 933–951.

Parrott, D. J. (2009). Aggression toward gay men as gender role enforcement: Effects of male role norms, sexual prejudice, and masculine gender role stress. *Journal of Personality, 77*, 1137–1166.

Parrott, D. J., & Peterson, J. L. (2008). What motivates hate crimes based on sexual orientation? Mediating effects of anger on antigay aggression. *Aggressive Behavior, 34*, 306–318.

Parrott, D. J., & Zeichner, A. (2005). Effects of sexual prejudice and anger on physical aggression toward gay and heterosexual men. *Psychology of Men and Masculinity, 6*, 3–17.

Parrott, D., Zeichner, A., & Hoover, R. (2006). Sexual prejudice and anger network activation: Mediating role of negative affect. *Aggressive Behavior, 32*, 7–16.

Parry, R. (2008, November 11). 'Emperor Akihito should apologise for Japan', says Lee Myung-Bak. *The Times Online.* Retrieved from http://www.timesonline.co.uk/tol/news/world/asia/article5126148.ece

Parsons, R. D. (1989). Forgiving-not-forgetting. In E. M. Stern (Ed.), *Psychotherapy and the remorseful patient* (pp. 259–274). Binghamton, NY: The Haworth Press.

Paulhus, D. L., & John, O. P. (1998). Egoistic and moralistic bias in self-perceptions: The interplay of self-deceptive styles with basic traits and motives. *Journal of Personality, 66*, 1025–1060.

Perdue, C. W., Dovidio, J. F., Gurtman, M. B., & Tyler, R. B. (1990). Us and them: Social categorization and the process of intergroup bias. *Journal of Personality and Social Psychology, 59,* 475–486.

Philpot, C., & Hornsey, M. (2008). What happens when groups say sorry: The effect of intergroup apologies on their recipients. *Personality and Social Psychology Bulletin, 34,* 474–487.

Piazza, J., Holbrook, C., & Fessler, D. M. T. (2011). *Empirical challenges to the 'authentic' and 'hubristic' appraisal model of pride.* Unpublished manuscript. University of Kent.

Pinter, B., Insko, C. A., Wildschut, T., Kirchner, J. L., Montoya, R. M., & Wolf, S. T. (2007). Reduction of interindividual–intergroup discontinuity: The role of leader accountability and proneness to guilt. *Journal of Personality and Social Psychology, 93,* 250–265.

Pizarro, D. A., & Bloom, P. (2003). The intelligence of the moral intuitions: A reply to Haidt (2001). *Psychological Review, 110,* 193–196.

Plant, E. A., & Devine, P. G. (1998). Internal and external motivation to respond without prejudice. *Journal of Personality and Social Psychology, 75,* 811–832.

Plant, E. A., Devine, P. G., & Peruche, B. M. (2010). Regulatory concerns for interracial interactions: Approaching egalitarianism versus avoiding prejudice. *Personality and Social Psychology Bulletin, 36,* 1135–1147.

Polivy, J., & Herman, C. P. (1985). Dieting and binging: A causal analysis. *American Psychologist, 40,* 193–201.

Pratto, F., & Glasford, D. E. (2008). Ethnocentrism and the value of a human life. *Journal of Personality and Social Psychology, 95,* 1411–1428.

Prinz, J. (2007). *The emotional construction of morals.* Oxford, UK: Oxford University Press.

Pryor, J. B., Reeder, G. D., Yeadon, C., & Hesson-McInnis, M. (2004). A dual-process model of reactions to perceived stigma. *Journal of Personality and Social Psychology, 87,* 436–452.

Pyszczynski, T., Greenberg, J., & Solomon, S. (1999). A dual-process model of defense against conscious and unconscious death-related thoughts: An extension of Terror Management Theory. *Psychological Review, 106,* 835–845.

Quigley, B. M., & Tedeschi, J. T. (1996). Mediating effects of blame attributions on feelings of anger. *Personality and Social Psychology Bulletin, 22,* 1280–1288.

Raggio, R. D., & Folse, J. A. G. (2009). Gratitude works: its impact and the mediating role of affective commitment in driving positive outcomes. *Journal of the Academy of Marketing Science, 37,* 455–469.

Rawls, J. (1971/1999). *A theory of justice.* Oxford: Oxford University Press.

Rawsthorne, L. J., & Elliot, A. J. (1999). Achievement goals and intrinsic motivation: A meta-analytic review. *Personality and Social Psychology Review, 3,* 326–344.

Ray, R. D., Wilhelm, F. H., & Gross, J. J. (2008). All in the mind's eye? Anger rumination and reappraisal. *Journal of Personality and Social Psychology, 94,* 133–145.

Rhodewalt, F., & Eddings, S. K. (2002). Narcissus reflects: Memory distortion in response to ego-relevant feedback among high- and low-narcissistic men. *Journal of Research in Personality, 36,* 97–116.

Richard, N., & Wright, S. (2010). Advantaged group members' reactions to tokenism. *Group Processes & Intergroup Relations, 13,* 559–569.

Richard, R., de Vries, N. K., & van der Pligt, J. (1998). Anticipated regret and precautionary sexual behavior. *Journal of Applied Social Psychology, 28,* 1411–1428.

Roccas, S., Klar, Y., & Liviatan, I. (2006). The paradox of group-based guilt: Modes of national identification, conflict vehemence, and reactions to the in-group's moral violations. *Journal of Personality and Social Psychology, 91,* 698–711.

Rokeach, M. (1973). *The nature of human values*. New York: Free Press.

Roseman, I. J. (1984). Cognitive determinants of emotion: A structural theory. *Review of Personality & Social Psychology, 5*, 11–36.

Roseman, I. J., & Evdokas, A. (2004). Appraisals cause experienced emotions: Experimental evidence. *Cognition & Emotion, 18*, 1–28.

Roseman, I. J., Spindel, M. S., & Jose, P. E. (1990). Appraisals of emotion-eliciting events: Testing a theory of discrete emotions. *Journal of Personality and Social Psychology, 59*, 899–915.

Roseman, I. J., Wiest, C., & Swartz, T. S. (1994). Phenomenology, behaviors, and goals differentiate discrete emotions. *Journal of Personality and Social Psychology, 67*, 206–221.

Rous, T., & Hunt, A. (2004). Governing peanuts: the regulation of the social bodies of children and the risks of food allergies. *Social Science & Medicine, 58*, 825–836.

Royzman, E. B., & Sabini, J. (2001). Something it takes to be an emotion: The interesting case of disgust. *Journal for the Theory of Social Behavior, 31*, 29–59.

Rozin, P. (1999). The process of moralization. *Psychological Science, 10*, 218–221.

Rozin, P. (2008). Hedonic 'adaptation': Specific habituation to disgust/death elicitors as a result of dissecting a cadaver. *Judgment and Decision Making, 3*, 191–194.

Rozin, P., & Fallon, A. E. (1987). A perspective on disgust. *Psychological Review, 94*, 23–41.

Rozin, P., & Singh, L. (1999). The moralization of cigarette smoking in America. *Journal of Consumer Behavior, 8*, 321–337.

Rozin, P., Haidt, J., & McCauley, C. R. (1993). Disgust. In M. Lewis & J. M. Haviland (Eds.), *Handbook of emotions* (pp. 575–594). New York: The Guilford Press.

Rozin, P., Haidt, J., & McCauley, C. R. (1999a). Disgust: The body and soul emotion. In T. Dalgleish & M. Power (Eds.), *Handbook of cognition and emotion* (pp. 429–445). Chichester: Wiley.

Rozin, P., Haidt, J., & McCauley, C. R. (2008). Disgust. In M. Lewis, J. M. Haviland-Jones, & L. F. Barrett (Eds.), *Handbook of emotions* (3rd ed., pp. 757–776). New York: Guilford.

Rozin, P., Lowery, L., & Ebert, R. (1994). Varieties of disgust faces and the structure of disgust. *Journal of Personality and Social Psychology, 66*, 870–881.

Rozin, P., Lowery, L., Imada, S., & Haidt, J. (1999b). The CAD triad hypothesis: A mapping between three moral emotions (contempt, anger, disgust) and three moral codes (community, autonomy, divinity). *Journal of Personality and Social Psychology, 76*, 574–586.

Rozin, P., Millman, L., & Nemeroff, C. (1986). Operation of the laws of sympathetic magic in disgust and other domains. *Journal of Personality and Social Psychology, 50*, 703–712.

Ruoff, K. J. (2003). *The people's emperor: Democracy and the Japanese monarchy, 1945–1995*. Volume 211 of Harvard East Asian Monographs. Cambridge, MA: Harvard University Asia Center.

Russell, J. A. (2003). Core affect and the psychological construction of emotion. *Psychological Review, 110*, 145–172.

Russell, J. A., & Barrett, L. F. (1999). Core affect, prototypical emotional episodes, and other things called emotion: Dissecting the elephant. *Journal of Personality and Social Psychology, 76*, 805–819.

Russell, J. A., & Fehr, B. (1994). Fuzzy concepts in a fuzzy hierarchy: Varieties of anger. *Journal of Personality and Social Psychology, 67*, 186–205.

Russell, P. S., & Giner-Sorolla, R. (2011a). Moral anger, but not moral disgust, responds to intentionality. *Emotion, 11*, 233–240.

Russell, P. S., & Giner-Sorolla, R. (2011b). Social justifications for moral emotions: When reasons for disgust are less elaborated than for anger. *Emotion, 11*, 637–646.

Russell, P. S., & Giner-Sorolla, R. (2011c). Moral anger is more flexible than moral disgust. *Social Psychological and Personality Science, 2*, 360–364.

Ryan, R. M., & Deci, E. L. (2000). Self-determination theory and the facilitation of intrinsic motivation, social development, and well-being. *American Psychologist, 55*, 68–78.

Sabini, J., & Silver, M. (1997). In defense of shame: Shame in the context of guilt and embarrassment. *Journal for the Theory of Social Behaviour, 27*, 1–15.

Sachdeva, S., Iliev, R., & Medin, D. L. (2009). Sinning saints and saintly sinners: The paradox of moral self-regulation. *Psychological Science, 20*, 523–528.

Sacks, O. (1995). *An anthropologist on Mars: Seven paradoxical tales*. London: Picador.

Saltzstein, H. D., & Kasachkoff, T. (2004). Haidt's moral intuitionist theory: A psychological and philosophical critique. *Review of General Psychology, 8*, 273–282.

Samuelson, S. (1980). The cooties complex. *Western Folklore, 39*, 198–210.

Sartre, J.-P. (1965/1938). *Nausea* (trans. R. Baldick). Harmondsworth, UK: Penguin.

Sayers, D. (1936). *Gaudy night*. London: Gollancz.

Schachter, S. (1964). The interaction of cognitive and physiological determinants of emotional state. *Advances in Experimental Social Psychology, 1*, 49–80.

Schadewaldt, H. (1940). *Polish acts of atrocity against the German minority in Poland*. Berlin: Volk und Reich Verlag.

Schaich Borg, J., Lieberman, D., & Kiehl, K. A. (2008). Infection, incest, and iniquity: Investigating the neural correlates of disgust and morality. *Journal of Cognitive Neuroscience, 20*, 1529–1546.

Schatz, R., & Staub, E. (1997). Manifestations of blind and constructive patriotism: Personality correlates and individual-group relations. In D. Bar-Tal & E. Staub (Eds.), *Patriotism in the lives of individuals and nations* (pp. 229–246). Chicago: Nelson-Hall.

Scheff, T. J., & Retzinger, S. M. (2001). *Emotions and violence: Shame and rage in destructive conflicts*. Bloomington, IN: iUniverse.

Scher, S. J., & Darley, J. M. (1997). How effective are the things people say to apologize? Effects of the realization of the apology speech act. *Journal of Psycholinguistic Research, 26*, 127–140.

Scherer, K. R. (1994). Emotion serves to decouple stimulus and response. In P. Ekman & R. J. Davidson (Eds.), *The nature of emotion: Fundamental questions* (pp. 127–130). New York: Oxford University Press.

Scherer, K. R. (2001). Appraisal considered as a process of multilevel sequential checking. In K. R. Scherer, A. Schorr, & T. Johnstone (Eds.), *Appraisal processes in emotion: Theory, methods, research* (pp. 92–120). Oxford: Oxford University Press.

Scherer, K. R., Shorr, A., & Johnstone, T. (Eds.). (2001). *Appraisal processes in emotion: Theory, methods, research*. Canary, NC: Oxford University Press.

Schimel, J., Simon, L., Greenberg, J., Pyszczynski, T., Solomon, S., Waxmonsky, J., & Arndt, J. (1999). Stereotypes and terror management: Evidence that mortality salience enhances stereotypic thinking and preferences. *Journal of Personality and Social Psychology, 77*, 905–926.

Schmitt, M. T., Miller, D. A., Branscombe, N. R., & Brehm, J. W. (2008). The difficulty of making reparations affects the intensity of collective guilt. *Group Processes & Intergroup Relations, 11*, 267–279.

Schnall, S., Haidt, J., Clore, G. L., & Jordan, A. H. (2008). Disgust as embodied moral judgment. *Personality and Social Psychology Bulletin, 34*, 1096–1109.

Schnall, S., Roper, J., & Fessler, D. M. T. (2010). Elevation leads to altruism, above and beyond general positive affect. *Psychological Science, 21*, 315–320.

Schneider, M. E., Major, B., Luhtanen, R., & Crocker, J. (1996). Social stigma and the potential costs of assumptive help. *Personality and Social Psychology Bulletin, 22*, 201.

Schoorman, F. D., Mayer, R. C., & Davis, J. H. (2007). An integrative model of organizational trust: Past, present, and future. *Academy of Management Review, 32*, 344–354.

Schruijer, S., Blanz, M., Mummendey, A., & Tedeschi, J. T. (1994). The group-serving bias in evaluating and explaining harmful behavior. *Journal of Social Psychology, 134*, 47–53.

Schwartz, S. H. (1992). Universals in the content and structure of values: Theory and empirical tests in 20 countries. In M. P. Zanna (Ed.), *Advances in experimental social psychology* (pp. 1–65). New York: Academic Press.

Schwarz, N., Bless, H., & Bohner, G. (1991). Mood and persuasion: Affective states influence the processing of persuasive communications. *Advances in Experimental Social Psychology, 24*, 161–199.

Segal, Z. V., Kennedy, S., Gemar, M., Hood, K., Pedersen, R., & Buis, T. (2006). Cognitive reactivity to sad mood provocation and the prediction of depressive relapse. *Archives of General Psychiatry, 63*, 749.

Sell, A., Tooby, J., & Cosmides, L. (2009). Formidability and the logic of human anger. *Proceedings of the National Academy of Sciences, 106*, 15073–15078.

Shaver, K. G. (1985). *The attribution of blame: Causality, responsibility, and blameworthiness*. New York: Springer.

Shaver, P., Schwartz, J., Kirson, D., & O'Connor, C. (1987). Emotion knowledge: Further exploration of a prototype approach. *Journal of Personality and Social Psychology, 52*, 1061–1086.

Sheikh, S., & Janoff-Bulman, R. (2010). The 'shoulds' and 'should nots' of moral emotions: A self-regulatory perspective on shame and guilt. *Personality and Social Psychology Bulletin, 36*, 213–224.

Shelton, J. N., & Richeson, J. A. (2006). Interracial interactions: A relational approach. *Advances in Experimental Social Psychology, 38*, 121–181.

Shelton, J. N., Richeson, J. A., Salvatore, J., & Trawalter, S. (2005). Ironic effects of racial bias during interracial interactions. *Psychological Science, 16*, 397–402.

Sherman, D. K., & Cohen, G. L. (2006). The psychology of self-defense: Self-affirmation theory. In M. P. Zanna (Ed.), *Advances in experimental social psychology* (Vol. 38, pp. 183–242). San Diego, CA: Academic Press.

Shiota, M. N., Campos, B., & Keltner, D. (2003). The faces of positive emotion: Prototype displays of awe, amusement, and pride. *Annals of the New York Academy of Sciences, 1000*, 296.

Shiota, M. N., Keltner, D., & Mossman, A. (2007). The nature of awe: Elicitors, appraisals, and effects on self-concept. *Cognition and Emotion, 21*, 944–963.

Shnabel, N., & Nadler, A. (2008). A needs-based model of reconciliation: Satisfying the differential emotional needs of victim and perpetrator as a key to promoting reconciliation. *Journal of Personality and Social Psychology, 94*, 116–132.

Shweder, R. A. (1990). Ethical relativism: Is there a defensible version? *Ethos, 18*, 205–218.

Shweder, R. A., Much, N. C., Mahapatra, M., Park, L., Brandt, A. M., & Rozin, P. (1997). The 'big three' of morality (autonomy, community, and divinity) and the 'big three' explanations of suffering. Morality and health. In A. Brandt & P. Rozin (Eds.), *Morality and health* (pp. 119–169). New York: Routledge.

Silvers, J. A., & Haidt, J. (2008). Moral elevation can induce nursing. *Emotion, 8,* 291–295.

Simner, M. L. (1971). Newborns' response to the cry of another infant. *Developmental Psychology, 5,* 136–150.

Simpson, J., Carter, S., Anthony, S. H., & Overton, P. G. (2006). Is disgust a homogeneous emotion? *Motivation & Emotion, 30,* 31–41.

Sinha, S. (2009). Empathy, not sympathy. Liliavati's Daughters (pp. 301–304). Retrieved from http://www.ias.ac.in/womeninscience/LD_essays/301–304.pdf

Skitka, L. J., & Houston, D. A. (2001). When due process is of no consequence: Moral mandates and presumed defendant guilt or innocence. *Social Justice Research, 14,* 305–326.

Slavin, M. O., & Kriegman, D. H. (Eds.). (1992). *The adaptive design of the human psyche: Psychoanalysis, evolutionary biology, and the therapeutic process.* New York: The Guilford Press.

Smith, C. A., & Ellsworth, P. C. (1985). Patterns of cognitive appraisal in emotion. *Journal of Personality and Social Psychology, 48,* 813–838.

Smith, C. A., Haynes, K. N., Lazarus, R. S., & Pope, L. K. (1993). In search of the 'hot' cognitions: Attributions, appraisals, and their relation to emotion. *Journal of Personality and Social Psychology, 65,* 916–929.

Smith, D., Loewenstein, G., Rozin, P., Sherriff, R. L., & Ubel, P. A. (2007). Sensitivity to disgust, stigma, and adjustment to life with a colostomy. *Journal of Research in Personality, 41,* 787–803.

Smith, E. R., Seger, C. R., & Mackie, D. M. (2007). Can emotions be truly group level? Evidence regarding four conceptual criteria. *Journal of Personality and Social Psychology, 93,* 431–446.

Smith, M. M. (2006). *How race is made: Slavery, segregation, and the senses.* Chapel Hill: University of North Carolina Press.

Smith, R. H., Webster, J. M., Parrott, W. G., & Eyre, H. L. (2002). The role of public exposure in moral and nonmoral shame and guilt. *Journal of Personality and Social Psychology, 83,* 138–159.

Solomon, R. C. (1993). The philosophy of emotions. In M. Lewis, J. M. Haviland-Jones, & L. Feldman Barrett (Eds.), *Handbook of emotions* (pp. 3–15), 1st edition. New York: Guilford.

Solomon, S., Greenberg, J., & Pyszczynski, T. (1991). A terror management theory of social behavior: The psychological functions of self-esteem and cultural worldviews. In M. P. Zanna (Ed.), *Advances in experimental social psychology* (Vol. 23, pp. 93–159). San Diego, CA: Academic Press.

Sontag, S. (1977). *Illness as metaphor.* New York: Picador.

Spencer, S. J., Fein, S., Wolfe, C. T., Fong, C., & Dunn, M. A. (1998). Automatic activation of stereotypes: The role of self-image threat. *Personality & Social Psychology Bulletin, 24,* 1139–1153.

Staats, A., & Staats, C. (1958). Attitudes established by classical conditioning. *The Journal of Abnormal and Social Psychology, 57,* 37–40.

Steenhuis, I. (2009). Guilty or not? Feelings of guilt about food among college women. *Appetite, 52,* 531–534.

Steins, G., & Weiner, B. (1999). The influence of the perceived responsibility and personality characteristics on the emotional and behavioral reactions to people with AIDS. *Journal of Social Psychology, 139,* 487–495.

Stevenson, R. J., Oaten, M. J., Case, T. I., Repacholi, B. M., & Wagland, P. (2010). Children's response to adult disgust elicitors: Development and acquisition. *Developmental Psychology, 46*, 165–177.

Stipek, D. (1998). Differences between Americans and Chinese in the circumstances evoking pride, shame, and guilt. *Journal of Cross-Cultural Psychology, 29*, 616–629.

Stouten, J., de Cremer, D., & van Dijk, E. (2006). Violating equality in social dilemmas: Emotional and retributive reactions as a function of trust, attribution, and honesty. *Personality and Social Psychology Bulletin, 32*, 894–906.

Stouten, J., de Cremer, D., & van Dijk, E. (2009). Behavioral (in)tolerance of equality violation in social dilemmas: When trust affects contribution decisions after violations of equality. *Group Processes and Intergroup Relations, 12*, 517–531.

Strack, F., Martin, L. L., & Stepper, S. (1988). Inhibiting and facilitating conditions of the human smile: A nonobtrusive test of the facial feedback hypothesis. *Journal of Personality and Social Psychology, 54*, 768–777.

Sturmer, S., Snyder, M., Kropp, A., & Siem, B. (2006). Empathy-motivated helping: The moderating role of group membership. *Personality and Social Psychology Bulletin, 32*, 943–956.

Sukhodolsky, D. G., Golub, A., & Cromwell, E. N. (2001). Development and validation of the anger rumination scale. *Personality and Individual Differences, 31*, 689–700.

Sunstein, C. R. (1996). *Legal reasoning and political conflict*. New York: Oxford University Press.

Tagar, M. R., Federico, C. M., & Halperin, E. (2010). The positive effect of negative emotions in protracted conflict: The case of anger. *Journal of Experimental Social Psychology, 47*, 157–164.

Tajfel, H., & Turner, J. C. (1979). An integrative theory of intergroup conflict. In W. G. Austin & S. Worchel (Eds.), *The social psychology of intergroup relations*. Monterey, CA: Brooks-Cole.

Tamir, M., Mitchell, C., & Gross, J. J. (2008). Hedonic and instrumental motives in anger regulation. *Psychological Science, 19*, 324–328.

Tanghe, J., Wisse, B., & van der Flier, H. (2010). The role of group member affect in the relationship between trust and cooperation. *British Journal of Management, 21*, 359–374.

Tangney, J. P., & Dearing, R. (2002). *Shame and guilt*. New York: Guilford.

Tangney, J. P., Wagner, P. E., Fletcher, C., & Gramzow, R. (1992). Shamed into anger? The relation of shame and guilt to anger and self-reported aggression. *Journal of Personality and Social Psychology, 62*, 669–675.

Tanis, M., & Postmes, T. (2005). A social identity approach to trust: Interpersonal perception, group membership and trusting behaviour. *European Journal of Social Psychology, 35*, 413–424.

Tapias, M. P., Glaser, J., Kelther, D., Vasquez, K. & Wickens, T. (2007). Emotions and prejudice: Specific emotions towards outgroups. *Group Processes & Intergroup Relations, 10*, 27–39.

Tavuchis, N. (1991). *Mea culpa: A sociology of apology and reconciliation*. Stanford, CA: Stanford University Press.

Taylor, S. E., & Lobel, M. (1989). Social comparison activity under threat: Downward evaluation and upward contacts. *Psychological Review, 96*, 569–575.

Terrizzi Jr., J. A., Shook, N. J., & Ventis, W. L. (2010). Disgust: A predictor of social conservatism and prejudicial attitudes toward homosexuals. *Personality and Individual Differences, 49*, 587–592.

Tetlock, P. E. (1981). Personality and isolationism: Content analysis of senatorial speeches. *Journal of Personality and Social Psychology, 41*, 737–743.

Tetlock, P. E. (1984). Cognitive style and political belief systems in the British House of Commons. *Journal of Personality and Social Psychology, 46*, 365–375.

Tetlock, P. E. (1986). A value pluralism model of ideological reasoning. *Journal of Personality and Social Psychology, 50*, 819–827.

Tetlock, P. E. (2003). Thinking the unthinkable: sacred values and taboo cognitions. *Trends in Cognitive Sciences, 7*, 320–324.

The Onion (2011, February 25). Marauding gay hordes drag thousands of helpless citizens from marriages after Obama drops Defense of Marriage Act. Retrieved from http://www.theonion.com/articles/marauding-gay-hordes-drag-thousands-of-helpless-ci,19325/

Thoits, P. A. (1990). Emotional deviance: Research agendas. In T. D. Kemper (Ed.), *Research agendas in the sociology of emotions* (pp. 180–203). Albany, NY: State University of New York Press.

Thomaes, S., Bushman, B. J., Stegge, H., & Olthof, T. (2008). Trumping shame by blasts of noise: Narcissism, self-esteem, shame, and aggression in young adolescents. *Child Development, 79*, 1792–1801.

Thompson, R. A., & Hoffman, M. L. (1980). Empathy and the development of guilt in children. *Developmental Psychology, 16*, 155–156.

Tice, D. M., Bratslavsky, E., & Baumeister, R. F. (2001). Emotional distress regulation takes precedence over impulse control: If you feel bad, do it! *Journal of Personality and Social Psychology, 80*, 53–67.

Tiedens, L. Z., & Linton, S. (2001). Judgment under emotional certainty and uncertainty: The effects of specific emotions on information processing. *Journal of Personality and Social Psychology, 81*, 973–988.

Townend, L. (2009). The moralizing of obesity: A new name for an old sin? *Critical Social Policy, 29*, 171.

Tracy, J. L., & Matsumoto, D. (2008). The spontaneous expression of pride and shame: Evidence for biologically innate nonverbal displays. *Proceedings of the National Academy of Sciences, 105*, 11655–11660.

Tracy, J. L., & Robins, R. W. (2004). Show your pride. *Psychological Science, 15*, 194.

Tracy, J. L., & Robins, R. W. (2006). Appraisal antecedents of shame and guilt: Support for a theoretical model. *Personality and Social Psychology Bulletin, 32*, 1339–1351.

Tracy, J. L., & Robins, R. W. (2007). The psychological structure of pride: A tale of two facets. *Journal of Personality and Social Psychology, 92*, 506.

Tracy, J. L., Cheng, J. T., Robins, R. W., & Trzesniewski, K. H. (2009a). Authentic and hubristic pride: The affective core of self-esteem and narcissism. *Self and Identity, 8*, 196–213.

Tracy, J. L., Robins, R. W., & Schriber, R. A. (2009b). Development of a FACS-verified set of basic and self-conscious emotion expressions. *Emotion, 9*, 554–559.

Tracy, J. L., Shariff, A. F., & Cheng, J. T. (2010). A naturalist's view of pride. *Emotion Review, 2*, 163.

Trawalter, S., & Richeson, J. A. (2006). Regulatory focus and executive attention after interracial interactions. *Journal of Experimental Social Psychology, 42*, 406–412.

Trawalter, S., Richeson, J. A., & Shelton, J. N. (2009). Predicting behavior during interracial interactions: A stress and coping approach. *Personality and Social Psychology Review, 13*, 243–268.

Trivers, R. L. (1971). The evolution of reciprocal altruism. *Quarterly Review of Biology, 46*, 35–57.

Tso, N. (2009). Edible excretions: Taiwan's toilet restaurant. *TIME magazine* online. Retrieved from http://www.time.com/time/arts/article/0,8599,1882569,00.html

Turiel, E. (1983). *The development of social knowledge: Morality and convention.* Cambridge, UK: Cambridge University Press.

Turner, C. W, Simons, L. S., Berkowitz, L., & Frodi, A. (1977). The stimulating and inhibiting effects of weapons on aggressive behavior. *Aggressive Behavior, 3*, 355–378.

Turner, J. C., & Oakes, P. (1989), Self-categorisation theory and social influence. In D. Paulus (Ed.), *Psychology of group influence* (pp. 233–275). Hillsdale, NJ: Erlbaum.

Tybur, J. M., Lieberman, D., & Griskevicius, V. (2009). Microbes, mating, and morality: Individual differences in three functional domains of disgust. *Journal of Personality and Social Psychology, 97*, 103–122.

Tyler, T. R., & Blader, S. (2003). Procedural justice, social identity, and cooperative behavior. *Personality and Social Psychology Review, 7*, 349–361.

Uhlmann, E. L., Brescoll, V. L., & Paluck, E. L. (2006). Are members of low status groups perceived as bad, or badly off? Egalitarian negative associations and automatic prejudice. *Journal of Experimental Social Psychology, 42*, 491–499.

US Department of Defense (2004, May 4). Deputy Secretary Wolfowitz interview on the Pentagon Channel. Retrieved from http://www.defense.gov/transcripts/transcript.aspx?transcriptid=2970

Vaes, J., Heflick, N. A., & Goldenberg, J. L. (2010). 'We are people': In-group humanization as an existential defense. *Journal of Personality and Social Psychology, 98*, 750–760.

Valdesolo, P., & DeSteno, D. (2007). Moral hypocrisy. *Psychological Science, 19*, 689–690.

Vallone, R. P., Ross, L., & Lepper, M. R. (1985). The hostile media phenomenon: Biased perception and perceptions of media bias in coverage of the Beirut massacre. *Journal of Personality and Social Psychology, 49*, 577–585.

Vandello, J. A., Bosson, J. K., Cohen, D., Burnaford, R. M., & Weaver, J. R. (2008). Precarious manhood. *Journal of Personality and Social Psychology, 95*, 1325–1339.

van den Bos, K., Poortvliet, P. M., Maas, M., Miedema, J., & van den Ham, E.-J. (2005). An enquiry concerning the principles of cultural norms and values: The impact of uncertainty and mortality salience on reactions to violations and bolstering of cultural worldviews. *Journal of Experimental Social Psychology, 41*, 91–113.

van Kleef, G. A., de Dreu, C K. W., & Manstead, A. S. R. (2006). Supplication and appeasement in conflict and negotiation: The interpersonal effects of disappointment, worry, guilt, and regret. *Journal of Personality and Social Psychology, 91*, 124–142.

van Kleef, G. A., de Dreu, C. K. W., & Manstead, A. S. R. (2010). An interpersonal approach to emotion in social decision making: The emotions as social information model. *Advances in Experimental Social Psychology, 42*, 45–96.

van Vugt, M., & van Lange, P. (2006). The altruism puzzle: Psychological adaptations for prosocial behavior. In M. Schaller, D. Kenrick, & J. Simpson (Eds.), *Evolution and social psychology* (pp. 237–261). Hove: Psychology Press.

van Zomeren, M., Postmes, T., & Spears, R. (2008). Toward an integrative social identity model of collective action: A quantitative research synthesis of three socio-psychological perspectives. *Psychological Bulletin, 34*, 504–535.

Vartanian, L. R. (2010). Disgust and perceived control in attitudes toward obese people. *International Journal of Obesity, 34*, 1302–1307.

Vasquez, K., Keltner, D., Ebenbach, D. H., & Banaszynski, T. L. (2001). Cultural variation and similarity in moral rhetorics. *Journal of Cross-Cultural Psychology, 32*, 93.

Vauclair, C.-M., & Fischer, R. (2011). Do cultural values predict individuals' moral attitudes? A cross-cultural multi-level approach. *European Journal of Social Psychology*, *41*, 645–657.

Victor, G. (1998). *Hitler: The pathology of evil*. Washington, DC: Brassey's.

Viki, C. T., Winchester, L., Titshall, L., Chisango, T., Pina, A., & Russell, R. (2006). Beyond secondary emotions: The infrahumanization of outgroups using human-related and animal-related words. *Social Cognition*, *24*, 753–775.

Vitaglione, G. D., & Barnett, M. A. (2003). Assessing a new dimension of empathy: Empathic anger as a predictor of helping and punishing desires. *Motivation and Emotion*, *27*, 301–325.

Vorauer, J. D. (2006). An information search model of evaluative concerns in intergroup interaction. *Psychological Review*, *113*, 862–886.

Vorauer, J. D., & Sasaki, S. J. (2009). Helpful only in the abstract? Ironic effects of empathy in intergroup interaction. *Psychological Science*, *20*, 191–197.

Vrana, S. R. (1993). The psychophysiology of disgust: Differentiating negative emotional contexts with facial EMG. *Psychophysiology*, *30*, 279–286.

Vytal, K., & Hamann, S. (2010). Neuroimaging support for discrete neural correlates of basic emotions: A voxel-based meta-analysis. *Journal of Cognitive Neuroscience*, *22*, 2864–2885.

Wainryb, C. (1993). The application of moral judgments to other cultures: Relativism and universality. *Child Development*, *64*, 924–933.

Weber, M. (2009/1904). *The Protestant ethic and the spirit of capitalism: The Talcott Parsons translation*. New York: W. W. Norton.

Weiner, B. (1985). An attributional theory of achievement motivation and emotion. *Psychological Review*, *92*, 548–573.

Weiner, B. (1995). *Judgments of responsibility: A foundation for a theory of social conduct*. New York: Guilford Press.

Weiner, B. (2005). Motivation from an attribution perspective and the social psychology of perceived competence. In A. J. Elliot & C. S. Dweck (Eds.), *Handbook of competence and motivation* (pp. 73–84). New York: Guilford Press.

Wells, B. E., & Twenge, J. M. (2005). Changes in young people's sexual behavior and attitudes, 1943–1999: A cross-temporal meta-analysis. *Review of General Psychology*, *9*, 249–261.

Wheatley, T., & Haidt, J. (2005). Hypnotically induced disgust makes moral judgments more severe. *Psychological Science*, *16*, 780–784.

Widen, S. C., & Russell, J. A. (2003). A closer look at preschoolers' freely produced labels for facial expressions. *Developmental Psychology*, *39*, 114–128.

Wierzbicka, A. (1999). *Emotions across languages and cultures: Diversity and universals*. Cambridge: Cambridge University Press.

Wilcox, K., Kramer, T., & Sen, S. (2011). Indulgence or self-control: A dual process model of the effect of incidental pride on indulgent choice. *Journal of Consumer Research*, *38*, 151–163.

Wilkowski, B. M., & Robinson, M. D. (2007). Keeping your cool: Trait anger, hostile thoughts, and the recruitment of limited capacity control. *Personality and Social Psychology Bulletin*, *33*, 1201–1213.

Williams, L. A., & DeSteno, D. (2008). Pride and perseverance: The motivational role of pride. *Journal of Personality and Social Psychology*, *94*, 1007–1017.

Williams, M. (2001). In whom we trust: Group membership as an affective context for trust development. *Academy of Management Review*, *26*, 377–396.

Wilson, T., Lindsey, S., & Schooler, T. (2000). A model of dual attitudes. *Psychological Review, 107*, 101–126.

Wohl, M. J. A., & Reeder, G. D. (2004). When bad deeds are forgiven: Judgments of morality and forgiveness for intergroup aggression. In J. P. Morgan (Ed.), *Focus on aggression research* (pp. 59–74). New York: Nova Science Publishers.

Wohl, M. J. A., Branscombe, N. R., & Klar, Y. (2006). Collective guilt: Justice-based emotional reactions when one's group has done wrong or been wronged. *European Review of Social Psychology, 17*, 1–37.

Wolf, S. T., Cohen, T. R., Panter, A. T., & Insko, C. A. (2010). Shame proneness and guilt proneness: Toward the further understanding of reactions to public and private transgressions. *Self and Identity, 9*, 337–362.

Wubben, M. J. J., de Cremer, D., & van Dijk, E. (2009). How emotion communication guides reciprocity: Establishing cooperation through disappointment and anger. *Journal of Experimental Social Psychology, 45*, 987–990.

Yamazaki, J. W. (2006). *Japanese apologies for World War II: A rhetorical study* (Vol. 3). Abingdon: Routledge.

Yuki, M., Maddux, W. W., Brewer, M. B., & Takemura, K. (2005). Cross-cultural differences in relationship- and group-based trust. *Personality and Social Psychology Bulletin, 31*, 48–62.

Yzerbyt, V. Y., Dumont, M., Gordijn, E. H., & Wigboldus, D. (2002). Intergroup emotions and self-categorization: The impact of perspective-taking on reactions to victims of harmful behavior. In D. Mackie & E. Smith (Eds.), *From prejudice to intergroup emotions* (pp. 67–68). Philadelphia, PA: Psychology Press.

Yzerbyt, V. Y., Dumont, M., Mathieu, B., Gordijn, E. H., & Wigboldus, D. (2006). Social comparison and group-based emotions. In S. Guimond (Ed.), *Social comparison and social psychology: Understanding cognition, intergroup relations, and culture* (pp. 174–205). New York: Cambridge University Press.

Zahn-Waxler, C. (2010). Socialization of emotion: Who influences whom and how? *New Directions for Child and Adolescent Development, 128*, 101–109.

Zaiser, E., & Giner-Sorolla, R. (2011). *Image repair and obligation shifting explain satisfaction with own-group apologies.* Unpublished manuscript, University of Kent.

Zajonc, R. B. (1968). Attitudinal effects of mere exposure. *Journal of Personality and Social Psychology*, Monograph Supplement, *9*, 1–27.

Zajonc, R. B. (1980). Feeling and thinking: Preferences need no inferences. *American Psychologist, 35*, 151–175.

Zajonc, R. B. (1984). On the primacy of affect. *American Psychologist, 39*, 117–123.

Zak, P. J., Stanton, A. A., & Ahmadi, S. (2007). Oxytocin increases generosity in humans. *PLoS ONE, 2*, e1128.

Zanna, M. P., & Rempel, J. K. (1988). Attitudes: A new look at an old concept. In D. Bar-Tal & A. Kruglanski (Eds.), *The social psychology of knowledge* (pp. 315–334). New York: Cambridge University Press.

Zeelenberg, M., & Breugelmans, S. M. (2008). The role of interpersonal harm in distinguishing regret from guilt. *Emotion, 8*, 589–596.

Zeichner, A., & Reidy, D. E. (2009). Are homophobic men attracted to or repulsed by homosexual men? Effects of gay male erotica on anger, fear, happiness, and disgust. *Psychology of Men and Masculinity, 10*(3), 231–236.

Zemack-Rugar, Y., Bettman, J. R., & Fitzsimons, G. J. (2007). The effects of nonconsciously priming emotion concepts on behavior. *Journal of Personality and Social Psychology, 93*, 927–939.

Zimbardo, P. G. (1971). The power and pathology of imprisonment. Congressional Record. (Serial No. 15, 1971–10–25). Hearings before Subcommittee No. 3, of the Committee on the Judiciary, House of Representatives, Ninety-Second Congress, First Session on Corrections, Part II, Prisons, Prison Reform and Prisoner's Rights: California. Washington, DC: U.S. Government Printing Office.

Zucker, G. S., & Weiner, B. (1993). Conservatism and perceptions of poverty: An attributional analysis. *Journal of Applied Social Psychology, 23*, 925–943.

Author Index

Subject Index

Judging Passions

European monographs in social psychology
Sponsored by the European Association of Experimental Psychology

Series Editor:
Professor Rupert Brown, Department of Psychology, University of Kent, Canterbury, Kent CT2 7NP

The aim of this series is to publish and promote the highest quality of writing in European social psychology. The editor and the editorial board encourage publications which approach social psychology from a wide range of theoretical perspectives and whose content may be applied, theoretical or empirical. The authors of books in this series should be affiliated to institutions that are located in countries which would qualify for membership of the Association. All books will be published in English, and translations from other European languages are welcomed. Please submit ideas and proposals for books in the series to Rupert Brown at the above address.

Published

The Quantitative Analysis of Social Representations
Willem Doise, Alain Clemence, and Fabio Lorenzi-Cioldi

A Radical Dissonance Theory
Jean-Léon Beauvois and Robert-Vincent Joule

The Social Psychology of Collective Action
Caroline Kelly and Sara Breinlinger

Social Context and Cognitive Performance
Jean-Marc Monteil and Pascal Huguet

Conflict and Decision-Making in Close Relationships
Erich Kirchler, Christa Rodler, Erik Hölzl, and Katja Meier

Stereotyping as Inductive Hypothesis Testing
Klaus Fiedler and Eva Walther

Intergroup Relations in States of the Former Soviet Union
Louk Hagendoorn, Hub Linssen, and Sergei Tumanov

The Social Psychology of Ethnic Identity
Maykel Verkuyten

Consumer Culture, Identity and Well-Being
Helga Dittmar

Judging Passions: Moral emotions in persons and groups
Roger Giner-Sorolla

Forthcoming Title
The Passionate Intersection of Desire and Knowledge
Gregory Maio